**DO NOT REMOVE
CARDS FROM POCKET**

**ALLEN COUNTY PUBLIC LIBRARY
FORT WAYNE, INDIANA 46802**

You may return this book to any agency, branch,

or bookmobile of the Allen County Public Library.

DEMCO

Negotiating Health Insurance in the Workplace

A Basic Guide

Negotiating Health Insurance in the Workplace

A Basic Guide

Suzanne S. Taylor

The Bureau of National Affairs, Inc., Washington, D.C.

Copyright © 1992
The Bureau of National Affairs, Inc.

Library of Congress Cataloging-in-Publication Data

Taylor, Suzanne Saunders.
   Negotiating health insurance in the workplace : a basic guide /
Suzanne S. Taylor.
      p. cm.
   Includes bibliographical references and index.
   ISBN   0-87179-731-3
     1. Insurance, Health—United States.   2. Collective bargaining–
–United States.   I. Title.
HG9396.T39   1992
331.89—dc20   92–11190
                                            CIP

Published by BNA Books, 1250 23rd St., N.W.
Washington, D.C. 20037

Printed in the United States of America
International Standard Book Number 0-87179-731-3

Preface

A guidebook for health insurance in today's rapidly changing environment of modified health plans is an ambitious undertaking, but one that is a necessary tool for both union and management personnel charged with developing a cost efficient and effective health plan. What is ultimately written in the contract must also be enforced and often litigated through grievance arbitration or the courts.

Very little has been published that provides a clear route through the maze of medical and insurance jargon. The busy benefits manager or union negotiator must be knowledgeable about pensions, salaries, and various leave policies, as well as all the factors affecting conditions of employment. None of this is easy. To clarify this complex area, this book (1) provides codification and organization of the basic elements of insurance; (2) includes specific suggestions for workable and unworkable items in negotiations; (3) lists resources for seeking additional help; (4) presents examples of dispute resolution in the area of health insurance; and (5) discusses future legislative proposals for improving access to and reducing costs of health care. Both the first-time negotiator and the experienced negotiator should find this book a valuable reference in negotiating health insurance contracts.

The author's experience in this field has been from the perspective of advocating union positions, but an effort has been made to make this discussion a balanced one, taking into account the needs of both union and management, and covering as well the needs of nonunion workplaces. It is the author's belief, in fact, as will be obvious from the text, that in many situations the needs of union and management are aligned rather than opposed, with the opposing party, so to speak, being the health care system. To the extent a given reader feels a pro-union bias is evident on occasion, the author takes sole responsibility for it, and anticipates that readers will understand that it simply results from her background in the field, rather than from any attempt to "slant" the presentation of information.

Contents

Chapter 1

Evolution of the Health Care Crisis

In both union and non-union shops, management and labor are frustrated with today's high costs of insurance. The reasons for these cost increases are complex, but knowing how to control them is even more complex. This book will offer some insight into the problem and suggest some steps that both labor and management can use to reduce costs.

As a domestic issue, the topic of health insurance probably ranks second only to the problem of the U.S. economy; indeed, these two issues are directly linked. Health care benefits played a major role in strikes during the 1980s, and the issue continues as a major topic of bargaining in the 1990s. Headline news in Boston, August 4, 1991: "Over 5,000 union employees of the Price Shopper Food Stores have agreed not to strike at the last minute as management backed off their stand to force employees to pay for part of the costs of their health insurance."[1]

Proposals for national health insurance or a national health care system draw hot debate everywhere, and numerous bills before Congress and state legislatures purport to offer the definitive solution. As yet, however, no solution has emerged, and experts predict it will take another decade for a real remedy to appear.

The first step in achieving any remedy is to understand the problem. To that end, the remainder of this chapter provides a brief historical sketch of the insurance industry in America, and then outlines the reasons for and impact of today's rapidly escalating health insurance costs.

Historical Overview

The origins of health insurance date back more than 100 years, and union involvement in health care began even earlier. The following discussion summarizes past developments leading up to the current state of affairs.

Labor Involvement

In the 1800s, unions often started out as "benevolent societies" whose main interest was to provide health and pension protection for their members.[2] The major model of health care bargaining, however, did not develop until World War II, when wage stabilization policies promoted non-wage forms of compensation.

Health care bargaining became further entrenched in 1948, when the courts upheld the National Labor Relations Board's ruling in the Inland Steel case.[3] This decision established that under the National Labor Relations Act,[4] employers had to bargain on "other conditions of employment as well as wages and hours." Following this ruling, two major unions settled contracts which included health insurance benefits: In 1948, the United Mine Workers developed its first contract providing health insurance for members, while one year later, the United Auto Workers negotiated one of the premier policies with Ford Motor Company.

Insurance Industry Origins

Prior to these labor developments, the availability of health insurance came about through health care providers who viewed insurance as a social necessity. Several religious and other nonprofit organizations were established during the early 1900s to offer health insurance. One of the first of these plans was the Baylor University Hospital prepayment plan, established in 1920. Even today, many religious organizations continue to provide health care. For example, the Catholic Archdiocese maintains two nonprofit hospitals in Providence, RI.

Blue Cross/Blue Shield, a major insurer in the field today, also began as a nonprofit insurer for hospital care and later expanded to cover other types of medical treatment. Today many of the separate Blue Cross entities across the country still maintain a nonprofit designation. Many others, however, have changed their charters and have become incorporated as mutuals.

Current Trends

The national network of Blue Cross/Blue Shield today is a loose affiliation of more than 70 organizations. To continue with an example from Rhode Island, its Blue Cross, founded by an enabling act of the legislature in 1939, today consists of a 1700-provider network of Rhode Island doctors and state hospitals, with some 600,000 plan participants. Numerous variations on this model exist in other states. Larger states usually have more than one Blue Cross/Blue Shield company, although in states like Pennsylvania and West Virginia, for example, recent mergers have taken place.

Typical of some Blue plans, the nonprofit Rhode Island Blue Cross/Blue Shield is a "service" insurance plan. The difference between this plan and a commercial insurance plan is that the Blues pay all medical costs sustained by a serious illness or injury, while commercial carriers reimburse only a predetermined portion of these costs. As long as a service is provided under Blue Cross guidelines, all expenses are covered. For providers, following Blue Cross/Blue Shield guidelines usually means agreeing to accept the company's rates as full payment.

While the Blues remain the industry leaders, other companies have entered the field offering variations on the traditional Blue service plan. Nontraditional health care plans also have multiplied, with the proliferation of health maintenance organizations (HMOs), preferred provider organizations (PPOs), and individual practice associations (IPAs). (For fuller discussion of these different types of insurance offerings, see Chapter 3).

The Current Cost Crisis

Increased competition among insurance companies has not led to price breaks for consumers, and over the last decade, health insurance rates have escalated rapidly. As Exhibit 1–1 illustrates, health care spending consumed almost 12 percent of the U.S. gross national product (GNP) in 1991, compared to only 9.1 in 1980.[5] Costs for health care have risen even faster than the overall rate of inflation (see Exhibit 1–2), and the trend shows no signs of abating. According to one recent study, health insurance costs rose by 46 percent from 1988 to 1990, reaching an average cost of $3,161 per

Exhibit 1-1 National Health Expenditures and Gross National Product (1950–1988)

YEAR	NATIONAL HEALTH EXPENDITURES AMOUNT (BILLIONS)	ANNUAL RATE OF GROWTH (PERCENT)	GROSS NATIONAL PRODUCT AMOUNT (BILLIONS)	ANNUAL RATE OF GROWTH (PERCENT)	NATIONAL HEALTH EXPENDITURES AS PERCENT OF GNP
1950	$ 12.7	12.2	$ 288.0	10.7	4.4
1955	17.7	7.0	406.0	7.0	4.4
1960	27.1	8.7	515.0	3.9	5.3
1961	29.1	7.1	534.0	3.6	5.4
1962	31.6	8.8	575.0	7.6	5.5
1963	34.4	8.9	607.0	5.6	5.7
1964	38.1	10.5	650.0	7.1	5.9
1965	41.6	9.4	705.0	8.5	5.9
1966	45.9	10.2	772.0	9.5	5.9
1967	51.7	12.6	816.0	5.8	6.3
1968	58.5	13.2	898.0	9.3	6.6
1969	65.7	12.4	964.0	7.9	6.8
1970	74.4	13.1	1016.0	5.4	7.3
1971	83.5	10.7	1103.0	8.6	7.5
1972	94.0	12.1	1213.0	10.0	7.6
1973	104.4	11.0	1659.0	12.1	7.5
1974	116.1	13.3	1473.0	8.3	7.9
1975	132.9	14.5	1598.0	8.5	8.3
1976	150.7	14.5	1783.0	11.5	8.5
1977	169.9	13.1	1991.0	11.7	8.6
1978	189.7	12.4	2250.0	13.0	8.6
1979	214.7	12.0	2508.0	11.5	8.6
1980	249.1	14.9	2732.0	8.9	9.1
1981	287.0	15.9	3053.0	11.7	9.5
1982	323.6	12.2	3166.0	3.7	10.2
1983	357.2	9.9	3406.0	7.6	10.5
1984	388.5	8.7	3772.0	10.7	10.3
1985	420.1	8.1	4015.0	6.4	10.5
1986	450.5	7.3	4232.0	5.4	10.6
1987	488.8	8.5	4516.0	6.7	10.8
1988	539.9	10.5	4874.0	7.9	11.1

Source: U.S. Department of Health and Human Services, Health Care Financing Administration and the U.S. Department of Commerce, *Survey of Current Business*, July 1989.

employee in 1990, a 21.6 percent increase over 1989.[6] At this rate, the study predicted, the cost per employee for health insurance will total $22,000 by the year 2000. The figures in Exhibit 1–3, while somewhat lower, illustrate similar, proportionately rapid increases in per-capita costs.

The factors underlying this inflationary trend, and the responses of management and labor to health care cost containment, are discussed in the following sections.

Exhibit 1-2 Health Care Cost Increases in the United States

CUMULATIVE PERCENT CHANGE SINCE 1980

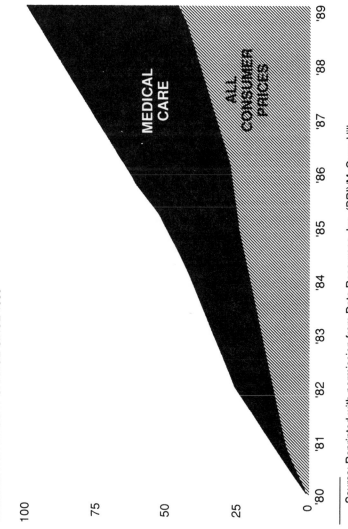

Source: Reprinted with permission from Data Resources, Inc. (DRI)/McGraw-Hill.
*First Nine Months, Annualized

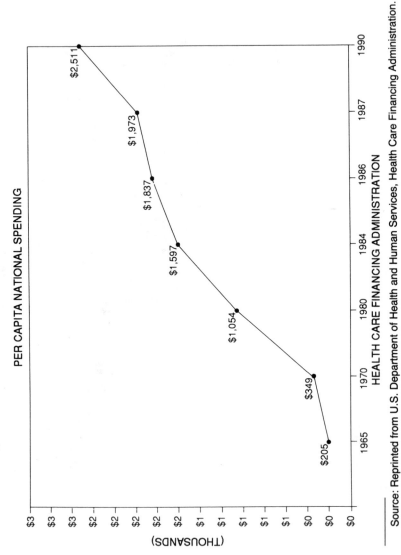

Exhibit 1-3 Rising Health Cost Per Person

PER CAPITA NATIONAL SPENDING

(THOUSANDS)

$2,511

$1,973

$1,837

$1,597

$1,054

$349

$205

1965 1970 1980 1984 1986 1987 1990

HEALTH CARE FINANCING ADMINISTRATION

Source: Reprinted from U.S. Department of Health and Human Services, Health Care Financing Administration.

Causes of Insurance Inflation

Five major factors have contributed to the increased costs of health care. These causes will be examined more fully in Chapter 2, but they merit brief discussion here.

A positive factor underlying health insurance price increases is that due to medical and technological advance, Americans are living longer and more productive lives. As a result, many more people are getting more medical attention, using more advanced and expensive treatments, over long periods of time.

A second factor increasing the cost of insurance is the overall acceleration of medical inflation. The annual rate of inflation for the cost of hospital services was 11 percent in 1989, compared with 6.6 percent in 1987.[7] Annual increases in doctors' fees and nurses' salaries, medical malpractice premiums, and advances in technology also contribute to inflation.

Third, utilization of health care services has increased significantly. This increase is due in part to more physician referrals for tests, medication, and treatment. The rising use of outpatient services, especially for surgery, has driven up some of these costs, although this trend also has reduced the number of overnight hospital stays.

A fourth reason for the rise in insurance rates relates to insurance company profitability, or more precisely, lack of profits. Both commercial insurance companies and Blue Cross/Blue Shield plans have experienced large losses in the last few years, and logic dictates passing these losses on to consumers through rate hikes. Some profit losses for traditional insurers may reflect increased competition from other forms of health care plans, such as HMOs and PPOs. Underpricing of premiums and inadequate management have also contributed to these losses. (Even HMOs have not proven profitable; only now are they merging and becoming more cost-efficient.)

A final factor is the shifting of health care costs, especially from the federal and state governments to business and labor. Restrictions on Medicare and Medicaid payment mean other insurance coverage must be utilized as the first payer. The most recognized form of cost shifting occurs when hospitals, doctors, and pharmacists raise the price of their services to the insured in order to cover the cost of treating the uninsured.

Impact on Management and Labor

While the problem of escalating health insurance costs has no one right answer, management has come up with three standard responses. One response is to require employees to share in the costs of health insurance so as to distribute the economic impact. The second response is to encourage employees to become more thoughtful and prudent users of health care. A third response is to redesign health insurance plans to offer either less dollar protection or less expensive benefits.

The management philosophy underlying these responses is that if employees share the increased costs of insurance, they will work harder at keeping costs down. All too often, however, this belief leads to an adversarial approach to bargaining, with management asserting that health insurance costs have been going up and that this spiral must stop. The 40 percent rate hikes have had devastating economic effects on companies, so employers naturally opt to shift some costs to employees.

The increasing management demands that employees should bear more of the burden of medical care has found little support among labor. Its bargaining position has held: "We never paid much for health insurance before, and we're not going to budge this year either." Employees have come to expect health insurance as a mainstay of their employment, and they often are willing to sacrifice salary increases in order to maintain fully paid benefits.

Costs of Non-Cooperation

The net result of these differing responses is polarization at the bargaining table. When neither side budges, strikes and bitter disagreements occur, with give-backs as a frequent result. Union leaders have lost elections when members lost or had to pay more for some health insurance benefits. Employers often underestimate future health insurance costs, and when rates increase, they must raise prices or cut services, staff and planned improvements to make ends meet. On the other hand, employees have very little influence on the health care industry and its costs, so the employer becomes the target of strikes when workers feel their benefits are threatened.

Recent contract negotiations illustrate the heightened importance of health care benefits to both labor and management. The United Auto Workers avoided a strike against the Big Three automakers in the fall of 1990, and members did not give back any of their health insurance benefits. In early 1991, a year-long dispute between American Airlines and the Allied Pilots Association was settled with respect to wages, but disagreement persisted over what amount pilots should pay for health coverage. The issue eventually went to arbitration under the auspices of the National Mediation Board.

Two of the more famous strikes over health care benefits involved the Pittston Company and NYNEX (the New York/New England Exchange Telephone Company). The Pittston settlement, reached after an 18-month strike, maintained a completely employer-paid health insurance plan, while NYNEX employees, after a long and bitter strike, accepted lower salary increases in order to maintain their health insurance benefits. In other negotiations, Bell Atlantic's management convinced its unions to accept an increase in their deductibles, including an additional $200 deductible for any treatment outside a prescribed network of doctors and hospitals. This telephone company settlement involved more than 160,000 telephone operators, installers, and repair workers in 15 states from two unions (the Communications Workers of America, and the International Brotherhood of Electrical Workers), and three regional phone companies (Bell Atlantic, NYNEX, and Pacific Telesis).

Benefits of Cooperation

Despite this polarization over benefits, employees and employers share a common goal on which they should be working cooperatively: controlling health insurance costs. A joint approach to understanding the nature of health care and health insurance can only improve bargaining results; equal knowledge is advantageous to both sides in this instance. Both management and labor can agree that healthy employees make for a better and more productive work force and that buying cost-effective medical protection benefits both sides.

Unlike salary negotiations, where the medium is dollars and bargaining alternatives are limited, bargaining over health care benefits also offers numerous and varied options. The choices range from preventative medicine to terminal and catastrophic illness protection, from a comprehensive, all-inclusive insurance policy to a mélange of add-on and cafeteria benefits. Close scrutiny of these choices and cooperation on cost control will serve everyone's best interests. After all, the fewer dollars spent on health care, the more "profit" for both management and labor.

For labor, less spending on health care means more take-home pay, or at least more salary dollars over which to negotiate. For management, controlling medical costs maximizes profits and helps the business to compete with companies in countries which have socialized health care and commensurately lower labor costs. Indeed, the impact of health care costs on U.S. companies' ability to compete globally often gets overlooked. The high wages paid U.S. workers are compounded by expensive fringe benefits like medical insurance. Aside from South Africa, the United States is the only country in the global market that has a capitalist, private-enterpirse type of health insurance.

In addition to improved labor-management negotiations, a shared understanding of health care costs can lead to more informed bargaining with health care providers and insurers. This book will attempt to provide some insight into ways labor and management can jointly negotiate more reasonably priced, quality health care. The negotiating strategies discussed will emphasize teamwork against and with health care providers. No doubt, any insurance dollars saved will prompt unions to ask for higher salaries while management will seek to get more work for less cost. This age-old struggle will not change, and this book is not intended as a guide to give either management or labor an edge. Instead, the intent is to offer guidelines for providing the best health care in the most efficient and economical manner.

While management does not need reminding of the astronomical costs of providing health care, union employees, for the most part, have only recently begun to take notice. Labor needs to understand that these costs have risen fivefold since 1960. Regardless of whether employers or employees foot the tab, the consumer continues to pay for the higher costs of health care.

Although both management and labor are losing dollars in profits and wages as a result of rising health care costs, physicians do not seem to have suffered. According to a recent study by the Employee Benefits Research Institute,[8] physicians' salaries have remained unchanged, even when accounting for the effects of inflation. As shown in Exhibit 1–4, increases in physician fees exceeded changes in the Consumer Price Index for three years, from 1985 to 1988. The supply of doctors, however, increased from 153 per 100,000 people in 1970 to 214 per 100,000 people in 1985.[9] Per capita medical costs obviously must increase for this heightened competition for patients to have no negative impact on doctors' incomes. By the year 2000, the supply of doctors should increase another 20 percent.[10] Whether prices will continue to increase along with the utilization of doctors remains to be seen, but the medical profession no doubt will strive at least to hold the line on income.

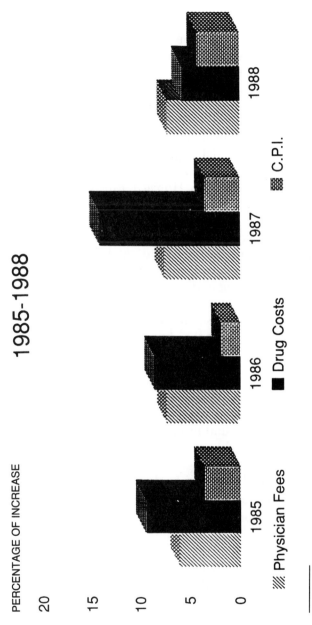

Exhibit 1-4 Increases in Physician Fees and Prescription Drug Costs vs. The Consumer Price Index

1985-1988

PERCENTAGE OF INCREASE

Physician Fees ▪ Drug Costs ▨ C.P.I.

Source: Reprinted with permission from D.R.I./McGraw-Hill.

Summary

Costs are of paramount concern in negotiating health insurance, yet understanding the nature of these costs can be a daunting task. Nonetheless, this understanding is essential to effective negotiations between labor and management, as well as between the buyers and suppliers of insurance products. This book will attempt to demystify much of the jargon and industry practices in order that both labor and management can get the most for their money.

During the initial stages of studying this process, both unions and management should realize that there is no quick fix to the problem. According to Howard Furman, commissioner of the Federal Mediation and Conciliation Service in Birmingham, AL, labor and management too often look only for the short-term solution and fail to consider what they will do in three years when the contract comes up for renegotiation.[11] Thus, any management proposals to share health care cost increases with workers without a cooperative effort at cost reduction will prove unrealistic in the long run.

The intent of this book is to provide some answers that will not only help in the short run, but also assist with long-term solutions. Informed and cooperative efforts to take advantage of health benefits at minimum cost poses a new challenge for labor and management in the last decade of the 20th century. To that end, this book provides chapters focusing on the following issues:

- the nature and pricing of health insurance;
- tactics used to shift or contain costs;
- bargaining strategies;
- data collection and other efforts to maintain and monitor health care contracts;
- education and available resources;
- the effects of government regulations;
- recommendations for responses to the five major causes of rising health care costs; and,
- an extensive discussion of proposed legislative changes on the national and state levels, as well as some new cooperative ventures by labor and management.

Notes

1. Channel 7 News, WHOH-TV, CBS, Boston, August 4, 1991.
2. Labor Institute of Public Affairs, AFL-CIO Department of Occupational Safety, Health, and Social Security, *Health Care Cost Containment*, Publication No. 175 (Washington, DC), 1.
3. *Inland Steel Co. v. NLRB*, 170 F2d 246, 22 LRRM 2506 (CA 7, 1948).
4. National Labor Relations Act, also known as the Wagner Act, was passed Jan. 5, 1935. It established the right of employees to self-organization, the machinery for holding elections to determine union preference, and the provision of exclusive bargaining rights for the union. Major amendments, passed in 1946 and collectively known as the Taft-Hartley Act, added many provisions spelling out the collective bargaining rights between employers and unions.
5. U.S. Department of Health and Human Services, Health Care Financing Administration, and U.S. Department of Commerce, *Survey of Current Business* (July 1989).
6. Bureau of National Affairs, Inc., *Pension Reporter* 18 (Feb. 4, 1991): 186. Article cites A. Foster Higgins & Co., Inc. "Medical Survey 1990," and quotes John Erb in news release of Jan. 19, 1991.
7. "CPI Pulse," *Medical Benefits* 7, no. 9 (May 15, 1990): 8. See also Exhibit 1-4.
8. Employee Benefits Research Institute, *Brief* 87 (February 1989): 5.
9. *Ibid.*
10. *Ibid.*
11. Howard Furman, discussion at Industrial Relations Research Association annual meeting, Dec. 29, 1990; also quoted in Bureau of National Affairs, Inc., *Daily Labor Report* (Jan. 3, 1991): A8–9.

Chapter 2

Understanding the Problem

The issue of rising health care costs is like a giant balloon that never deflates and almost never seems to stop expanding. Nonetheless, one of the most important ways to keep down health care costs is for labor and management to come to a joint understanding of the nature of the problem. They also should know what promises made by insurers will work and what will not work. Toward this end, this chapter supplies more details on the five major causes of soaring health care costs. (See Exhibit 2-1 for an overview of the factors contributing to rising health insurance costs.)

Improved Technology and Longevity

The first and most obvious reason for higher health care costs is that improved medical technology has lengthened the life spans of Americans (see Exhibit 2-2). It is wonderful that, as actuaries put it, "our mortality losses are increasing." However the consequence is costly when health care must be provided over a longer life span and on a more complex basis. Those who retire at or after age 65 now may enjoy another 20 to 30 years of life; 15 years ago, the life expectancy was much shorter. With increasing age, medical problems mount, and the increase in health care costs after age 65 contrasts dramatically with that of persons under 65. Providing health care protection for retirees is a problem of increasing concern to many labor unions and of special significance to management. However, this topic is not a major focus of this book. Others have written extensively on this topic and the reader is directed to Chapter 8 for a listing of several pertinent studies.

Aside from longer life expectancy, new diseases (like AIDS) and the availability of more medical technology to save lives contributes

Exhibit 2-1 The Forces Driving Health Care Costs

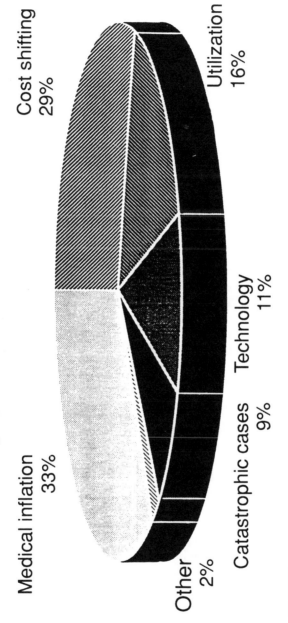

Medical inflation
33%

Cost shifting
29%

Utilization
16%

Technology
11%

Catastrophic cases
9%

Other
2%

Source: Reprinted with permission from New England Critical Care, 1989 Annual Report.

Exhibit 2-2 Trends in Death Rates (1920–1987)

DEATH RATES AND CAUSES (per 100,000 population)	1920	1940	1960	1980	1987
Death rates	1,298.9	1,076.4	954.7	874.1	872.4
Major causes of death					
Pneumonia and influenza	207.3	70.3	37.3	23.2	28.4
Diseases of the heart	159.6	292.5	369.0	335.9	312.4
Tuberculosis	113.1	45.9	6.1	*	*
Cerebrovascular diseases	93.0	90.9	108.0	75.0	61.6
Malignant neoplasms	83.4	120.3	149.2	182.4	195.9
Accidents	71.0	73.6	52.3	46.9	39.0
Infant mortality (per 1,000 live births)	NA	47.0	26.0	12.5	10.1
Maternal mortality (per 100,000 live births)	NA	376.0	37.1	6.9	6.6

---

*Not listed as a major cause of death.

Source: National Center for Health Statistics, Monthly Vital Statistics Report, September 26, 1989.

to expenses. More premature babies are surviving at earlier stages than ever before. The bill for one infant born three months premature can well exceed $1 million. MRI (magnetic resonance imaging), ultrasound, laser treatments, and arthroscopy are all new, effective, and expensive breakthroughs on the medical front. Exhibit 2-3 illustrates the costs associated with these new procedures.

In some cases, these technologies can actually help to reduce costs. For example, the use of laser surgery to remove kidney stones and arthroscopy for knee surgery has reduced recovery time by many days, with commensurate savings in costs. On the other hand, some new technologies may be used more often than necessary. For a variety of reasons—be it unfamiliarity with a new technique, desire to practice defensive medicine, or the need to bring in more dollars—physicians may order more diagnostic tests than are necessary. Employees need to be trained to ask the practitioner, "Is this really necessary? Will it make a difference?" One physician's response to this question, when asked by the father of an eleven year old with respect to an MRI test, was: "Well, it would not make much difference in the treatment and would not change the outcome." The test would have cost $325, so the father naturally chose to forgo the expense and saved his son the discomfort and inconvenience of the test.

Exhibit 2-3 Cost of High-Technology Medical Procedures (1989)

PROCEDURE	COST OF THE PROCEDURE TO THE PATIENT
Cardiovascular	
Thrombolytic agents (blood clot dissolver)	$ 8,000
PTCA (coronary angioplasty)	4,000
Pacemaker (advanced)	7,000
Implantable defibrillator	12,000
Orthopedics	
Bone growth devices for spinal surgery	6,000
Bone growth stimulator	2,000
Ear, nose, throat	
Cochlear implants	4,000
Urological	
Penile prosthesis	4,000
Drug delivery	
Implantable drug infusion pumps	1,800
Diagnostic imaging	
MRI (Magnetic resonance image)	850
High-speed Cine-CT	700
Other technologies	
Peripheral vascular angioplasty	4,000
Lithotripsy	10,000
Valvuloplasty (opening blocked aorta valve)	6,000

*Estimated costs of procedures include hospital costs only. Physicians' fees are not included.

Source: Reprinted with permission from Health Insurance Association of America, *Source Book of Health Insurance Data,* Washington, D.C. Based on information from The Wilkerson Group Project Hope, 1989.

Medical Cost Inflation

Advanced medical technology contributes to the second major cost increase factor—medical inflation. Other components of medical inflation include increased doctors' fees and nurses' salaries, as well as higher hospital rates (while vacancy rates are often at 40 percent). As shown in Exhibit 2-4, the rate of inflation for medical costs in some years has run almost double the inflation rate for other components of the Consumer Price Index.

In part, this inflation reflects the highly labor-intensive nature of the industry, as well as the extraordinary expenses of medical technology and equipment. Rationing quantities of equipment or limiting equipment sites is not popular with hospitals or clinics that want to retain the competitive edge by owning the latest medical technology. However, a portion of the medical inflation results from the administrative and processing costs of billing for medical treatment. The amount of paperwork and computer tracking required in this country has been cited as one of the major causes of the cost differences between Canadian and American health care.[1] Some 22 percent of health care costs in the United States is due to records processing, while in Canada, administrative costs make up only 9 percent of the total health care tab.

Proposals for regulation and review of rates have been one response to this medical inflation. Demands for a national form of health care plan similar to the one in Canada, are another response. Chapter 10 provides further discussion of these proposals, and of unions' efforts to form lobby groups to support state and national health care reform.

Utilization

The third factor contributing to rising health care costs is that utilization of health care services is provider-driven. That is, the

Exhibit 2-4 Percent Change in Major Components of Consumer Prices, Urban Consumers (1982–1991)

	1982	1983	1984	1985	1986	1987	1988	1989	1990	1991
All items	6.2	3.2	4.3	3.6	1.9	3.6	4.1	4.8	5.8	4.4
Food/beverages	4.1	2.3	3.7	2.3	3.3	4.0	4.1	5.7	4.8	2.8
Housing	7.2	2.7	4.1	4.0	3.0	3.0	3.8	3.8	4.3	2.8
Apparel/upkeep	2.6	2.5	1.9	2.8	0.9	4.4	4.3	2.8	10.5	4.6
Transportation	11.6	8.8	6.2	6.3	7.5	6.6	6.5	5.0	5.3	4.8
Medical care	11.6	8.8	6.2	6.3	7.5	6.6	6.5	7.7	9.9	11.6
Entertainment	6.5	4.3	3.7	3.9	3.4	3.3	4.3	6.4	7.9	5.5
Other goods and services	10.3	11.0	6.7	6.1	6.0	5.8	6.3	7.8	9.8	8.7

Source: U.S. Department of Labor, Monthly Labor Review.

medical community, not the consumer, decides what services to provide to the "consumer." As a result, services are offered more often to those who can afford them through health insurance than to those who are uninsured. (Those who have insurance or who can pay also subsidize what services the uninsured and indigent do receive.) A congressional staff report released in 1989 estimated that upwards of 20 percent of medical services, costing $125 billion a year, may be unnecessary.[2] The suggested antidote was to encourage development of standards of effectiveness based on research of various tests and procedures.

Some cost-containment measures have worked so well that the medical community has developed ways to get around them. Thus charges for medical care have simply shifted from hospital stays to outpatient services. In 1987, to give an example, the decreasing number of inpatient admissions was indicative of the increasing popularity of outpatient procedures. Thus outpatient treatment and emergency patient volume made up for losses in other areas.[3] Preadmission and concurrent reviews of hospital stays, incentives for outpatient testing and surgery, and requirements for second surgical opinions have resulted in fewer hospital admissions and shorter stays. However, providers have been creative in making up for lost revenues by charging more for outpatient facility usage, which rarely requires preadmission certification or authorization of treatment. Implementing more controls over outpatient services would provide a short-term solution, but the health insurance balloon probably would inflate somewhere else. Future chapters discuss this problem in more detail.

Another aspect of provider-driven cost increases concerns the diagnostic or treatment facilities to which patients are referred. A growing prevalence of x-ray clinics and diagnostic labs are owned by physician investors who stand to profit by referring their patients for services. Indeed, these physician-owned centers tend to prescribe more tests per patient and charge higher costs for these tests than similar labs and centers that are not physician owned.[4] The federal government has attempted reform in this area by issuing regulations restricting referrals of Medicaid and Medicare patients to facilities in which the doctor has a financial stake.

Profit Margins

Another reason for increased costs is the lack of profitability associated with health insurance. Not only has the health insurance industry been hard hit by the recession of the early 1990s, but other aspects of the business, such as life and casualty insurers, have also been undergoing difficult times.[5] In fact, some companies are leaving the health insurance business and fewer are interested in entering the field. Consolidation often occurs. In terms of health insurance companies, many of the Blues have faced staggering losses, even those that are non-profit. In trying to keep afloat, insurers have increased their product rates quite rapidly. While the 20 to 60 percent increases of the last several years may slow down somewhat in the mid-1990s, many in the business feel that this moderating trend is a cyclical phenomenon as prices are not coming down.

HMOs and PPOs have offered some cost containment, but these organizations also have raised their rates almost as fast as other health care providers. The inability of discount fee arrangements to reduce overall costs is believed by some consultants to reflect the "usual, customary, and reasonable" (UCR) rates and/or the "customary, prevailing, and reasonable" (CPR) limits used under Medicare. While UCR and CPR rates disallow a small portion of the highest physicians' fees, they have no effect in containing the escalating annual increases. In addition, expensive procedures eventually become commonplace and less expensive, so thus are rarely challenged by Medicare. As a result, UCR and CPR rates are "rewarding complicated surgical procedures over services that require more diagnostic and management skill, providing disproportionately high reimbursement for inpatient services, and encouraging physicians to break down treatment into a greater number of billable services."[6]

While the discount fee providers in PPOs and HMOs have not always been profitable, recent consolidations, reforms made by the 1988 HMO Reform Act (see Appendix 1 for a summary), and some stricter state regulations of HMOs, have helped turn some around. Others, however, have been forced to go out of business or consolidate. One notable example of consolidation involved the acquisition of EQUICORP by CIGNA, which should produce the largest health insurance network in the country. Measures beyond mergers and reorganizations, however, are needed to effect reform in this area. Further discussion of efforts that management and unions can undertake are provided in later chapters.

Cost Shifting

The fifth cause of cost increases is the shifting sands of who must bear the cost—government, the independent entity, or the individual. Of late, the government has shifted more of the burden from itself to other payers. While management and labor have little control over this trend, both sides must be informed about government regulations so as to avoid any unnecessary penalties and to take advantage of tax breaks. Moreover, the lack of state regulations in self-funded plans means that management may prefer this less regulated option. Labor may have to exercise oversight to ensure such plans provide comparability and effective coverage. (For a fuller discussion of government regulations, see Chapter 9).

Some government regulations currently serve as an incentive for employers to provide medical insurance because the benefits are not taxable to the employees and the provision of health insurance by the employer is an allowable and deductible business expense with the Internal Revenue Service. However, Congress may not continue to provide this tax incentive in its present full form. Instead of a direct tax, Congress may levy a surtax on premiums as it looks to increase revenues to avoid a larger deficit.

Covering Retirees and Older Workers

Recent accounting mandates that will cause problems for business require disclosure on a company account balance sheet for the employer's financial obligation to provide promised health care to its retirees. Both the Financial Accounting Standards Board,[7] whose standards affect private-sector employers, and the Government Accounting Standards Board,[8] which advises the public sector, recently have adopted such requirements. The standards specify that retiree health benefits are a form of deferred compensation and no longer should be funded on a pay-as-you-go (cash) basis or on a terminal accrual (accrue at retirement) basis. Private-sector companies will be required to begin the process by 1993, while public-sector employers may have to implement the regulations by 1994. Actual recording of a minimum liability is essential by 1997 in the private sector.[9]

At present, 80 percent of employers who offer retiree benefits fund the program on a pay-as-you-go basis.[10] For companies with a significant number of retirees, this health care cost would increase by three to six times in the first year of the rule change.[11] Even if companies have only a small number of retirees, the accrual method would increase costs by 30 times the present amount spent on a pay-as-you-go basis.

The Omnibus Budget Reconciliation Act of 1990 provided a way to avoid part of the anticipated financial crisis, permitting employers to transfer some excess pension assets to retiree health insurance accounts. The law allows a pension or annuity plan to pay benefits for sickness, accident hospitalization, and medical expenses of retired employees, their spouses, and dependents under certain conditions, which include subordinating those benefits to retirement benefits and establishing a separate account for them.

Medicare also involves cost shifting. When first instituted, Medicare provided most of the medical insurance for individuals over age 65 who were employed. Now, however, Medicare requires the employer's plan to pay before Medicare does. Again, Chapter 9 provides a more detailed discussion of this issue.

Providing for the Unemployed and Uninsured

Another example of the federal government shifting costs to the private payer is a requirement that employers continue to cover laid-off or terminated workers and their families under company plans for as long as 18 to 36 months. Some state regulations also require coverage continuation of retired workers under state or municipal health insurance plans on the same basis as active employees. All of these requirements increase premiums since former workers who avail themselves of the plan usually have higher health risks and are more likely to use the plan with greater frequency than the active work force. (For a more detailed discussion of this problem, see Chapter 9.)

Treating the uninsured is the most expensive aspect of cost shifting. Although many of the uninsured go without treatment under ordinary circumstances, when an emergency exists, the uninsured are given treatment under the requirements of the Hill Burton Act that helps finance hospitals.[13] The cost of treatment is born by the caregiver: the hospital, the physician, the clinic, the pharmacy, or the psychologist. Naturally, this requirement affects providers' profits as they receive no reimbursement. In turn, providers pass these costs on to others who do pay the bills.

In 1989, the Pepper Commission estimated that between 30 to 37 million Americans were without health insurance,[14] today, some estimate the figure to be nearly 54 million.[15] The largest category of uninsured persons are full-time workers, followed, in order, by students and preschool children, homemakers and part-time workers, and, more recently, the newly unemployed. An analysis done for the state of Rhode Island revealed that only 23 percent of the state's uninsured were considered to be impoverished; in fact, some 12 percent were considered to be in a high economic class.[16]

Summary

Cost shifting from management to labor may defray the health care bill for management. Given the many causes of escalating health insurance costs discussed here, cost shifting, used alone, will do little to bring down the high costs of medical care. Many other answers must be found to solve the overall problem. The remaining chapters of this book concentrate on the essentials of how to shop for a plan and negotiate with each other and with providers for the best and least expensive healthcare insurance. Readers will find that there is no one right solution to health care costs nor is there any one strategy for negotiating the best health insurance protection.

What works today will be ineffective tomorrow, and new solutions must be sought and tried each year. As a result, management and labor need to work together in an ongoing partnership to deal with health care issues. Cooperative efforts by management and national trade unions should focus on the overall problem as it exists on both the state and national levels. The concluding chapter of this book offers more insight into these broader efforts to address healthcare issues. Since many predict that true reform will take at least 10 years, the following chapters offer a practical guide on how to get the best deal today.

Notes

1. David U. Hemmelstein, M.D., speech before National Education Association Health Benefits Forum (April 30, 1990), Hollywood, FL.
2. Democratic Staff of Joint Economic Committee and Rep. James H. Scheuer (D-NY), chairman of the Health subcommittee, report released Oct. 3, 1989. See also "Medicare Reform, Waste Cutting Needed to Avoid Crisis, Report Says," *New London Day* (10/3/89):_____.
3. Landmark Medical Center, 1989 Report, Appendix G.
4. Health Insurance Association of America, *Source Book of Health Insurance Data 1990*, Table 2.14 "Underwriting Results for Insurance Companies and Blue Cross/Blue Shield Plans (1984-1988)," Washington, DC. HIAA, 1991), 30.
5. Ron Winslow, "AT&T's Plan on Health Insurance May Set Pattern," *Wall St. Journal,* July 19, 1990. p B1.
6. Robert Krinsky, president, Martin Segal Co., "Health Benefits and Rising Costs," *Pension World* (August 1989): 47–51.

7. Financial Accounting Standards Board statement no. 106, "Employers; Accounting for Post Retirement Benefits Other than Pensions," requires many companies to record a liability for retiree health benefits on their balance sheets, beginning with the fiscal year following Dec. 15, 1992. See also *EBRI Issue Brief* no. 112 (March 1991).
8. Government Accounting Standards Board, statement no. 12. See Charles D Spencer and Associates, Inc., *Spencer's Research Reports on Employee Benefits* 303 (Feb. 22, 1991): 3–13.
9. Coopers and Lybrand, "NAA Study of Retiree Health Benefits: How to Cope with the Accounting, Actuarial, and Management Issues," *Actuarial Benefits and Compensation Information Release* (Jan. 23, 1991). See also Murray S. Akresh, Barbara S. Bald, Harold Dankner, Lee E. Launer, Teresa A. McKenna, and Richard J. Poccia of Coopers and Lybrand, "NAA Study of Retiree Health Benefits: How to Cope with the Accounting, Actuarial, and Management Issues," (Washington, DC: National Association of Accountants, 1990).
10. *Ibid.*
11. *Ibid.*
12. ERISA Section 401(h). See *ERISA, The Law and the Code, 1991 Ed.*, p. 352. See also Coopers and Lybrand, "Reversion of Excess Pension Assets," *Actuarial Benefits and Compensation Information Release* (Nov. 8, 1990): 1–5.
13. Hill Burton Act
14. U.S. Bipartisan Commission on Comprehensive Health Care (The Pepper Commission), assorted reports (10 in all) (Washington, DC: GPO, 1990).
15. Mel Glassner, speech before the National Education Association Health Benefits Strategy Conference, St. Petersburg, FL, April 26, 1991.
16. Rhode Island Department of Health, Office of Data Evaluation, *NEWSLETTER* (May 1988): 3.

Appendix A

Landmark Medical Center—Data Through the Decades

Nothing protrays the unparalleled increases in health care costs more clearly than an inspection of medical records from an historical perspective. Below is a table that illustrates how sharp those increases have been at Landmark Medical Center.

Fiscal Year	Number of Patients	Average Length of Stay	Average Daily Census	Patient Days
1893	97	41.8	11.2	4,088
1903	150	24.8	10.8	3,944
1913	492	20.0	27.0	9,855
1923	1,365	10.5	39.2	14,312
1933	1,997	9.3	51.0	18,633
1943	4,743	8.6	112.0	40,801
1953	8,170	6.0	134.3	49,020
1963	9,729	7.9	209.8	76,560
1972	10,664	8.1	234.6	85,873
1987	8,168	7.4	148.0	56,480

The recent trend toward a decreasing number of inpatient admissions is indicative of the increasing popularity of outpatient procedures and outpatient testing. Conversely, the Average Length of Stay has risen since 1953. This represents the fact that those patients who are actually admitted to the hospital are much sicker than in previous decades. The overall decrease in patient days reflects the impact of technological advances.

Furthermore, outpatient admissions and a large emergency patient volume make up for the losses in other areas. In 1987 alone, the emergency department at Landmark's Woonsocket Unit treated over 33,000 patients.

****

Number and Cost of Hospital Beds

Year	Number of Beds	Room Rates: Intensive Care	Semi-Private
1926–1940	102	$7.00	$7.00
1959–1962	181	$30.00	$25.00
1965–1975	267	$179.00	$79.50
1989	315	$775.00	$335.00

(The information available for years prior to 1926 is incomplete. Records indicate, however, that as many as 25 beds may have been available.)

Chapter 3

Selecting a Type of Health Insurance

Four major types of health insurance plans can be purchased today, and the following discussion describes each type in detail and gives guidelines to consider prior to purchasing a particular plan. Before proceeding to this discussion, however, a caveat regarding nomenclature is merited. The terms attached to these plans often vary, much in the way "Kleenex" can be used as either a brand name or a synonym for tissue. While this book utilizes the more common terminology, no one name is universally accepted as the proper term for each of the four general classes of health insurance. Moreover, various gradations of each type exist, and no one product is a pure distillation of the general categories as described below.

Types of Insurance

With the preceding caveats in mind, the four types of plans that exist today include the following:

Traditional insurance or a basic indemnity plan that provides first-dollar coverage is the type most preferred by unions. It also is the most expensive but generous of the plans offered.

A *comprehensive or wraparound plan* is similar to a basic indemnity plan. It has some deductibles and co-payment requirements, but it still provides comprehensive coverage in that it protects employees against serious financial loss. It also costs less than first-dollar coverage.

Managed care plans began many years ago as health maintenance organizations (HMOs). Now some physician consortiums, known as preferred provider organizations (PPOs) and individual (or independent) practice associations (IPAs), have been formed to manage costs by offering discounts. More preventative in nature, managed care plans generally provide full protection in that subscribers incur no additional expenses other than their premiums (and a co-pay charge if specified). These plans, however, severely limit the choice of hospitals and doctors, and may or may not cost less than traditional first dollar plans. (Note: Some IPAs function as HMOs.)

A *flexible benefit or cafeteria plan* provides a predetermined amount of employee benefit dollars, paid by the employer, and a menu of benefits from which an employee selects the types of coverage desired. This plan offers a more customized fit of insurance; however, it may cost employees more since they pay for any additional benefits or cost increases beyond the employer's original contribution.

Details of these plans, as well as their relative advantages and disadvantages (summarized in Exhibit 3-1), are discussed below. For comparative purposes, Exhibit 3-2 provides a simplified example to illustrate how differences between plans might affect an actual claim.

Exhibit 3-1 Comparison of the Four Categories of Insurance Plans

PLAN FEATURE	PLAN TYPE			
	TRADITIONAL	COMPREHENSIVE	MANAGED CARE	CAFETERIA
Choice of Provider	unrestricted	unrestricted	limited	depends
Cost	most costly type for management, least costly type for employees	less costly to employers, more costly to labor, compared to traditional	some saving for management, none for labor	savings for both vary
Quality of Care	depends on employee's choice of providers	depends on employee's choice of providers	depends on network's selection of doctors	depends on employee's choice of providers
Ease of Access	depends on employee's choice of providers	depends on employee's choice of providers	depends on network's selection of doctors	depends on employee's choice of providers
Administration and Paperwork	very little, if a Blue plan is used	some	none	depends on type of plan

Exhibit 3-2 Comparison of Claim Coverage Under Four Different Plans

EXAMPLE: Jane's knee troubles have made it painful to work out, so she visits her physician. The doctor suggests that Jane have some exploratory arthroscopy done to determine what is wrong, and this minor surgical procedure is performed on an outpatient basis the next day.

TRADITIONAL INSURANCE PLAN

Jane's indemnity plan provides first-dollar coverage of the "usual, customary, and reasonable" rates charges for office visits and surgery. Since Jane's surgical costs exceed the UCR by $150, she submits the remainder to her major medical plan, which has a $100 deductible and 20 percent copayment feature. The costs to Jane and the insurance plan break down as follows:

SERVICE	CHARGE	JANE PAYS	PLAN PAYS
Doctor visit	$ 50	$ 0	$ 50 (UCR allowed)
Arthroscopy	$500	$100 (deductible)	$350 (UCR allowed)
		$ 10 (20% of $50)	$ 40 (80% of $50)
Totals	$550	$110	$440

COMPREHENSIVE PLAN

Under a comprehensive plan, Jane has no first-dollar coverage. Instead, all costs from the outset are subject to the plan's $100 deductible and 20 percent copayment features. As a result, Jane pays $80 more than she would under the traditional indemnity plan:

SERVICE	CHARGE	JANE PAYS	PLAN PAYS
Doctor visit	$ 50	$ 50 (toward $100 deductible)	$ 0
Arthroscopy	$500	$ 50 (remainder of deductible)	$360 (80% of $450)
		$ 90 (20% of $450)	
Totals	$550	$190	$360

MANAGED CARE

Jane belongs to an HMO that provides full coverage of office visits and medically necessary surgery, provided the network's physicians are used. Since Jane utilized her HMO's doctors, the plan pays all costs and Jane has no out-of-pocket expenses.

FLEXIBLE BENEFIT PROGRAM

Jane has a "core plus" flexible benefit package that provides basic and major medical insurance. Like the comprehensive plan, Jane's flexible benefit program offers no first-dollar coverage, and all costs are subject to a $100 deductible and 20 percent copayment requirement. As a result, Jane's cost under this program are identical to those under the comprehensive plan. [Note: For ready comparison, the deductibles and copay requirements have been kept the same. In real life, however, both features may vary, with higher out-of-pocket costs as a potential result.]

Traditional Insurance or Basic Indemnity Plan

The first type of medical insurance, which may or may not provide true first-dollar coverage, is often called a basic indemnity or traditional insurance plan. This plan usually provides three categories of benefits: (1) hospital, (2) medical/surgical, and (3) supplemental major medical, which provides protection for medical care not covered under the two categories. Variations and riders to these plans may offer coverage for maternity care, prescription drugs, home and office visits, and other medical expenses.

In most instances, copayment requirements and deductibles do not apply to expenses covered under the hospital or medical/surgical benefit categories. Thus, traditional insurance plans provide some first-dollar coverage, since employees may receive full reimbursement of all expenses covered by the hospital or medical/surgical benefit categories. The only exception would arise if the claim exceeded the "usual, customary, and reasonable" (UCR) charge for a particular benefit. In this case, most policies reimburse only the UCR charge, and the patient would submit the remainder of the bill for payment under the major medical category.

For the major medical component, most traditional plans do have copayment and deductible requirements, with maximum family limits. Deductibles can vary from $50 to $250 or more per person, while copayment provisions usually require an employee to pay 20 percent of the first $2,000 to $5,000 or more of expenses. Under most basic indemnity plans, the deductible must be met every year. Some policies, however, may allow a two-year period for fulfilling the deductible, while others with annual deductibles may extend the year by three months, thus allowing employees to apply expenses toward the deductible over 15 months.

This type of plan is often called the Cadillac of insurance policies since it supplies first-dollar coverage for major expenses without restricting choice of providers. It offers a great deal of protection to employees, who pay little out-of-pocket for their medical care.

Comprehensive Plans

The second alternative is a comprehensive plan, also sometimes called a wraparound plan. Despite the name, comprehensive plans do not supply coverage as extensive as that of traditional insurance. Instead, these plans are labelled "comprehensive" because they have no separate categories of insurance coverage. Workers will foot more out-of-pocket medical expenses under these plans, but their premiums will usually be lower since the insurer provides less dollar payout.

A comprehensive plan operates basically like a full major medical plan, with per-person and per-family deductibles, as well as copayment requirements. Under a comprehensive plan, an employee must pay the first dollars of any medical expenses and fulfill the deductible before the insurer pays anything. Deductible amounts can vary from $50 to $500 or more per individual, and may or may not have a family cap over a one- or two-year period. The co-payment requirement in a comprehensive plan applies immediately to *all* costs incurred after the deductible is met. Typical co-payment provisions require the employee to pay 20 percent of the first $2,000 to $5,000 or. more of expenses.

Thus, the primary difference between comprehensive and basic indemnity plans is the lack of any first-dollar coverage in a comprehensive plan. Employees covered by a comprehensive plan will always pay a portion of any medical costs incurred during the plan year. In contrast, basic indemnity plans fully reimburse the UCR charges for hospital and medical/surgical expenses, and only excess charges are subject to the major medical co-payment deductible requirements.

Managed Care Plans

As of 1989, over 2.5 million persons were enrolled in 47 multi-state HMOs, the most popular form of a managed care plan.[1] Kaiser Permanente, one of the earliest HMOs, now ranks as one of the best-known and largest managed care plans in the country, accounting for nearly one of every four HMO members.[2]

Managed care plans come in two basic forms. The first type, sometimes referred to as a staff or group model health maintenance organization, encompasses the traditional HMO model used by organizations like Kaiser Permanente. This model operates as a group practice of physicians teamed in one or more clinic(s). The physicians are salaried employees of the HMO, and a patient's choice of doctors is often determined by who is on call when the patient visits.

The second type of managed care plan is known as an individual (or independent) practice association (IPA) or a preferred provider organization (PPO), each of which is a network of doctors who work individually out of their own offices. This arrangement gives the patient some degree of choice within the group. If a patient goes outside the network, however, the plan reimburses at a lower percent. Thus, enrollees' freedom of choice is limited by their willingness or ability to incur higher costs. Generally an IPA may be prepaid, while a PPO is similar to an indemnity plan, in that claims may be filed and reimbursed at a predetermined rate if the services of a participating doctor are utilized. Some IPAs function as HMOs.

Unlike many traditional insurance and comprehensive plans, HMOs emphasize preventative care and routinely cover annual checkups. Most staff models also provide a significant amount of services on the premises, thus eliminating trips to specialized labs, outpatient clinics, or diagnostic groups. Many, however, offer only limited resources for mental health or substance abuse treatment.

Some experts contend that HMOs provide inferior care to that offered by independent physicians, while others believe that HMOs offer care equal to, if not better than, that of traditional providers. Major disadvantages of an HMO are that patients must give up their usual doctor and deal with more bureaucracy. The offsetting advantage is that most HMOs do not exclude pre-existing health problems or place other time or cost limitations on the services offered.

For many years, HMOs were not very profitable, but their finances are once again becoming healthy. This upswing partly reflects recent mergers and improvements in the overall management of HMOs. In addition, 1988 modifications to the original HMO Act of 1973 have loosened restrictions and allowed HMOs to become more competitive.[3] While the 1988 amendments are discussed more fully in Chapter 9 and summarized in Appendix 1, the following discussion highlights some of the federal regulations governing HMO operations.

Federal and State HMO Regulations

Managed care groups that are federally qualified under the HMO Act must meet standards requiring:

- A wide scope of inpatient, outpatient, and physician services.
- Fiscally sound operations, with set financial reserves or guarantees from a parent company to protect against insolvency.
- Satisfactory administrative and managerial arrangements, with adequate delivery capabilities to care for the HMO's anticipated enrollment, and a system to meet its goals.
- HMO member participation on the board of directors.
- Ongoing quality assurance programs.
- Reporting and disclosure procedures.

The HMO Act also requires that an employer's contribution to an HMO plan must not discriminate against the HMO. Thus, the employer's contribution to the HMO plan must equate in some form—such as equal dollar amounts, equal percentage contributions, and so on—with the contribution that the employer would have made to another type of insurance.

Other federal HMO requirements, which apply until 1995 under the 1988 amendments, allow employees a dual-choice option. This option is also mandated under some state laws, including those in Connecticut, Michigan, New York, Ohio, Rhode Island, Tennessee, Washington, and West Virginia.[4] Under a dual-choice requirement, an employer with 25 or more employees must, upon the request of an HMO, offer the HMO as an alternative to the standard benefit coverage. If workers' health care is subject to a collective bargaining agreement, the offer must be made to the bargaining unit (the union), which can accept or reject the offer on behalf of employees.

The federal dual-choice requirement, until the 1988 amendments were enacted, applied only if the employer's contribution to the HMO would be the same as that paid for other types of insurance. Since many HMOs, when first instituted, had costs higher than those of regular insurance plans, a significant number were unable to compete and were excluded from consideration.

Today, cost-competitive HMOs are proliferating and many no longer seek to become federally qualified, thus avoiding some regulatory requirements. Other forms of managed care that are not federally regulated have also arisen. One such innovation, known as a point-of-service plan, consists of various consortiums which may include providers, insurance companies, or, in some instances, consumer groups. Exhibits 3-3 and 3-4 (see pp. 38–39) provide more information on this growth in the managed care field.

For managed care operations that are not federally qualified under the HMO Act, ERISA (The Employee Retirement Income Security Act),[5] or state laws governing insurance companies may apply. Ongoing jurisdictional disputes have arisen regarding the regulation of HMOs, and as yet, no definitive answer has come from the courts. In general, state laws are allowed to ensure the quality of care and regulate an HMO's financial solvency. According to the federal government, states can apply their regulations governing insurance companies to HMOs, unless the HMO involves an employee welfare plan. In the latter case, the federal government

Exhibit 3-3 47 Multistate HMO Networks Now Operating in U.S.

MULTISTATE HMO COMPANIES AND NETWORKS

COMPANY NAME	1989 HMOs	1989 ENROLLMENT	1988 HMOs	1988 ENROLLMENT	1987 HMOs	1987 ENROLLMENT	'88-'89 ENROLLMENT PERCENTAGE CHANGE	'87-'88 ENROLLMENT PERCENTAGE CHANGE
Aetna Life & Casualty	24	773,079	4	527,067	6	398,136	46.7%	31.6%
Amer. Health Network	2	6,300	—	4,892	—	62	28.8%	7790.3%
Amer. Healthcare Prov.	3	64,100	—	57,200	—	24,557	12.1%	132.9%
American Medical Intl.	1	181,116	3	161,672	3	146,464	12.0%	10.4%
Blue Cross/Blue Shield	85	4,244,242	97	4,159,051	99	3,874,978	2.1%	7.3%
Capital Area Comm. HP	6	171,810	5	169,813	5	184,631	1.2%	−8.0%
CIGNA Healthplan(a)	29	1,484,677	31	1,431,071	28	1,206,655	3.7%	18.6%
Complete Health Inc.	2	121,900	—	79,750	—	39,914	52.9%	99.8%
Coventry Corp.	2	142,000	—	131,615	—	131,226	7.9%	0.3%
Equicor Health Plans(a)	21	435,119	19	424,086	24	413,324	2.6%	2.6%
Family Health Plan	2	111,146	2	108,210	2	96,445	2.7%	12.2%
FHP International Corp.	3	182,800	4	166,974	4	125,410	9.5%	33.1%
Foundation Health Corp.	3	544,629	6	450,277	6	187,932	21.0%	139.6%
Group Health (Puget S.)	3	65,467	4	53,810	5	45,128	21.7%	19.2%
Health Power	3	46,000	3	43,850	3	24,281	4.9%	80.6%
HealthCare Corp. of Am.	3	144,687	3	159,298	3	145,037	−9.2%	9.8%
Healthsource	4	66,183	—	64,600	—	40,684	2.5%	58.8%
Heritage Health System	2	122,184	2	109,450	2	89,107	11.6%	22.8%
Heritage National HP	1	168,000	3	167,000	3	94,882	.6%	76.0%
HIP of Greater NY	3	1,030,708	3	1,058,500	3	966,605	−2.6%	9.5%

HMO America	2	167,341	2	148,836	2	140,453	12.4%	6.0%
Humana Health Care	14	627,974	13	517,113	19	584,931	21.4%	−11.6%
Independent Health	3	231,239	2	195,759	2	169,868	18.1%	15.2%
Kaiser Foundation HP(b)	14	6,144,927	14	5,638,824	14	5,174,280	9.0%	9.0%
Lincoln Natl. Life Ins.	17	401,465	17	329,855	12	269,948	21.7%	22.2%
Maxicare HP Inc.(c)	7	356,074	24	760,597	44	843,209	−53.2%	−9.8%
Mercy Alternatives	5	108,330	5	88,960	4	49,697	21.8%	79.0%
MetLife Healthcare	23	525,033	22	451,229	21	264,412	16.4%	70.7%
Ochsner Medical Corp.	2	65,910	2	61,108	2	57,957	7.9%	5.4%
PacifiCare Health Syst.	5	746,670	5	424,162	4	299,977	76.0%	41.4%
Partners National HP	5	179,525	24	123,390	18	100,130	45.5%	23.2%
Physician Corp. of Amer.	2	79,594	—	68,480	—	49,405	16.2%	38.6%
Physicians Health Svc.	2	129,800	—	115,103	—	94,660	12.8%	21.6%
Principal Financial Grp.	5	98,379	—	75,296	—	35,490	30.7%	112.2%
Prucare (Prudential Ins.)	25	703,099	23	787,681	24	799,022	−10.7%	1.4%
Qual Med Inc.	7	104,908	5	95,443	5	66,529	9.9%	43.5%
Sanus Health Plan	5	529,100	5	461,863	5	263,237	14.6%	75.5%
Santa Fe Healthcare	5	276,391	—	119,496	—	97,374	131.3%	22.7%
Sentara Health System	2	102,304	2	71,772	2	63,106	42.5%	13.7%
Sisters of Providence	2	66,841	—	41,595	—	26,835	60.7%	55.0%
The HMO Group (e)	15	1,855,700	15	1,759,090	14	1,565,748	5.4%	12.3%
The Wellcare Mgmt. Grp.	2	28,869	2	18,616	2	13,103	55.0%	42.1%
Travelers Health Netwk.	10	116,669	10	142,303	15	104,897	−18.0%	35.7%
United Healthcare Corp.	14	1,030,662	20	981,650	36	1,007,505	5.0%	−2.6%
United Healthcare Corp./ Omnicare	3	110,909	3	95,717	3	79,357	15.9%	20.6%
U.S. Healthcare Inc.	7	970,862	7	853,876	8	557,566	13.7%	53.1%
Wausau Insurance	6	75,818	6	70,284	6	73,393	7.9%	−4.2%
TOTAL U.S.	411	25,863,946	417	24,026,284	458	21,087,547	7.6%	13.9%

Exhibit 3-3   *Continued*

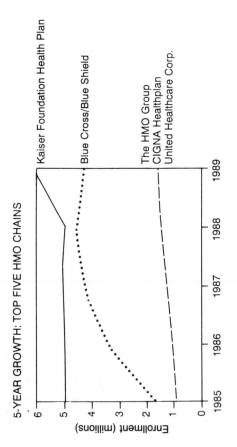

5-YEAR GROWTH: TOP FIVE HMO CHAINS

Kaiser Foundation Health Plan

Blue Cross/Blue Shield

The HMO Group
CIGNA Healthplan
United Healthcare Corp.

NOTES:
a. CIGNA Healthplan acquired 19 Equicor Health Plans that enrolled 450,000 members on March 29, 1990. CIGNA and Equicor operated overlapping plans in 9 markets when they merged. As of April 27, no action had been taken to merge, combine or close any of the 18 overlapping plans.
   Markets in which CIGNA and Equicor plans duplicated each other were in Phoenix/Tucson, Los Angeles, Denver, Ft. Lauderdale/Miami, Tampa, Chicago, Kansas City, Dallas and Houston
b. Kaiser Foundation Health Plan enrollment for 1988 has been revised to correct an inaccuracy in the 1989 Digest.
c. Maxicare Health Plans Inc. sold many of its plans during 1989 after filing for protection under the bankruptcy laws March 15, 1989.
d. John Hancock Health Plan HMOs, which appeared on this list in the 1989 Digest, were sold during February, 1989 to several different companies.
e. The HMO Group, begun in 1984, is a membership organization, owned by its members, that operates as a national HMO network on national accounts.

Source: Reprinted with permission from *Managed Care Digest, HMO Edition 1990*, Marion Merrell Dow, Inc., Kansas City, MO.

believes ERISA and other relevant standards of the federal HMO Act should apply.

These legal ambiguities and liability issues present an ongoing concern for employers looking into enrolling in an HMO plan. At a recent conference on these topics sponsored by the National Health Lawyers Association,[6] the main conclusion was that the HMO field is still vaguely defined and in need of better organization. While conference participants agreed that the proliferating variations of HMOs offer greater choice and responsiveness to individual needs, most cited the need for more comparative data and information.

Flexible Benefit or Cafeteria Plans

Flexible benefit plans operate rather like a defined contribution pension plan in that the employer pays a fixed and predetermined amount. Employees generally share some portion of the plan's premium costs and thus are at risk if costs go up. An employee's contributions, however, can be paid from gross salary before taxes are applied (i.e., in pretax dollars).

Since flexible benefit plans allow employees to pick what benefits they want, labor-management negotiations may focus more on the employer's dollar contributions than on plan design. Unlike other forms of insurance, the employer's annual payment is fixed, and employees must shop to buy the best benefits for this fixed amount. Any benefits costing more than the employer has contributed must be purchased at the employee's cost. In addition, when the costs of current benefits increase, the employee must decide whether to spend more money or to sacrifice benefits—unless the employer agrees to share a portion of the rising costs. As a result of this fixed-contribution feature, unions tend to view flexible benefit plans as an easy way for management to control its expenditures for health insurance.

To give a practical example, instead of paying premiums to an insurance company, an employer can simply agree to allocate a fixed sum of, say, $3,000 per employee for health-related benefits. Employees then may choose which benefits to purchase from several options. Any benefits that bring the plan's cost to more than $3,000 will be paid by the employee. The employer also can stipulate how much its contribution in future years will increase. If the employer stipulated that its contribution would not increase by more than 10 percent and benefit costs rise by more than 10 per-

Exhibit 3-4 HMO Distribution as of 12/31/89

BY STATE[1]

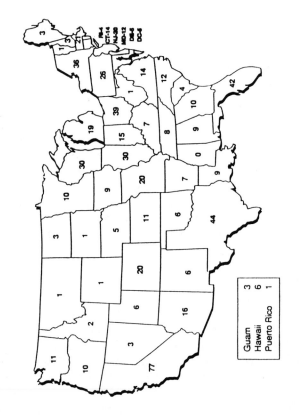

Guam	3
Hawaii	6
Puerto Rico	1

[1]Excludes HMOs of adjoining states with contiguous service areas.

Source: Reprinted with permission from AMCRA, 1990.

Exhibit 3-4 *Continued*

HMO Market Penetration in 27 Metropolitan Areas, 1989, Sorted by HMO Penetration

METROPOLITAN STATISTICAL AREA OR COMPLEX AND STATE[2]	12/31/89 HMO ENROLLMENT	HMO PENETRA- TION RATE	NUMBER OF HMOs SERVING[3]
1 San Francisco-Oakland-San Jose/Sacramento (Calif.)	3,396,986	46%	24
2 Minneapolis-St. Paul (Minn., Wis.)	1,049,258	44	8
3 Milwaukee-Racine (Wis.)	553,261	35	8
4 Portland-Vancouver (Ore., Wash.)	474,388	34	6
5 Los Angeles-Anaheim-Riverside/San Diego (Calif.)	5,107,719	32	28
6 Boston-Lawrence-Salem (Mass., N.H.)	1,136,271	28	15
7 Denver-Boulder/Colorado Springs/Ft. Collins/Greeley (Colo.)	668,809	26	13
8 Phoenix (Ariz.)	518,639	26	11
9 Seattle-Tacoma (Wash.)	581,706	24	9
10 Washington, D.C. (Md., Va.)/Baltimore (Md.)	1,355,737	22	21
11 Kansas City (Mo., Kan.)	344,585	22	11
12 Miami-Fort Lauderdale (Fla.)	628,588	21	17
13 Philadelphia-Wilmington-Trenton (Pa., N.J., Del., Md.)	1,224,930	21	24
14 Detroit-Ann Arbor (Mich.)	882,247	19	9
15 Columbus (Ohio)	243,083	18	8
16 St. Louis (Mo., Ill.)	420,349	17	12
17 Chicago-Gary-Lake County (Ill., Ind., Wis.)	1,341,497	16	25
18 Cleveland-Akron-Lorain (Ohio)	452,455	16	10
19 Cincinnati-Hamilton (Ohio, Ky., Ind.)	268,573	16	8
20 Tampa-St. Petersburg-Clearwater (Fla.)	244,640	12	7
21 Houston-Galveston-Brazoria (Texas)	429,611	12	8
22 Atlanta (Ga.)	305,826	11	7
23 Dallas-Fort Worth (Texas)	416,447	11	10
24 New York-Northern N.J.-Long Island (N.Y., N.J., Conn.)	1,934,541	11	24
25 San Antonio (Texas)	136,844	10	4
26 Norfolk-Virginia Beach-Newport News (Va.)	138,313	10	5
27 Pittsburgh-Beaver Valley (Pa.)	226,322	10	7

[2]Slashes (/) separate metropolitan statistical areas that have been combined to form a market.

[3]Some HMOs serve more than one area, particularly in New Jersey and California.

cent, then the employee must either pay more or cut back on coverage.

The above example, while presenting the union's perspective, accurately illustrates some of the concerns management can expect to encounter when proposing implementation of a flexible benefits plan. Indeed, most studies of successful flexible benefit accounts emphasize the need for good communication and preplanning.[7] Prior to implementation, both the employer and the union should work to inform employees of the nature of flexible benefit programs and of the options available. Surveying employees to determine their interest in any or all aspects of the program also might prove helpful. The Landmark Plan in Appendix 2 illustrates a well-designed flexible benefit plan that provides clear guidelines regarding benefit options and costs. (Readers should note, however, that the terminology in this example may be confusing: Landmark's basic insurance is actually a classic Blue plan and its "deductible" plan is a form of a comprehensive plan.)

The following discussion outlines some of the primary types of flexible benefit programs, as well as mechanisms for funding flexible benefits through salary reduction plans. In general, the more options available, the more complex the program is to operate. As a result, large companies, such as Continental Can, and medical providers, such as Landmark Medical Center, have been the most successful in providing these complex plans.

Types of Flexible Benefit Programs

Several types of flexible programs exist, and three of the more popular forms include modular packages, core-plus plans, and full cafeteria plans.

Modular plans offer a set number of predetermined policy options. All policies have equal dollar value, but include different benefits. For example, policy A might provide basic medical/surgical insurance accompanied by a major medical plan, dental coverage, and some life insurance. As an alternative, policy B might offer a different type of basic medical/surgical and major medical insurance, covering both dental and vision care, but charge higher deductibles. Exhibit 3-5 gives additional examples of various plan modules, each costing the same amount, but one of which offers additional benefits with less generous coverage.

Exhibit 3-5 Example of Modular Plan Options

BENEFITS	MODULE ONE	MODULE TWO	MODULE THREE
Life/Accidental Death or Dismemberment Coverage	$25,000	$25,000	$50,000
Medical Care Coverage	Full hospital, medical/surgical, & major medical	Same	Same, but with cost containment requirements
Deductible	None	$200/person $400/family	$200/person $600/family
Co-payment	None	20% of first $2,000	20% of first $4,000
Maximum	None	$1 million lifetime	$1 million lifetime
Dental Care Deductible	$ 50/person $150/family	$25/person $75/person	$25/person $75/person
Co-payment Options	20/20/50% of all costs	0/20/40% of all costs	0/20/40/50% of all costs
Maximum	$1,000/year (all costs)	$1,000/year (all costs)	$1,000/year (dental) $1,000/year (ortho)
Vision Care	None	None	Scheduled plan

Full cafeteria plans feature employer-paid "benefit dollars" which employees can use to purchase the type of coverage desired. In some instances, employees can opt to convert benefit dollars to cash. Exhibit 3-6 illustrates the range of possible medical and dental benefits that a cafeteria plan might offer. In addition, Appendix 2 gives an example of an actual plan (the Landmark Medical Plan) which offers employees a variety of benefit options.

Core-plus plans have a set "core" of employer-paid benefits, which usually include basic hospitalization, physician, and major medical insurance. Other benefit options, such as dental and vision, can be added on at the employee's expense, using either pre- or post-tax dollars. Exhibit 3-7 illustrates how one core-plus program might operate. Unlike cafeteria and modular programs, core-plus plans can be introduced incrementally. They also are somewhat

Exhibit 3-6 Example of Cafeteria Plan Options

PAYMENT CHOICES	MEDICAL PLAN OPTIONS			DENTAL PLAN OPTIONS		
	A	B	C	A	B	C
	Individual Plan					
Total Cost	$ 800	$ 700	$ 500	$ 60	$ 50	$30
Employer-Paid Credits	$ 500	$ 500	$ 500	none	none	none
Employee's Payment*	$ 300	$ 200	none	$ 60	$ 50	$30
	Family Plan					
Total Cost	$1500	$1350	$1000	$120	$100	$65
Employer-Paid Credits	$1000	$1000	$1000	none	none	none
Employee's Payment*	$ 500	$ 350	none	$120	$100	$65

*If benefits selected exceed employer-paid credits, the employee can pay the balance through a section 125 salary reduction plan. Thus, the employee's actual cost, when offset by the tax savings, is somewhat lower than the figures shown.

easier to administer, modify, and budget for than the other two types of flexible benefit programs.

Funding Options and Federal Regulations

When setting up a flexible benefit program, employers have a number of design options that provide certain financial advantages under Internal Revenue Code regulations. Conforming to these federal requirements can prove complicated, but the following discussion outlines the broad options available. The pros and cons of these options to labor and management are summarized in Exhibit 3-8.

Salary Reduction Plans. An advantage of cafeteria or flexible benefit plans is that employees' contributions can be made in pretax dollars, provided the program is set up as a salary reduction plan under section 125 of the Internal Revenue Code. Employees' premium payments to the other three types of plans also can be made in this fashion, provided the salary reduction is implemented as a type of flexible benefit plan.

Exhibit 3-7 Example of a Core-Plus Program

BENEFIT	CORE PROGRAM—EMPLOYER PAID	OPTIONS—EMPLOYEE PAID
Life/Acciden-tal Death & Dismem-berment	$25,000	A: One times salary B: Two times salary C: Three times salary
Medical Care Coverage	$200/individual, $600/family deductible 80% co-payment provision with cost containment $1 million lifetime maximum	D: HMO or other first-dollar coverage E: Same as core, but no cost containment
Dental Care Coverage	$ 50/individual, $150/family deductible 20% (individual/spouse) 50% (family) co-payment $1,000 annual maximum	F: $25/individual $50/family deductible G: 0% (individual), 20% (spouse), 40% (family) co-payment
Vision Care Coverage	None	H: Scheduled Plan

By paying premiums in pretax dollars, employees can save some 15 to 28 percent of additional taxes on their total salary. This payment option is not actually a benefit, just a less expensive way of charging employees for premium sharing. However, employers often advertise this feature to employees, since it reduces the net effect of premium sharing on pay loss.

The Landmark example in Appendix 2 cites how this feature might work, but to illustrate the tax savings, consider the case of an employee whose annual premium contributions amount to $316 (10 percent of the total $3,161 annual premium). If these premiums are paid in pretax dollars, the employee would save by lowering his or her tax liability percentage. If the employee's salary falls in the 28 percent tax bracket, then the employee would save $88.48 in annual income taxes. In addition, since the employer and employee each pay social security taxes amounting to 7.65 percent of total salary, the salary reduction would produce savings in this area as well.

Setting up such a plan is complex, but standard documents can be purchased from either accounting or legal firms. One major

Exhibit 3-8 Pros and Cons of Section 105 and Section 129 Flexible Benefit Accounts

	ADVANTAGES	DISADVANTAGES
T O		
E M P L O Y E E S	Lower income and social security taxes Nondeductible medical costs payable with pretax dollars	Lost money if expenses over-estimated

E M P L O Y E R S	Lower social security taxes
	
	Increased employee morale
	
	Pilot-testing of plans to expand flexible
	  benefits
		Unexpected costs if employees leave
		  with account deficits
		
		Poor employee morale if employees
		  overpay
		
		Higher administrative costs possible

requirement is that an employer must establish a bookkeeping system and have employees sign authorization forms allowing a salary reduction (rather than deduction) to fund their contributions to the insurance plan. To simplify insurance renewal, employers can notify staff that unless they act to revoke their waiver at the time of renewal, the waivers will remain in effect each year. Further discussion of salary reduction plans occurs in Chapter 5, and Appendix 2 provides an example of a standard salary reduction agreement.

Health Reimbursement Accounts. A second funding option is a reimbursement account, which comes under section 125 of the Internal Revenue Code. This arrangement allows employees to set aside a predetermined amount of dollars, in the form of a salary reduction, to use for funding certain qualifying health care expenses. The Landmark Plan in Appendix 2 also illustrates how this option works.

Qualifying expenses for which the reserved funds can be used include medical, dental, and vision care; physical exams; and other health maintenance programs. The account is a type of "use it or lose it" plan, since unused contributions revert back to the plan, not the employee. On the other hand, if an employee incurs a cost in the first part of the year before sufficient funds have accrued in the account, the employer must advance the necessary funds, up to the amount that will accrue in the employee's account by year's end. Should this employee leave before contributing the amounts owed, the employer is out the money advanced.

Thus, reimbursement accounts involve some financial risk for both employers and employees. The employee needs to anticipate his or her medical expenses to avoid overpayment, and the employer needs to avoid liability for covering excessive claims. In most cases, an employer will have a small amount of excess assets in the plan at year's end. These assets are often used to offset expenses, although some companies may decide to donate these excess account funds to a worthy cause.

Dependent and Child Care Reimbursement Accounts. A third arrangement is a dependent care and qualifying child care account. Under section 129 of the Internal Revenue Code, employees can set aside dollars to cover their annual expected expenses for care of children, elderly/dependent parents, or spouses. Limits restrict the amount of funds that can be set aside for these purposes, so employees may save more by using instead the child care credits allowed when filing income taxes. In 1990, limits under section 129 established that qualifying children had to be under age 13, while the maximum annual allowance ranged from $2,500 to $5,000, depending on marital status.

In sum, the cost of the care will determine whether an employee should take the income tax credit or use a section 129 salary reduction plan to cover expected expenses. For some employees, the salary reduction option may prove more attractive and useful. Once again, readers can refer to Appendices 2 and 3 for examples of actual plans containing this option.

Guidelines for Purchasing an Insurance Plan

After weighing the pros and cons of each category of insurance and deciding which type to purchase, employers then must decide on a particular company and policy. For all types of insurance, employers should investigate the company's reputation and background to determine if it compares favorably to that of others in the field. The policy also should be compared to others with regard to:

definitions of "accident," "disability," and other terms; exclusions and inclusions; dismemberment provisions; the nature of cosmetic or restorative surgery covered; disability income benefit periods; renewal and cancellation provisions; medical expense coverage; and cost.

To facilitate such comparisons, some states gather and publish data about available insurance products and/or information on how to be a knowledgeable consumer of medical care. The Pennsylvania Insurance Department, for example, compiles data on insurance products and comparative medical rates, while the state of Maryland publishes "A Health Care Shopper's Guide."[8]

In addition to these broad comparisons, other considerations will vary depending on whether the plan involves some form of traditional or comprehensive insurance plan, or whether it employs a form of managed care. The following discussion highlights guidelines to consider for each of these forms of insurance programs.

Traditional or Comprehensive Plans

Despite their differences, both traditional and comprehensive plans have certain common elements that merit review prior to purchase of a particular one. These common elements also can be found in flexible benefit programs, since most offerings include some form of a basic insurance program. The kinds of questions to ask concern each of the four major components: hospital care, surgical benefits, medical expenses, and major medical provisions.

Hospital Care

Check the amount of maximum daily coverage, as well as the maximum number of days allowed. Some policies have no specified daily dollar limit for certain types of rooms (such as a semi-private room), while others will pay up to a stated maximum dollar amount.

Understand the variations and maximums allowed. For example, some policies impose a limit on maternity benefits that differs from the limit on other types of hospital stays. Limitations may be expressed as a lump-sum dollar maximum or be based on the type of service rendered.

Determine the basis for listed rates for certain homogeneous groups of hospital services. Some plans base rates using a category known as DRGs (diagnosis-related groups) or some other commonly used rate standard developed within the state or area. A DRG rate reflects the amount Medicare reimburses for hospital stays. Originally developed in 1975 as a planning tool at Yale University, DRG rates have grown in usage to become the basis for the "prospective payment system for hospital services."[9] Many states use this rate as a guideline for allowable reimbursement. Other allowable rates may reflect the going rate, the negotiated rate, or some other agreed-upon system.

Know what, if any extras are covered, and be aware of specified limitations or other exceptions. For example, reimbursement for emergency room treatment of accidental injuries may vary according to whether or not the patient is admitted. Nursing expense reimbursement may vary depending on whether the nursing care takes place at home or in the hospital.

Surgical/Medical Benefits

Review how surgical procedures are grouped. If more than one surgical procedure is performed during an operation, some plans may reimburse only one at the full rate. Or the opposite could occur, in which case the physician may "unbundle" what used to be a single comprehensive procedure and bill several different procedures separately in order to get full reimbursement.

Determine if application of usual, customary, and reasonable (UCR) rates will be made and on what basis (i.e., the particular rate or percent used). In most instances, insurance companies set a benchmark dollar limit on what they will pay for various surgical procedures. This amount is usually based on a UCR rate that reflects average charges in the state or geographical area. Although it is possible to learn these rates in advance, rates change frequently. Other plans use percentage limits that typically reimburse only 75 to 95 percent of surgical costs.

Know what limits exist on medical expense coverage for surgery-related costs, such as pre-surgery appointments, diagnostic visits, and post-operative treatments. Some plans restrict these benefits by limiting the number of physician calls or the amount payable per visit/day, or by imposing a total overall limitation.

Major Medical Policies

Determine the amount of deductible charged. Deductibles can vary from $50 to $500 or more in costs that must be paid by the employee before the insurer pays anything.

Know what limits are placed on the deductible. For example, a policy could have a $50 deductible per person but a family maximum of $200. Thus, if a family paid out deductibles for four members totalling $200, then the fifth family member would not be charged a deductible.

Find out the time period over which the deductible is applied. Deductibles can be applied monthly, yearly, and/or to each instance. If the deductible is applied over a 12-month period, does the policy extend coverage into the following plan year to provide reimbursement for a full 12 months after the deductible is fulfilled? Or does the plan place a calendar year's limitation on paying, even though the condition is ongoing?

Understand what overall limits on expense reimbursement exist and how are these limits applied. It is the rare policy that is unlimited. Many plans place overall limits ranging from $1 million to $5 million over a lifetime, with aggregate limits set by calendar or benefit years. (Some are lower and some have no maximum limit.) Some plans even have special limits dependent on the nature of the illness or disability. For example, many policies have lower reimbursement rates for expenses related to mental illness or alcohol and drug rehabilitation.

Determine what the plan's copayment requirements are. For example, a copay provision could require participants to pay 20 percent of the first $2,000 per individual and have a $5,000 maximum per family out-of-pocket expense limitation. Some policies, however, do not specify a maximum cap per individual or family. In this case, the potential costs to an employee could be considerable.

Understand the extent of coverage provided, and whether the major medical policy applies to all additional costs or only to UCR charges. The policy should clearly delineate what is covered and what is not covered as major medical benefits. For example, most plans would not cover charges for a television and phone in a hospital room. Will a cane or crutches be covered? Does the plan cover only services or supplies that are prescribed?

Know whether the policy has special provisions for particular diseases. With the prevalence of AIDS today, for example, the plan should be examined to see if it places a dollar limit on reimbursement, or excludes coverage completely, for this type of treatment.[10] More liberal major medical policies are written so as to extend the time period for application of the deductible for special diseases.

Managed Care Plans

When considering an HMO or some other form of managed care program, a different set of considerations arises. The following discussion lists some questions to ask concerning costs, rates, benefits, services, organizational structure, member rights, and stability.[11]

Costs

- What are the current membership fees?
- For how long are these membership fees guaranteed? What is the projected annual increase? What has been the past history of annual increases?
- How do these fees compare with individual premiums of other types of insurance?
- Can laid-off employees pay the HMO directly to maintain coverage? Are such direct payments higher than group rates?

Rates

- What method and data are used to calculate premium rates? If necessary, negotiate with the HMO to obtain rates that are reasonable and advantageous to your group.
- Are multiple-year rates available? Would use of these rates reduce premiums?

Benefits

- What is and is not covered? If benefits do not match those found in a basic plan, negotiate additional coverage to bring coverage up to par.
- What services are available for treating mental illness, alcoholism, and substance abuse?
- What emergency services are offered?
- What happens if a non-designated emergency room is used? How are these charges reimbursed?
- What are the arrangements for consulting specialists and obtaining second opinions?
- What happens if a member needs service while some place outside the area covered by the HMO?
- What is the policy regarding coverage of annual physicals?

Service

- Where are the facilities located? Are they easily accessible?
- What are the hours of operations?
- What is the average waiting time to get an appointment?
- What is the average waiting time in waiting rooms? Are there sufficient physicians?
- Do the doctors and nurses seem to spend enough time with each patient?
- Is sufficient information provided each patient about his or her medical problem?
- With what hospital is the HMO affiliated?

Organization

- Is the HMO a group or individual practice?
- Is it qualified under federal or state law, or both?
- Are there any restrictions on or pending reviews of the HMO's license to operate?
- Who are the physicians, what are their specialities, and how many are board-certified, board-eligible, or neither?
- Is the HMO organized to serve any special population? For example, some HMOs provide only critical care; others may or may not provide pediatric services.
- What criteria are used to select participating physicians?

Member Rights

- What are the complaint or grievance procedures?
- How many grievances were filed and resolved during previous years?
- Under what conditions may an enrollee terminate membership in the HMO and return without penalty?
- Under what conditions can the HMO terminate members?
- What protection do members have if the HMO should dissolve?

Stability

- What is the HMO's current enrollment? What has enrollment been over the past several years?

- What major employer groups are currently enrolled and which ones were enrolled in the past?
- What has the withdrawal rate averaged in the preceding two years?

Notes

1. Marion Merrell Dow, Inc., *Marion Managed Care Digest, HMO Edition 1990* (Kansas City, MO: Marion Merrel Dow, Inc., 1990).
2. *Ibid.*
3. Changes to the HMO Act of 1973 (P.L. 93-222) made by the HMO Act of 1988 (P.L. 100-51) are summarized in Appendix 1.
4. Author's own research.
5. For more information on ERISA, see Barbara J. Coleman, *Primer on Employee Retirement Income Security Act*, 2nd ed. (Washington, DC: Bureau of National Affairs, Inc., 1987).
6. Bureau of National Affairs, Inc., *Benefits Today* 8, 1 (1/11/91): 12–14.
7. See Coopers and Lybrand, "Cafeteria Plans and Flexible Spending Arrangements," ABC 89/4 (3/23/89), and Wyatt Co., *1989 Survey of Flexible Benefits* (Washington, DC: Wyatt Co, 1980).
8. Belita H. Cowan, *Health Care Shopper's Guide, 59 Ways to Save Money* (Baltimore, MD: Consumer Protection Division of Maryland Attorney General's Office, 1987).
9. John D. Reynolds and Robin N. Bischoff, *Health Insurance Answer Book*, 3rd ed. (New York: Panel Publishers, 1991), p. 365.
10. A recent federal appeals court ruling, allowing employers with self-insured health plans to restrict benefits for AIDS-related illnesses, may lead to exclusions of other types of catastrophic illness. See "AIDS Case Ruling Favors Self-Insured Companies," *Hartford Courant* (11/27/91): 1.
11. *The Labor Management Guide To Health Care Cost Containment*, published by The United States Conference of Mayors, The American Federation of State, County and Municipal Employees, AFL-CIO and the National Public Employer Labor Relations Association under a grant from the Federal Mediation and Conciliation Service, no date, but about 1988. Questions were adapted from this document pp. 38–40.

Chapter 4

Pricing and Marketing of Insurance

Understanding how insurance is priced and marketed can provide helpful preliminary data for bargaining with insurance carriers or for negotiating a management-labor contract. Knowing how to get the best deal for your money will result in either lower costs or better benefits. The marketing process is usually pitched to the employer, unless the insurance is provided by a union or through a multi-employer or union trust. Some insurance companies, however, will provide comparable data to the union's bargaining agent, if the employer certifies release of such information. In any event, both sides should know the same information and review it together.

For all types of insurance, some funds must be set aside to cover for projected claim payments and administrative costs. These funds can be called "premiums" or "contributions," and they can be assessed against individuals or groups. The funding method determines who banks the premium dollars and who will carry the risk if claims exceed available revenue or, on the other hand, if claims are less than expected.

Two major methods are used to fund insurance plans: (1) an individual or group can purchase insurance from an insurance company, or (2) an employer or group of employees can self-fund and manage claims reimbursement internally or hire an external administrator. To illustrate how most insurance companies operate, the bulk of this chapter is devoted to the first method of funding. Cost considerations involved in this funding method apply to basic indemnity insurance, as well as to comprehensive and even flexible benefit plans. Managed care insurance provided through an HMO or PPO also might use some of these general principles. However, managed-care plans usually have other pricing options to consider as well. These options, as well as cost considerations unique to self-insurance, will be discussed later in this chapter.

Standard Insurance Pricing Practices

Setting health insurance rates operates in a manner similar to the process used by auto insurers, except that the risk factors are typically assessed for each separate policy holder, rather than for all clients covered by the company. Thus, the same insurance company may set different rates for many small groups based on their differing experiences and risk factors. Although some insurers will combine several small groups into one large group for rate-setting purposes, most companies rate groups of 50 to 200 or more individuals separately.

Along with the experience rating of the particular group, other factors enter into the pricing of an insurance product. The methods used by the insurance company to calculate rates, assess administrative costs, hedge against losses and medical inflation, and reimburse claims all affect premium charges. Other cost variables involved in purchasing an insurance policy can arise when an employer turns to salespersons or brokers for assistance in selecting a product. All of these cost variables are discussed below.

Experience Ratings

Experience ratings will take into account members' overall usage of the plan, along with trends in use of particular benefits funded. Other factors used to calculate experience ratings reflect broader demographic variables that have been determined by actuaries to affect the health of plan users. These demographic variables include geographic location, sex, age, income, occupation, lifestyles, and the stability of the work force. Past reserves or liabilities on the health plan account also may be used to determine a plus or minus rating factor, depending on the method used to calculate premiums. Finally, group size and adverse selection can affect the experience rating.

Group size

Differences in group size can create variability that adversely impacts experience ratings of particular plans. The larger the group or "pool" over which to spread the risk, the less likely one major catastrophe will destroy profits. Under this "economy of size" calculation, a pool of 1,000 or more bears closer resemblance to "average" populations and its claims experience should come close to statistical predictions. Similar to the theory behind sampling, outcome predictions for a small group are less reliable, since they are not truly representative of the larger population and a few individual aberrations can cause large unanticipated expenses.

As a result, few insurance companies conduct separate experience ratings for very small groups—those with fewer than 50, or sometimes 100, individuals. Instead, these groups are usually combined and put into a general risk pool for purposes of insurance rating. In general, the rates of these "hybrid" groups are often higher than many other experience-rated groups. Although in theory, a larger group should reduce the likelihood that one major catastrophe will destroy profits, in actual practice, this theory does not hold up. In fact, those brought together to share in an artificially created pool may have higher utilization rates than other groups who have related members.

Adverse selection

Adverse selection also affects a plan's experience rating and, as a result, the cost of the plan. The theory of adverse selection holds that those who remain in a plan are adversely affected by the departure of other members, when or if those who quit the plan were using few of its benefits. As a result, the departure of these probable non-users adversely impacts the plan by creating higher usage rates and cost.

Some employers unwittingly encourage this phenomenon by paying financial incentives to employees to opt out of the plan. Employees who opt out are usually healthier and younger individuals who do not use the plan, or persons who belong to an HMO. Thus, the short-term economy to the employer of saving the expense of several premium contributions is offset by the likelihood of higher rates resulting from bad experience ratings and increased utilization of benefits. (For further discussion of the phenomenon of adverse selection, see Chapter 5.)

Rate-Setting Methods

In translating experience ratings into premium charges, insurance companies generally employ three basic types of rate-setting formulas: (1) a retrospective method, (2) a prospective method, and (3) a hybrid method that combines the first two.

A retrospective method, as its name implies, is subject to future adjustment if the premium rate charged, based on anticipated claims, does not reflect actual claims experience. Thus, both refunds or additional charges are possible under this rate-setting method.

Under a prospective plan, the insurance company does not directly levy additional charges when claims exceed expectations, nor does it provide direct refunds if premiums paid exceed actual claims. Instead, any difference between actual and anticipated claims experience is applied when calculating rates the following year. If claims were excessive, then the next year's premium will increase to reflect that experience. If claims were less than antici-pated, the insurance company may lower or, in the event of medical inflation, at least stabilize premiums the following year. In general, this rate-setting method is most favorable for small groups whose claims levels and experiences fluctuate due to the greater variability that occurs in small groups.

The third, hybrid, method calculates premiums on a prospec-tive basis, but allows some losses or profits to be debited or credited to the account. If claims exceed premiums paid, then the next year's rate usually is correspondingly higher and some percentage of the losses also will be tacked on to the total anticipated claims used to set premiums. The loss reserve thus becomes a past liability to be amortized over time through higher premiums. As the following example illustrates, however, this method allows some flexibility with regard to how past liabilities are amortized.

Example: Past year's claims exceeded premiums paid, creating a $100,000 deficit. As a result, the insurance company has increased rates by 25 percent and added on one-half of the deficit ($50,000) to the total claims projected for next year. The new annual premium to be charged totals $1,200,000.

Negotiation strategy: The amount of the deficit to be charged in one year can be negotiated. The employer may want to suggest some lesser amount, say only $25,000, be added on the next year. The hope is that a good plan experience will result in some savings and wipe out a portion of the past reserve. In any event, this strategy will allow the employer to amortize the $100,000 loss over four years, rather than two.

Administrative Expense Variations

When different insurance companies bid on a contract, varia-tions in the projected cost of the plan will depend not only on analysis of past claims experience, demographics, and projected future rates, but also on the way each company calculates and charges for the administrative costs of processing claims. These charges are usually calculated as a percentage of total anticipated claims, but the percentage used can vary from company to company.

Insurers also use administrative charges as a means to protect against higher than anticipated claims. The method used to calculate this buffer will affect total charges, as Exhibit 4-1 illustrates. In this example, the incumbent uses a credibility factor to account for possible variations in the rate it has projected. Like a standard deviation, a credibility factor bears a relationship to the size of the groups: the smaller the group, the less reliable the prediction, and the larger the charge needed to provide adequate protection. In contrast, the two competitors in Exhibit 4-1 use a considerably smaller "margin of error" to provide additional dollars to offset any miscalculations.

The cost comparison in Exhibit 4-1 is dependent on the assumption that all competitors offer equal coverage. To effect equal coverage, the initial bids or requests for proposals (RFPs) should specify the exact nature of the coverage desired, so the policies submitted will be as nearly alike as possible (see Appendix 4 for an example of a RFP.) In general, however, no two insurance companies provide identical coverage. Except when a very large group is involved, most insurers provide an "off the shelf" product rather than attempt to design coverage to a company's exact specifications. Exceptions to this rule can occur, and every case is susceptible to individual negotiations. Chapter 5 will provide additional tips for evaluating the coverage and costs of competing insurance policies.

Even when coverages differ, the administrative costs contained in competing plans deserve close scrutiny. Administrative expenses can vary significantly, not only among different companies but even from year to year within the same company. Knowing what the administrative charges are enables an employer to at least challenge these expenses and to suggest lower fees. The following example demonstrates one such negotiating tactic.

Example: A premium increase of 40 percent prompted a recent rate review case. This review revealed that administrative charges in the previous year had amounted to 18.3 percent of a $1 million-plus premium. For the upcoming year, administrative charges would be 18.6 percent of the new $1.4 annual

Exhibit 4-1 Renewal Comparisons

ITEM	AS PROPOSED BY INCUMBENT	COMPANY B	COMPANY C
Projected Incurred Claims claims that will develop***	$1,243,520	$1,243,520	$1,243,520
Credibility Adjustment provides a margin + or −	+ 79,121	0	0
Margin provides leeway + or −	0	124,352*	62,176*
Expense Charge (Retention)	+ 313,709	223,834**	149,222**
Miscellaneous Adjustment	− 4,761	0	0
New Premium	$1,631,589	$1,591,706	$1,454,918
Rate Increase	40.2%	36.7%	25%
"Savings" or Difference from current carrier		$ 39,883	$ 176,671
*The Margin or credibility		10%	5%
Expense Charge as % (Retention)	25.22%	15%	12%

*Margin of 10% and 5% of projected claims allows leeway in estimating rates
**Expense charge of 18% and 12% of projected claims
***Incurred claims are paid claims and current reserves less the prior reserves (Reserves are usually 25% of paid claims with a 3-month run out of time in the event of plan termination)

Source: Reprinted with permission from Old Saybrook Pension & Employee Benefit Board from a report prepared by Wyatt Co., June 1990.

premium, increasing administrative costs by $77,400 to total $260,400.

Negotiation Strategy: The policy holder should point out that this new rate includes some $77,000 in additional administrative costs, an increase of 42 percent over the prior year's administrative charges. A rate of 15 percent would still generate some $210,000, which is $27,000 (14.75 percent) higher than the previous year. Even if the past year's claims had exceeded premiums, the same rate of 18.3 percent, when applied to the higher premium charged, should cover the additional administrative work. In fact, the plan's bad claims experience may have resulted from fewer claims of larger magnitude, thus creating no additional administrative work.

As the above example illustrates, an investigation into the nature of any excessive claims should take place in order to evaluate the need for increased administrative fees. Such an investigation also may provide some insight into areas that may require different insurance protection.

Catastrophic Claims Protection

As noted above, lack of protection against unexpected catastrophic claims can cause premiums to increase. One case of cancer, an organ transplant, a premature baby, or a spinal cord injury easily could use up a normal pool of premiums. As an example of the high cost of life-saving medical technology, the first $1 million claim for a premature baby occurred in 1991 for Connecticut Blue Cross/Blue Shield. Some insurers build specialized insurance protection against these costs into their basic rates. Buyers, however, can purchase protection against such catastrophic costs through a separate "stop-loss" insurance, which comes in two basic types: aggregate and specific.

Aggregate "stop-loss" coverage limits an employer's or union's liability to a particular overall amount for the plan. After this limit is reached, then the stop-loss insurer must pick up the remaining expenses. A typical stop-loss limit is set at 120 percent to 135 percent of expected claims.

Specific stop-loss insurance limits the employer's liability on large, single claims for particular types of treatment, such as premature births or organ transplants. For example, the specific stop-loss level for a single claimant might be set at 10 percent to 15 percent of expected claims per policy year, up to a fixed dollar amount. This limit is usually based on claims actually paid, not those incurred but not yet paid.

> *Example:* In Connecticut, the Blue Cross/Blue Shield plan has organ transplant protection, so that if a claim for organ transplant exceeds $75,000 (as it surely will), the excess goes into the Blues' overall pool and the experience is not charged to the employer's plan. A similar pool for excess expenses exists in Rhode Island and is built right into the insurance premium charges.
>
> *Negotiation strategy:* Review claims experience data annually and calculate at least the number and type of catastrophic claims. If there are two or more transplants, "premies," and other catastrophes that have caused costs to exceed expectations, calculate the excess. Then determine the price to reinsure. If the excess claims are well over the amount for

reinsuring, then stop-loss insurance coverage would appear to be a necessary purchase. If, on the other hand, the reinsurance premium matches or is less than the excess claims, purchasing specific stop-loss insurance is probably not necessary.

Reimbursement Rates

In many areas, insurance providers have difficulty competing with the premiums charged by Blue Cross/Blue Shield plans due to the edge the Blues have with regard to reimbursement rates. Some Blues negotiate directly with hospitals and a large panel of doctors in a state or given territory concerning the amounts they will accept as reimbursement. Through these long-standing negotiations, Blue Cross/Blue Shield companies often get discounted rates that allow them to pay less to participating doctors and hospitals than other insurance companies must.

In essence, these arrangements transform the Blues into a type of preferred provider network, and the discounts they receive translate into lower premium rates. In fact, the competition from managed care plans, such as HMOs and PPOs, has prompted some Blues to tout their discount method as PPOs. In general, however, the Blues have held a historical market niche when it comes to discounting.

Factors considered by the Blues in determining the hospital rate of reimbursement include the hospital's rates and increases, operating expenses, recent improvement in medical technology, and renovations, among other variables. When the Blues negotiate discounted rates, other insurers and payers have to pay full prices and often more than they otherwise would, since health care providers want to make up for the money they do not receive from Blue Cross/Blue Shield. Blues that are no longer nonprofit carriers, however, usually lose the advantage of discounted hospital fees, sometimes as a result of state insurance regulations.

With respect to medical/surgical insurance, which covers physician fees and services, the not-for-profit Blues have a similar process which gives them a competitive edge. In setting reimbursable physician rates, the Blue Shield in Rhode Island, for example, conducts collective negotiations dependent upon a review of all rates charged by its participating physicians. Typical rate increases amount to only one-half to one percent over the preceding year. According to some participating physicians, these reimbursement rates are based on the lowest charges for services reported and do not take into account a physician's greater specialization or reputation. If a physician does not respond to the survey, then Blue Shield continues reimbursement at the old rate.

Many doctors refuse to accept this kind of price control and choose not to participate in the Blue network. For services supplied by nonparticipating doctors, patients covered by a Blue plan must pay the bill and then submit a claim for reimbursement of the allowable amount. That amount is usually set at a percentage of the actual charges, or the usual and customary rate (somewhere between 70 to 95 percent of charges). In most cases, the amount reimbursed is less than the physician's actual charges.

These discount arrangements only apply to nonprofit Blues, and not all Blue Cross/Blue Shield organizations have retained this designation. For example, in Connecticut, the local Blue company has become totally competitive with other for-profit health insurance carriers. As the nonprofit designation fades, the virtual monopoly enjoyed by the Blues has been slipping.

Other factors also have begun to erode the Blues' edge with regard to rates. Commercial insurers began to attract healthier clients in the 1960s, which increased the Blues' costs and caused rates for those left in the Blues' pool to rise. In addition, hospital discounts to the Blues were eliminated in many states, as was the federal tax-exempt treatment of the Blues. While Blue Cross/Blue Shield in Kentucky still receives a seven percent discount on its hospital rates, Connecticut's discount, which had been gradually decreasing, was phased out completely in 1992. Elimination of these tax breaks and discounts reflects changes in how the Blues operate. Besides dropping the nonprofit designation, many Blues also have abandoned the practice of providing coverage to everyone regardless of risk. Those few Blues that have retained this practice are primarily located in the Northeast.

Payment Alternatives

A variety of payment arrangements also can affect short-term and overall plan costs. For example, a deferred-payment arrangement would allow premium payments to begin three or more months after the contract year starts. Insurers, however, usually charge interest to the plan for the 30, 60, or 90 days of delay. The interest rate is usually based on the annual Treasury Bill rate.

Under a deferred payment arrangement, premium payments, if submitted on a monthly basis, would have to continue for three months after the plan year ends. Thus, a change in carriers would necessitate double payments during the first quarter of the new plan. As a result, while deferred payments can be an effective one-time savings device, this arrangement also serves as a disincentive to leave an insurance carrier.

The timing of the contract year also can impact on budget planning, both for the company and the employee. Insurance does not have to be purchased only on a calendar-year basis. It is available to match any budgetary year desired: a fiscal year, an October to October year (as with the federal government), a May to May scheme, or any other period.

Since renewal rates usually are known a few months prior to the start of a new plan year, selecting an insurance contract that begins before the business's fiscal year can facilitate the budgeting process. If the insurance plan involves premium sharing, however, then this arrangement will cause the employee's share of the premium to increase prior to any cost-of-living or other annual salary adjustments. The resulting loss of take-home pay may generate some objections from employees. In addition, payroll deductions will have to be recalculated, although today's sophisticated computer programs can make this adjustment without major expense to the employer.

Professional Sales Help

Although employers can deal directly with an insurance company, hiring a professional to assist with the purchase can prove helpful. Reasons for hiring help are similar to those suggested for using a real estate agent. While foregoing a commission may save some dollars, premium rates and underwriting practices are complex and an expert's ability to negotiate the best product variations, options, and combinations may offset the commission charged. Insurance prices often vary due to product differences as much as the group's experience, and an insurance professional is aware of these differences. A large company or labor union, however, that has an employee benefits department knowledgeable about insurance should have sufficient expertise to negotiate a deal on its own.

Types of Outside Assistance

For companies that need outside help, choices include four types of insurance sales assistants: a group or client sales representative, a broker, an agent, or an employee benefits consultant. These professionals differ from each other mainly in terms of the method by which they are paid and in the objectivity of their services.

A group sales representative is employed by the insurance company from which the insurance policy is purchased. This person is usually a salaried employee who does not earn a commission. An insurer also may employ some client service representatives who assist with the implementation, continuation, and renewal of the insurance policy. While this person can explain the insurer's policy rates, a sales representative is not able to help clients shop among other carriers.

Brokers and agents differ in the number of firms they represent. An agent represents a single insurance company and will sell most of that company's insurance products. A broker usually has a relationship with several insurance companies and will work with the customer to provide the best insurance at the most reasonable price. The salaries of both agents and brokers are provided through commissions paid by the insurance company whose product is bought. Brokerage firms vary from a single professional to a firm that employs many professionals and may operate on a national or international basis.

An employee benefits consultant usually specializes in working for a company which provides employers with an independent analysis of their benefit needs. These consultants analyze variations in types of insurance, recommend funding vehicles, suggest plan design changes, implement cost containment measures, and develop alternatives.

Fees and Commissions

Because consultants charge the buyer a fee for the consultation, they are not dependent on any insurance company for salary or commissions. As a result, the benefits consultant usually is considered the most objective of the four sales professionals. Some gray areas, however, can occur in almost any of these categories. For example, an employee benefits consultant can arrange either to be retained on a fee schedule or to be reimbursed by commissions at the time of the insurance purchase. In the same manner, if an agent's own company cannot meet a client's desires, the agent may utilize another company, becoming in effect a broker.

Examples of commission schedules in current use illustrate the general amount of compensation a broker may receive. The two most common schedules are a high-low schedule and the level schedule. As implied by the name, the high-low schedule provides higher commissions in the early years and less in renewal years. This system rewards brokers for having employers change carriers, but also recognizes that more work is generally required in the early years of a contract. The level schedule, on the other hand, provides the same percent commission each year the contract is renewed, as long as the premium is a similar amount each year. The level method supposedly encourages the broker to push clients to stay with the same carrier, since renewals entail less work. Exhibit 4-2 illustrates differences between these schedules in terms of rates charged over time.

The commission system comes into play primarily when shopping for traditional indemnity or comprehensive insurance plans. In some instances, a broker or an agent can earn added bonuses for convincing a client to switch from a basic first-dollar indemnity plan to a comprehensive or wraparound plan. Insurers offer this incentive since a plan with less first-dollar coverage has lower rates and increases the likelihood of the company staying with the provider. The purchaser, however, needs to understand that a comprehensive plan does not offer the same first-dollar coverage as basic indemnity plans. The differences between these two types of plans were outlined in Chapter 3, but are reemphasized here since buyers can become confused over what is a good deal. If the rates sound too good, the benefits provided may not be what the purchaser wanted.

Exhibit 4-2 Example of Commission Schedules

ANNUAL PREMIUM	HIGH-LOW SCHEDULE YEAR 1	YEARS 2–10	LEVEL SCHEDULE YEARS 1–10
First $1,000	25.0%	6.5%	7.5%
Next $8,000	20.0	3.0	5.0
Next $5,000	15.0	2.0	3.5
Next $10,000	10.0	2.0	3.2
Next $10,000	7.5	2.0	2.8
Next $25,000	5.0	2.0	2.0
Next $100,000	2.5	1.0	1.5

Source: Reprinted from the *Health Insurance Answer Book, Third Edition*, by John D. Reynolds and Robin N. Bischoff, by permission of Panel Publishers, Inc., 36 West 44th St., New York, NY 10036.

Special Cost Concerns for Flex Plans

While the preceding rate-setting factors affect the pricing of flexible benefit plans, a number of other cost considerations enter into the purchase of flexible benefit plans.

Liability for Price Increases

In most cases, the employee rather than the employer will be liable for any increases in the premiums. The only exception would occur if a bargaining agreement specified that higher plan charges will entail a percentage increase in the employer's dollar contribution. This increase is usually based on either the increase in benefit costs or the percent change in salary deductions.

Most employers will limit their financial risks by specifying a fixed amount of dollars that the company will pay for benefits. As noted in Chapter 3, a core or modular approach to flexible benefits provides employees with some guarantee as to the basic benefits for which the employer will pay. In such instances, only add-ons will increase the plan's costs for employees. In either case, the employer or employee is at risk for cost increases, and it is usually the employee who foots the bill.

Hidden Benefits and Costs

Flexible benefits are increasing in popularity with both management and employees. According to a survey by Wyatt Co.,[1] employers also use flexible benefit programs to recruit and retain workers in a competitive market. Of the employers surveyed, 30 percent offered flexible benefits and 41 percent of these employers had adopted the flex plan within the past two years. In addition, 52 percent of employers without a flex plan indicated that they would adopt one within the next five years. More large employers (those with 5,000 or more employees) than small employers (those with fewer than 500 employees) planned such a change. Given their popularity, flex plans may offer some cost savings through improving employee morale and reducing turnover.

In reference to problem areas, the survey found the nearly one-third of employers with flex plans said they had not experienced any implementation problems, despite expecting such difficulties. While 36 percent had anticipated administrative concerns, only

23 percent had actually experienced problems in administering the program. The largest problem cited by flex plan users concerned the need for communication and explanation to employees prior to implementation. Thus, during the start-up phase, employers should anticipate additional costs for education efforts.

Pricing Managed-Care Plans

Evaluating alternatives to standard insurance plans involves a variety of cost concerns beyond the issues discussed in Chapter 3. The following pointers may provide helpful pricing guidelines when considering a managed-care plan.[2]

As a first step, compare the rates offered by managed-care providers with those offered by more traditional insurers to determine if the deal is competitive. A cost-benefit analysis should be undertaken as well, given differences in coverage. Along with coverage differences, other quality comparisons involve checking the ratio of board-certified specialists to nonboard-certified specialists. A good guide would be to look for HMOs that have about 40 percent of their providers board certified.

As with other insurance plans, the nature of the rating method used by the managed-care plan will affect rates. Will the method utilize community ratings, that is, base rates on the total experience of the plan's entire membership within a given geographic area? Or will it employ the specific group experience, or some other combination method, to set rates? If the group's utilization and experience rates are favorable, then managed-care plans using these factors will offer more economical rates than those plans that employ community ratings.

For HMO plans, many nuances in rate setting are possible today. One of the newest arrangements allows for some "out of network" options in open-ended HMOs. These open-ended HMOs permit enrollees some choices in using outside providers. Options may be limited to various types of specialized care and usually are accompanied by deductibles, co-payments, or some kind of coinsurance. An example of one of these plans is the "Versatile HMO" offered by U.S. Healthcare in Pittsburgh, PA. Services provided outside the plan are reimbursed at 75 percent of the usual, customary, and reasonable (UCR) charges, with full reimbursement provided after $2,500 in out-of-pocket expenses. Another variation is

Health Plan Select in Greenbelt, MD which imposes a $250 deductible and pays only 80 percent of the UCR rate, with a higher out-of-pocket maximum.[3]

The managed-care plan's rate history will provide information on the percent increases over time. This data will help not only to predict future rates but also to evaluate whether the plan's current rates are as competitive with other insurers as they had been in previous years.

The HMO's rate history also should be examined to make certain that "shadow pricing" of regional carriers is not used by the HMO. An HMO's rates often are inflated when the annual percentage increase in its rates is the same as other regional carriers. The excess profit from these rates is usually hidden in management expenses, as the following example illustrates.

> *Example:* Jim Smith switches from an indemnity plan that had a monthly charge of $100 a person to an HMO that also charges $100 a person each month. However, the HMO's actual cost for providing services is only $50 per month, so the HMO is making a sizable profit. The following year, the regular insurance carrier raises its monthly rates to $125 per person, and the HMO shadows this price hike by raising its monthly rate to $112.50 per person. While the HMO's rate hike is only half that charged by the indemnity carrier, appearances are deceiving. The initial HMO monthly rate should have been only $50, and if raised by 12.5 percent, the second year's monthly premium should have totalled only $56.25 per person.

In a similar fashion, comparing the rates of a preferred provider organization to the usual, customary, and reasonable (UCR) rates charged by traditional insurers will help to determine whether the discount offered is real. For example, a PPO might advertise itself as offering a 20 percent discount compared to standard insurance plans. If the UCR charge paid by standard carriers for office visits is $30 and the PPO's proposed office visit charge is $36, then this rate obviously does not amount to a 20 percent discount. This example is fairly simple, but actual plan data may prove difficult to decipher. The assistance of a consultant may be necessary here.

A final cost factor for PPOs concerns the treatment styles of participating physicians. Conservative doctors, that is, ones who generally keep patients for longer terms of treatment than the average physician, will be more costly. The way to determine treatment characteristics of doctors is to review data on group and compare it to benchmark private practitioners. As will be discussed in the next chapter, obtaining an annual data analysis of network doctors also will prove helpful when monitoring other savings.

Self-Insurance Cost Considerations

An alternative to paying premiums to an insurance company or managed-care plan is for an employer to self-insure. Self-insurance programs have many different nuances, advantages, and disadvantages. Some consultants believe that self-funding is not a wise decision for companies with fewer than 500 employees since these small businesses usually cannot handle the large losses that might occur. Other analysts are concerned that employers will be tempted to put aside less than the required reserves, particularly as a cost-saving device during times of fiscal hardship or recession. Nonetheless, this option has become quite fashionable as a less expensive alternative to standard insurance.

Forms of Self-Insurance

One way to self-insure is to establish a section 501(c)(9) trust, commonly referred to as a VEBA (voluntary employee benefit association). The VEBA must represent employees' interests, and it may or may not have employee representation on the board. It is, in effect, a separate entity or trust devoted to providing life, illness, or accident benefits to members.

A modified form of self-insurance, called minimum premium, allows the insurance company to charge only a minimum premium that includes a specified percentage of projected annual premiums, plus administrative and legal costs (retention) and a designated percent of the annual premium. The employer usually holds the claim reserves and earns the interest paid on these funds. The insurer gets to avoid paying state taxes on these funds, which results in savings of 1.5 percent to 2.5 percent of total anticipated premiums. Despite these tax savings, some insurance companies adjust the amount charged for administrative costs to recoup some of the interest they lose. Nonetheless, employers who implement this modified form of self-insurance generally save between 3.0 to 10 percent of the premiums charged for standard insurance policies.

Other Cost Savings

Full self-insurance by an employer, with either an insurance company or a third-party administrator performing the administrative services, may provide some initial cash-flow relief at the time of implementation. This cash-flow relief results from the three-month or so delay before the employer has to pay any claims. The lag time occurs because the old insurance will pay for claims incurred during the period prior to self-insurance, while new claims will not be submitted and processed until well into the third month of the new arrangement. Thus, the employer may gain some short-term relief in its cash flow, although no real savings result.

Real savings can occur, however, if the employer had a large claims deficit with its old carrier that cannot be recouped from the insurer's reserves. This debt will never have to be repaid, since without a contract renewal, the old carrier cannot impose charges to cover the account deficit. In the earlier example of a $100,000 deficit, the half-charge of $50,000 will not be included in the initial premium reserves to be set aside for self-insurance, nor will the additional $50,000 be tacked on in the second plan year.

Additional savings could result from lower administrative fees. Charges for claims administration might be levied as a percentage of claims paid, the method commonly used by Blue Cross/Blue Shield and many insurance companies. As an alternative, some insurers and most third-party administrators use a per-employee, per-month rate. The employer may establish a benefit program account as a depository for funds which can be used, directly or indirectly, to pay claims arising under the benefit program. Under the direct payment method, an agent is authorized to make daily, weekly, or monthly drafts, usually by electronic fund transfer, to cover claims reimbursement.

Program Administration

A major concern regarding self-insurance is the quality of the program's administration. Claims administration may be done by the old insurance carrier, which virtually guarantees replication of the former insurance program's administration. Or the self-insurance program can be serviced through the employer's own benefits office, an option commonly employed by very large companies of 10,000 or more employees. The final option is to hire an outside third-party administrator (TPA) to process claims. This last option generates a number of quality and cost issues that employers should bear in mind.

Selecting a TPA

Anticipated cost savings is a common reason cited for hiring a TPA, rather than employing the former insurance carrier, to process claims. A variety of firms today specialize in this field and promise substantial savings, usually by guaranteeing their fees will not exceed a specific percent. Whether levied on a monthly or per employee basis, this percentage typically falls well below the traditional rates used for calculating administrative costs. For example, the per-employee cost charged by TPAs in the eastern United States during 1991 averaged about $13.00 per employee on a monthly basis.[4]

Despite guaranteed fee discounts, some hidden expenses are possible. One such expense relates to the commission charged by TPAs for providing stop-loss insurance. Earnings from these commissions can amount to about 10 percent of the total cost of the stop-loss insurance. As a result, TPAs sometimes earn more from the commission on stop-loss insurance than they do from performing administrative services. Employers may want to secure stop-loss insurance from another party to ensure the TPA selected makes administrative work a priority.

Employers also should select a TPA that is readily accessible to clients and provides expeditious claim turnaround time. The contract should ensure timely and accurate claims processing by specifying penalties if delays or errors exceed a certain tolerance. For example, a contract might state that if a claim is not paid within 30 days, a penalty amounting to one percent of the amount owed for the claim will be credited to the policy holder's account. Or the contract may specify that if upon annual or biannual review, more than five percent of submitted claims have not been paid within 20 days, then the fee paid to the TPA will be reduced by five percent. Of course, some exceptions for appeal or review of questionable or complex claims should be built into this penalty procedure.

In addition, the contract should ensure that the policy holder will receive accurate claims analysis information upon request (see Appendix 5 for examples of claims analyses). The company also should establish some mechanism to ensure regular auditing of claims handling and reimbursement procedures. These review mechanisms will add to overall costs, although the savings they produce may make the effort worthwhile.

A number of other costs are associated with using a TPA instead of performing administration in house or using the former insurance company. These expenses include the costs of installing the program, preparing legal documents and enrollment materials, as well as developing and disseminating education materials to ensure employees understand the new program.

Conclusion

Regardless of the type of insurance and its cost, some economies can be effected in the selection or financing methods used. The preceding discussion provided some general guidelines to use in shopping wisely, but the list offered is by no means definitive. Other alternatives can keep the price down or shift the cost elsewhere. The following chapters will discuss these various cost-sharing and cost-containment strategies.

Unions prefer to negotiate plans that are 100 percent employer-paid, and employees also expect medical insurance to be as integral to the employment contract as salary. The value and cost of this benefit, however, is not often understood or known by employees. Indeed, if a survey of employees were to be conducted today, few would probably know just how much their insurance costs.

Both management and labor bear the responsibility of educating employees about insurance costs. The most dramatic way to bring home this message is to have the employee pay some part of the medical insurance premium. This strategy, however, does not always result in employees helping to keep insurance costs down. A famous study by Rand posited this effect,[5] but other researchers have attacked the reliability of the data. They point out that the Rand data show that minor variations of $100 to $500 in employees' share of premium payments did not reduce overall insurance costs or the number of office visits, although employees' demand for drugs, outpatient surgery, X-rays, and lab work did decline.[6]

While employers expect a cost-sharing initiative to generate the most formidable objections during labor negotiations, these protests have not kept the use of cost-sharing from growing. According to an EBRI study,[7] employees' annual contributions to individual health insurance premiums went from $36 in 1984 to $105 in 1988, a rate of increase four times the change in employers' contributions. Employers' share of costs exceeded inflation by only 3.9 percent, even though overall medical inflation was running at 5.9 percent annually.

Thus, along with the cost-saving strategies discussed in this chapter, employers are turning to cost-sharing with employees to keep insurance expenses down. Some of the strategies that will be discussed in later chapters include direct premium sharing, increased use of co-payments, higher deductibles, and fixed spending accounts.

Notes

1. Wyatt Company, *The Compensation and Benefits File* 6, no. 2 (Feb. 1990): 5.
2. William E. Hembree, speech given May 5, 1988, National Education Association Health Insurance Conference, Miami, FL.
3. Bureau of National Affairs, Inc., "HMO 'Open-Ended' Products," *Benefits Today* (March 8, 1990): 76.
4. Arthur Giulietti, National Risk and Insurance Consultants, Inc., Waterbury, CT.
5. Karen Ignagni, Jeff McDonald, and Meredith Miller, *Health Care Cost Containment* (Washington, DC: AFL-CIO Department of Occupational Safety, Health and Social Security, Labor Institute of Public Affairs, George Meany Center for Labor Studies, no date).
6. William S. Custer, *Health Care Plan Design, Plan Costs, and Health Care Delivery*, an EBRI special report (Washington, DC: Employee Benefits Research Institute, 1989).
7. "Features of Employer-Sponsored Health Plans," *EBRI Issue Brief* no. 100 (Washington, DC: Employee Benefits Research Institute, 1990).

Chapter 5

Cost-Shifting or Cost-Sharing Strategies

To management, having labor bear part of the increasing costs of health insurance is cost sharing; to labor, this strategy is cost shifting. The strategy may not affect the overall price of insurance premiums, but rising costs have nonetheless prompted management to demand increased participation by labor in sharing the expenses. Ten different cost-sharing tactics, summarized in Exhibit 5-1, will be examined in detail in this chapter.

Premium Sharing

The use of premium sharing to offset employers' costs of providing health insurance has grown steadily in the past few years. In 1987, an A. Foster Higgins health care benefits survey found that 88 percent of plans included some type of deductible and only 31 percent of employers provided no-cost benefit coverage for dependents, although 61 percent paid the full premium for individuals.[1] Among employers who had collective bargaining agreements, 58 percent paid in full for dependent coverage, compared to 22 percent of all non-unionized employers. Three years later, another A. Foster Higgins survey found a considerable rise in the percentage of employees paying part of the premiums.[2]

Other surveys produce similar findings regarding the increasing use of premium sharing. In 1989, a *Time* survey of employees found that 70 percent of the companies required employees to pay at least some of the costs of insuring themselves and their families, up from 51 percent in 1984.[3] According to a nationwide EBRI/Gallup survey of employees,[4] 25 percent had to start paying part of their premiums for the first time between 1989 and 1990. Of those who had been paying a portion of their premiums, over 43 percent

Exhibit 5-1 Summary of 10 Cost-Sharing Tactics

TACTIC	IMPACT ON MANAGEMENT	IMPACT ON LABOR
Premium Sharing	Cuts overall contribution	Increases costs
Higher Deductible	Lowers plan's overall cost	Higher out-of-pocket expenses, but less costly than premium sharing
Coinsurance Requirements	Lowers plan's overall costs by small percentage	Lowers premium, but increases costs if care is used
Copayment for Certain Benefits	Reduces premium for benefits affected	Lowers benefit cost but raises out-of-pocket expenses
Coordination of Benefits	Considerable savings if UCR limit and carve-out approach is used	Lower premiums; may incur higher out-of-pocket cost if carve-out approach used
Opt-Out Incentives	Reduces premiums but can raise plan's costs if adverse selection results	May save costs but risky if need to reenroll arises; higher costs if coordination of benefit advantages are lost
Plan Census	Avoids overpayment of premiums for noneligible persons and legal liability for failure to cover eligible individuals	Reduces plan's costs (and individual premiums); ensures proper coverage
Subrogation of Benefits	Saves plan from paying some claims, thus lowering overall plan costs	Lower premiums through plan savings
Change of Carriers	May lower costs, but difficult to replicate former coverage	Same as for management
Plan Redesign	Savings if costly benefits eliminated	Reduces coverage and/or benefits; may increase out-of-pocket expenses in exchange for lower premiums

said their share of the monthly premium had increased, while one-third also had to pay higher deductibles.

Bargaining Options

All these statistics document the recent trend in labor negotiations focusing on premium sharing. Eliminating negotiated plans with no employee insurance contribution is the number one demand by management and the most emotional issue being resisted by labor. Any negotiations regarding premium sharing, however, should involve a thorough analysis of the current and past costs of insurance premiums, as well as projections of future costs and the impact of any proposed changes on both management and labor.

Case Illustration

Compiling data for this sort of analysis can have a significant impact at the bargaining table, as the example used in Exhibit 5-2 illustrates. In Exhibit 5-2, the percent of payroll devoted to premium payments almost doubled in five years, going from 6.5 percent in 1986-87 to 11.1 percent by 1991-92. At this rate, total premium costs would double again within three years.

Now consider a management proposal that would require employees to pay 20 percent of the premiums, starting in 1990-91. Twenty percent of $1,029,889 would amount to $205,978 in premiums to be paid annually by employees. The employees' share of premium contributions thus would represent 2.06 percent of the total payroll account. To management, reducing the company's expenditure by this amount means its contribution drops from 10.3 percent of payroll to 8.26 percent—close to the percentage paid in 1988-89.

Verifying the Data

In conducting this sort of analysis, the same basic data should be used each year for the salary account. For example, in Exhibit 5-2, the payroll figures did not include inflation factors or FICA contributions. If, on the other hand, pension contributions

Exhibit 5-2 Middletown Paper Company Medical Insurance Cost as Percent of Total Budget

	TOTAL BUDGET	MEDICAL INSURANCE EXPENDED	PERCENTAGE OF BUDGET
1986-87	6,072,966 Actual	395,169	6.5%
1987-88	6,893,543 Actual	520,148	7.6%
1988-89	8,001,098 Actual	645,077	8.1%
1989-90	8,910,764 Actual	802,872	9.0%
1990-91	9,979,337 Actual	1,029,889 Budgeted	10.3%
1991-92	11,306,589 Projected	1,257,361 Projected	11.1%
1992-93	12,810,365 Projected	1,571,701 Projected	12.3%
1993-94	14,514,144 Projected	1,964,626 Projected	13.5%
1994-95	16,444,525 Projected	2,455,783 Projected	14.9%
1995-96	18,631,647 Projected	3,069,727 Projected	16.5%

and/or FICA taxes paid by the employer are included one year, then the account figures for future years should include these adjustments. Similar agreement should be reached regarding whether future cost projections should include salary increases and inflation factors, and if included, at what rates.

Labor negotiators will need to verify that the salary and insurance expenses quoted by management are accurate. Most companies do not fully pay insurance plans in every category and for all dependents. For example, dental insurance often is partially paid for by the employee. Even more cost variations can occur with policies that go beyond simple first-dollar or comprehensive plans. A breakdown of the numbers of people enrolled in each category and type of insurance will make it easier for labor to price some counterproposals, as well as to verify and understand the nature of the medical costs. Exhibit 5-3 illustrates a method for calculating the costs of a first-dollar plan based on actual premium charges and enrollment figures for a fictional business, Company XYZ.

Impact on Employees

While management is interested in the overall effects of medical costs on the company's budget, premium sharing has a significant impact on the individual that employers must recognize. Any proposal for cost sharing should document the potential effect on each employee, as well as the per-employee cost increases in the past. Using the Company XYZ plan described in Exhibit 5-3, Exhibit 5-4 presents a detailed historical analysis of per-employee premium increases, while Exhibit 5-5 outlines how management's premium-sharing proposal would affect each employee for the 1991-92 plan year.

One of labor's major arguments against premium sharing is that an employee's share represents a larger contribution from salary than it initially would appear, since fringe benefits are not taxed. Consider, for example, a proposal for employees to begin paying 10 percent of premiums that had previously amounted to $5,190 in nontaxable fringe benefits. Depending on an individual's tax bracket, paying that $519 contribution also will cost up to 28 percent of the $519 in lost tax dollars, or another $145.

Thus, the net cost to the individual of this 10 percent premium-sharing proposal actually amounts to $664, not $519 as appeared at first glance. In addition, when paid as benefit dollars, fringe benefit compensation does not result in an increased salary base. Therefore,

Exhibit 5-3 Company XYZ Insurance Costs, 1990–91

BENEFIT PLAN	INDIVIDUAL COVERAGE			COUPLE COVERAGE			FAMILY COVERAGE		
	MONTHLY PER EMPLOYEE PREMIUM	NUMBER OF ENROLLEES	TOTAL MONTHLY PREMIUM FOR COMPANY	MONTHLY PER EMPLOYEE PREMIUM	NUMBER OF ENROLLEES	TOTAL MONTHLY PREMIUM FOR COMPANY	MONTHLY PER EMPLOYEE PREMIUM	NUMBER OF ENROLLEES	TOTAL MONTHLY PREMIUM FOR COMPANY
Blue Cross	$49.54	54	$2,675.15	$99.08	87	$8,619.96	$134.60	159	$21,401.40
Blue Shield C 96	$21.43			$42.86			$ 51.34		
Home & Office	$ 7.86			$15.72			$ 27.19		
Total	$29.29	51	$1,493.79	$58.58	76	$4,452.08	$ 78.53	156	$12,250.68
Dental¹ Co. Pays	$15.55			$41.02			$ 51.21		
Employee Pays	$14.00	116	$1,624.00	$34.26	62	$2,124.12	$ 41.15	69	$ 2,839.35
Category I	$ 7.55			$ 6.76			$ 10.06		
Major Medical Under Age 65	$10.00	NA	NA	$23.00	NA	NA	$ 23.00	NA	NA
Ages 65-69	$15.00	NA	NA	$34.05	NA	NA	$ 34.05	NA	NA
Life Insurance	(varies according salary)	all employees	$1,275.00						

	INDIVIDUAL COVERAGE		COUPLE COVERAGE		FAMILY COVERAGE	
	MONTHLY	YEARLY	MONTHLY	YEARLY	MONTHLY	YEARLY
Blue Cross Blue Shield & Dental Total Costs To Company	$5,792.95	$69,515.40	$15,196.16	$182,352.92	$36,491.43	$437,897.16
Life Ins.	$1275.00	$15,300	NA	NA	NA	NA

Total Benefit Costs to Company for 1990–91: $798,613.56, or 7.98% of $10 million salary account.

¹ For dental benefits, the company provides a flat $14.00 premium contribution to all employees, and pays 75 percent of the remaining premium for those with couple or family plans.

Exhibit 5-4 Company XYZ Medical Insurance Premiums History

BENEFIT PLAN COVERAGES	1987-88 MONTHLY RATES	1987-88 ANNUAL COST	1987-88 % INC.	1988-89 MONTHLY RATES	1988-89 ANNUAL COST	1988-89 % INC.	1989-90 MONTHLY RATES	1989-90 ANNUAL COST	1989-90 % INC.	1990-91 MONTHLY RATES	1990-91 ANNUAL COST	1990-91 % INC.	1991-92 MONTHLY RATES	1991-92 ANNUAL COST	1991-92 % INC.	Projected 1992-93 MONTHLY RATES	Projected 1992-93 ANNUAL COST	% INC.
Blue Cross I	25.68	308.16	NA	36.10	433.20	40	32.53	390.36	(-10)	49.54	594.48	52	82.98	995.76	68	90.98		10
Blue Cross II	67.07	804.84		72.20	866.40	8	65.06	780.72	(-10)	99.08	1188.96	52	165.96	1991.52	68	182.56		10
Blue Cross III	67.07	804.84		98.09	1177.08	46	88.38	1060.56	(-10)	134.60	1615.20	52	225.46	2705.52	67	248.01		10
Blue Shield I	15.93	191.16	NA	19.87	238.40	25	21.06	252.72	6	29.29	351.48	39	43.06	516.72	47	47.36		10
Blue Shield II	31.86	382.32		39.74	476.88	25	42.12	505.44	6	58.58	702.96	39	86.12	1033.44	47	94.73		10
Blue Shield III	42.36	508.32		52.43	629.16	24	56.54	678.48	8	72.53	942.36	39	116.63	1399.56	49	127.80		10
Dental I	11.96	143.52	NA	12.00	144.00	.7	13.09	157.08	9	15.55	186.60	18	17.00	204.00	10	19—		
Dental II	32.61	391.32		32.71	392.52	.3	34.52	414.24	6	41.02	492.24	19	44.83	537.96	9	49—		
Dental III	40.68	488.16		40.80	489.60	.2	43.10	517.20	6	51.21	614.52	19	55.97	671.52	9	60—		
Major Medical I							11.12	133.44		under age 65 10.00 Ages 65-69 15.00	120.00	35	under age 65 10.00 Ages 65-69 15.00	120.00	0	12 17		
Major Medical II							29.03	348.36		under age 65 23.00	180.00	17	under age 65 23.00	180.00	0	25		
Major Medical III										Ages 65-69 34.05	276.00	17	Ages 65-69 34.05	276.00	0	37		
											408.60			408.60				

Social Security and benefit payments based on the salary will be considered "lost."

Employees can avoid paying taxes on their share of premiums, provided the company funds the benefit program as a type of cafeteria plan using a salary reduction account. As described in Chapter 3, this arrangement involves a cooperative agreement whereby, with the employee's consent, an employer designates an agreed-on portion of the employee's salary as pretax dollars used to pay for benefits. (See Appendices 2 and 3 for examples.)

Other Management Proposals

Premium-sharing proposals can take a number of different forms. Some alternatives to the earlier proposal of Company XYZ are described below. The first three proposals offer different strategies for implementing a 20 percent premium-sharing requirement, while the last set of proposals looks at alternatives to a 20 percent premium-sharing requirement.

Alternative One

The company continues to pay in full to cover individuals, but requires a 20 percent contribution from employees opting for family coverage. The form of this cost sharing is usually calculated by subtracting the individual premium from the charge for the family premium. Rounding the figures shown in Exhibit 5-5, the total family premium is $5,190, of which the employer will pay an amount equivalent to the individual premium of $1,896. This leaves a premium of $3,294, of which the employee must contribute 20 percent ($659).

Thus, this proposal would spare any additional expenses to employees on individual plans, while those on family plans will pay $659 annually. This contribution amounts to considerably less than the $1,038 annual contribution that would have been paid by family plan subscribers under the original proposal.

Alternative Two

Employees could be required to pay 20 percent of the premiums for basic insurance coverage (i.e., hospital, medical/surgical, and dental benefits), but the company will pay the major medical premiums for all employees. Thus subtracting the employer-paid portion from the total premium, employees on individual plans will

Exhibit 5-5 Cost Summary of an Employee Premium-Sharing Proposal

	FULL PREMIUM AND COPAYMENT COSTS PER MONTH/YEAR		
	INDIVIDUAL	COUPLE	FAMILY
Hospital	$ 83.00 / $ 993.00	$166.00 / $1,992.00	$225.00 / $2,705.00
20% co pay	16.60 / 199.20	33.20 / 398.40	45.00 / 541.00
Medical/Surgical	43.00 / 516.00	86.00 / 1,032.00	117.00 / 1,404.00
20% co pay	8.60 103.20	17.20 / 206.40	23.40 / 280.08
Major Medical	15.40 / 180.00	34.05 / 408.60	34.05 / 408.60
20% co pay	3.08 / 36.00	6.81 / 81.72	6.81 / 81.72
Dental	17.00 / 204.00	45.00 / 538.00	56.00 / 672.00
20% co pay	3.40 / 40.80	9.00 / 108.00	11.20 / 134.40
TOTALS			
Full Premium	158.40 / 1896.20	331.05 / 3970.60	432.50 / 5189.60
Labor's costs	31.68 / 379.20	66.21 / 794.12	86.41 / 1037.92
Employer's costs	126.72 / 1517.00	164.84 / 3176.48	345.64 / 4151.68

Overall Cost of Plan: $894,209
Overall Costs to Labor: $178,842 (1.78% Payroll)
Overall Costs to Employer: $715,367 (7.15% Payroll)

pay 20 percent of the $1,713 premium for basic insurance, or $343.60 a year. Family plan subscribers would pay 20 percent of $4,781, or $956.20 a year.

Alternative Three

Employees could pay 20 percent of the non-basic premiums, such as dental, vision, drug, home and office, or some other combination, which may or may not include the major medical component. To continue with the earlier example, this proposal would require employees to pay only 20 percent of the dental benefit costs, since this is the only benefit supplied beyond the basic medical coverage. For an individual, this proposal would amount to $40.80 a year (20 percent of $204), while family plan participants would pay $134.40 a year (20 percent of $672).

Alternative Four

The percentage paid by employees can vary. Indeed, the 20 percent amount used in previous examples is generally the maximum paid by employees. Before proposing a cost-sharing rate, management should survey comparable industries or companies in the same geographical location to determine the "going rate." In addition, when initiating a cost-sharing arrangement, management may find it easier to phase in the percentage contribution, perhaps beginning at 5 percent the first year, then increasing to 7.5 percent and 10 percent in later years.

Alternative Five

Management could require employees to pay a set percentage of any increases in premium costs, either in addition to or in lieu of paying a regular percent of the premium. To continue with the example used earlier in Exhibit 5-5 if the per-employee premium of $1,896 increases 25 percent (by $474) the following year, the company could require employees to pay one-half of this increase ($237). When this $237 increase is added on to the 20 percent regular premium contribution ($379.20), an employee would wind up paying a total of $616.20 annually for individual coverage.

Alternative Six

Instead of a percentage contribution, the company could require employees to pay a fixed dollar amount. This figure may or may not be capped, and the arrangement also should specify what occurs if plan costs drop. For example, contract language might link the amount of the premium to be paid per employee to the amount of the increase or decrease in total plan costs. Or, the contract could provide that if plan costs decrease, a certain percentage of employees' contributions will be reserved in a fund to offset future increases or used to fund wellness programs.

If a cap is set, a figure equivalent to a percentage contribution might be used as the dollar limit. For example, if a 20 percent contribution totals $379, the contract language could specify that the amount of an employee's premium contribution will not exceed $400. For contracts of several years' duration, this language ensures some stability and protects against sharp increases in employees' premium payments. This system clearly favors employees, whereas using a percentage contribution is more beneficial to management.

Deductibles and Out-Of-Pocket Expenses

Other methods of reducing a plan's costs include increasing deductibles and/or the maximum out-of-pocket expenses paid by employees. Deductibles establish a sum that the employee must pay before the insurance company provides any reimbursement. Out-of-pocket expenses, known by the acronym OOPS, establish an additional sum that the employee must pay before the insurance provides full reimbursement. For example, many plans require an individual to pay 20 percent of the first $2,000 of expenses ($400), plus the deductible, before the insurer will begin full payment.

Potential Cost Savings

To illustrate the possible cost savings, consider a proposal that would raise the deductible from $50 to $200 per individual, and from $200 to $1,000 per family. The increased cost to employees would amount to $800 for those with family plans, and $150 for those on individual plans. Savings to management would result from a reduction in the plan's claims reimbursement expenditures, which would cause a small percentage drop in the major medical premium. On a $1 million total premium, the savings to management might come to only $3,000 or $4,000.

To continue with the example of Middletown Paper used in Exhibit 5-2, consider a management proposal to double the major medical deductibles, from $100 to $200 per individual and from $250 to $500 per family. This change was estimated to save $3,638 for the 1990-91 plan year and $4,406 or so for the 1991-92 plan year. These savings amount to a very small percentage (.35 percent) of the total annual plan costs.

An example of an increased out-of-pocket expense maximum might double the dollar limit on total expenses. Instead of paying 20 percent of the first $2,500 in medical costs, an employee would pay 20 percent of the first $5,000. This shift would increase an individual's maximum out-of-pocket expenses from $500 to $1,000. While employees' potential costs double under this proposal, management's savings are considerably less. Savings typically amount to less than one percent of the major medical premium, and a much lesser percentage of the total account.

Contractual Safeguards

As these examples illustrate, deductibles or out-of-pocket expenses should receive close scrutiny during labor-management negotiations. Sometimes, limits on these amounts are specified in the section of the bargaining contract that describes insurance benefits. If this is not the case, then language in the contract should refer to a master trust agreement or some other fairly specific agreement that details the exact parameters of the insurance coverage.

Otherwise, the insurance contract may fail to establish a maximum family deductible or a limit on out-of-pocket expenses. For large families, the lack of a maximum family deductible could increase their costs considerably, while the lack of a limit on out-of-pocket expenses will mean that the insurer never has to begin providing full reimbursement.

Other Co-Payment Requirements

Besides co-payments on initial medical expenses, other types of co-payment provisions require the patient to pay something each time a service is used. In general, this practice began with implementation of prescription drug coverage. For example, a co-payment requirement for prescription drugs might have the patient foot the first $3.00 or so of the medicine's cost. The policy might require even higher co-payments if non-generic brands are used, unless the prescribing physician specified the medicine by name. In general, co-payments for prescription drugs can vary from 75 cents to $5.00 and higher.

Estimates of cost savings for instituting this type of co-payment provision range from one to three percent of the premium for the particular benefit area affected. The main rationale behind establishing this requirement is not the actual dollar savings but the indirect cost control. By having employees pay an immediate out-of-pocket expense, overuse of plan coverage presumably will decline.

Coordination of Benefits

Coordination of benefits is a fairly universally accepted method used to prevent the duplication of payments for health care services when family employees have separate policies. Some insurers have used coordination of benefits since 1969 for hospital benefits, and since 1975 for physician coverage.

Coordination of benefits permits a determination as to whose insurance program will be the primary payer of a claim and whose will be the secondary payer. The primary plan initially covers all eligible expenses up to the limit of its contract. When necessary, the secondary plan will cover outstanding balances of allowable expenses, also up to the limit of benefits in its contract. In this manner, the total benefits provided by both plans do not exceed the total cost of covered services.

Methods for Determining Primary Plans

The following rules typify common methods used to determine which insurance policy is the primary plan:

- A policy that does not contain a coordination of benefits clause may automatically be considered the primary plan.
- A patient's primary plan is the one which lists him or her as the subscribing member.
- The plan of the parent whose birthday occurs first during the calendar year will usually serve as the primary plan for all children. A few states, however, assign charges first to the father's plan.
- In the rare event that an individual has two health plans which list him or her as the subscribing member, the one in effect the longest will be the primary one.

Potential Cost Savings

To illustrate how coordination of benefits operates, both partners of a married couple might receive family coverage under different employer-provided insurance plans. If both plans contain a coordination of benefits clause, Mrs. Jones' policy is the primary carrier for her claims and will pay $700 (the UCR charge) for a $1,000 medical/surgical claim. She can then submit the remaining $300 to Mr. Jones' plan for payment. Between the two plans, the total bill is paid and the savings of $400 to Mr. Jones' plan will be useful in rate stabilization. That is, by having lower utilization and expenditures, Mr. Jones' plan will have a more favorable experience rating, which will help keep costs down or stable.

In the above example, Mrs. Jones did not need to utilize her major medical benefit to cover the remainder of her bill, nor did she incur a deductible. In essence, since the major medical portion of Mrs. Jones' plan did not have to cover the excess costs, the coordination of benefits provision produced a savings to her overall insurance program as well. If an excess, however, had remained that neither plan would pay under the medical/surgical coverage, then the primary plan's major medical would have become operative.

While coordination of benefits has become fairly routine, a new variation, known as a "carve out" approach, is being introduced. Under this arrangement, the secondary plan will not reimburse for any amounts which exceed the total benefit that would have been payable under the program had it been the primary payer. In the Jones' case, if Mr. Jones' policy as a primary plan would allow expenses up to $800, then Mrs. Jones would have received only $100, not $300, when she submitted the remainder of her $1,000 bill. If Mr. Jones' plan allowed only $650, then Mrs. Jones would have received no additional reimbursement for her claim.

Caveats Regarding Duplicate Policies

In the preceding example of Mr. and Mrs. Jones, if they both worked for Company XYZ, some employers would automatically assume that the two single policies should have been replaced with one combined policy when the employees married. Thus, the two individual premiums of $1,896 could become either $3,990 or a family rate of $5,190. Yet each employee may want to keep a separate policy, either as a family policy or as a couple policy with coverage for the spouse.

Under state laws and federal equal opportunity guidelines, employers who automatically replace single policies with one combined policy, without the explicit consent of the affected employees, can be charged with sex discrimination and sued for damages. In today's informed world, such presumptive actions logically should never take place. Numerous examples of this mistake, however, still occur in the public sector.

In short, when two employees marry, the employer should continue to offer separate coverage to each one, but update it for the additional coverage of a spouse and/or children. The economy of saving a premium is hardly worth the risk of a lawsuit and the future obligation of paying damages for health-incurred claims.

Opt-Out Provisions

Since more than 80 percent of women are employed and most families have two wage-earners, duplication of coverage frequently occurs. Coordination of benefits, however, may not be the best answer to reducing costs. Instead, some employers offer a direct financial incentive to encourage employees to forego coverage, thus sparing the company the costs of insuring these employees. Opt-out incentives can vary from more than one-half the premium saved to some lesser amount. In general, the larger the incentive, the more likely the employee is to opt out.

Potential Cost Savings

Although opt-out incentives might appear to offer considerable savings to the employer, other factors can offset the savings. As discussed in Chapter 4, adverse selection can cause the premiums for employees left in the plan to rise at a faster rate than previously. Adverse selection results if those who opted out had lower than average plan usage, whether because their medical expenses were paid by another insurer or because they happened to be healthy. When this happens, the average utilization rate of the remaining pool goes up and premium rates increase accordingly.

Case Illustration

Nonetheless, most employers can save some money up front by instituting an opt-out provision. To illustrate the savings, consider the policy of Company XYZ (see Exhibits 5-3 through 5-5). It offers employees who opt out of family coverage a rebate of $2,500 and those who opt out of individual coverage a rebate of $1,000. Annual family coverage costs the employer $5,190 per employee, while individual coverage costs $1,896 per employee.

If 13 of the 54 people currently receiving individual coverage opt out, the company's premium payments drop by $24,648 (13 times $1,896). When offset by the $13,000 paid to those opting out of individual coverage, the company's net savings total $11,648. In addition, 21 of those eligible for family coverage opt out. Since the company no longer makes premium payments of $5,190 for these 21 persons, it saves $108,990. After adjusting for the $52,500 paid to those opting out of the coverage, the company realizes a net savings of $56,490 in this area.

The company's total net savings amount to $68,138. Since the anticipated premium for insuring all 300 employees would cost $924,697, the savings represent some 7.37 percent of the anticipated expenses, not counting any subsequent increase in premiums if the utilization rate rises.

Procedural Issues

When implementing an opt-out incentive program, employers will need to establish clear-cut procedural guidelines for the program. Contract language illustrative of the specific opt-out provisions discussed below can be found in Exhibit 5-6.

Payment Methods

The method of paying the opt-out incentive should be defined clearly. A common system is to make the payment in two equal installments. As an alternative, employers can opt to pay the incentive in full at the end of the plan year. This last option can simplify

Exhibit 5-6

10. Waiver of Coverage
   A. Notwithstanding the above, effective with the execution of this agreement, an employee may voluntarily elect to waive in writing all health insurance coverages outlined above and, in lieu thereof, shall receive an annual payment of three thousand dollars ($3,000) for family or member plus one *or* fifteen hundred ($1500) for individual in cash. Payment to those waiving such coverage shall be made at the conclusion of the fiscal year during which insurance was waived.
   B. Up to 25% of the total insurance group of all eligible employees may take advantage of the waiver of health insurance. If more than 25% apply, seniority will be utilized annually for all employees not yet receiving but desiring the waiver for any openings below 25% of eligible employees.
   C. Notice of intention to waive insurance coverage must be sent not later than April 1 to be effective in the following contract year.
   D. The following rules will apply:
      1. An employee electing provided insurances must stay with the provided insurances for at least one full year.
      2. All insurance waived employees who wish to return to provided insurances will have an open enrollment date annually of one month to return to the provided insurance coverage for any reason at no cost to the employee (with no penalty) under same criteria established for new hires. To qualify for the enrollment, an employee must have notified the employer not later than June 15 of the same year of his/her decision to return to the desired insurances.
      3. Employees who have a change in coverage status such as death of the spouse, divorce, or the loss of coverage through the spouse (not by selection), may return to all provided health insurance coverage at any time throughout the year as long as written evidence is provided which substantiates one of these special conditions.
      4. Restoration of insurance coverage shall be reinstated as soon as possible; subject, however, to any regulations or restrictions, including waiting periods, which may then be prescribed by the appropriate insurance carriers. Appropriate financial adjustments shall be made on a pro rated basis for any waiver elected in this section.
   E. Waiver of coverage procedures must be acceptable to all applicable insurance carriers.
   F. Waiver of premium does not apply to life insurance.

bookkeeping in the event an employee who opted out chooses to reenroll prior to the end of the plan year.

Eligibility Requirements

Another concern is how many employees will be allowed to opt out. In the previous example, 54 of 300 people opted out, or 18 percent of the plan's membership. Insurance companies often will not renew a policy if more than 25 percent of subscribers opt out of the program, so some limits may be necessary.

If a limit on the number of employees allowed to opt out is necessary, employers will have to set up some type of eligibility process. The Landmark plan in Appendix 2, for example, requires those opting out to show proof that they have some other form of insurance coverage. This proof of coverage should be reviewed at least annually before plan reenrollment time.

Seniority also might be used as a procedure for prioritizing which employees get first consideration for the opt-out incentive. Whether seniority is based on time served within the company or within some job category, the procedure should follow the guidelines established to determine seniority for other purposes under the collective bargaining agreement.

Reenrollment Provisions

Other issues to consider when implementing an opt-out incentive concern the procedures used to allow someone back into the plan. These procedures can differ depending on the reason for reenrollment, but clear-cut guidelines should be specified.

For involuntary loss of alternative insurance coverage due to the death of a spouse, loss of the spouse's job, divorce, or some other factor, provisions should allow the person to reenroll within 31 days of loss of coverage, without restrictions as to preexisting conditions or the ability to pass a physical. Negotiating such a provision with the insurance carrier may not always be possible, but in general, an attempt should be made.

For voluntary reinstatement into the plan, more stringent criteria can be employed. An insurer may require evidence of insurability (passing a physical), or preclude coverage for preexisting conditions until a year's time has passed, or limit coverage of costs for certain preexisting conditions to a specified dollar limit. Many states, however, prohibit plans above a certain size from excluding preexisting conditions. In New York, for example, the threshold is 300 employees.

The employer also should set up a clear procedure by which an employee gives notice of intent to reenroll in the plan on a voluntary basis. For example, an employer might require at least three months' notice.

Finally, the policy governing the opt-out program should specify that when an employee reenters the plan, a pro-rata refund of the bonus received must be repaid to the plan by the employee.

Plan Funding Methods

Prior to implementing an opt-out program, the employer should make sure the insurance plan is set up as a cafeteria plan conforming to section 125 of the Internal Revenue Code. This arrangement ensures that the health insurance plan will not be viewed as a taxable fringe benefit. Absent a cafeteria plan, the IRS will consider funds received under the opt-out provision to be "constructive receipt" of additional benefits, and employees will have to pay taxes on the value of the opt-out incentive received. A recent statement by the Pennsylvania State Education Association, contained in Exhibit 5-7, explains this tax issue in more detail.

Plan Census

One additional cost-saving measure that is often overlooked is a plan census. A plan census identifies which individuals should not be continued in the plan, as well as who should be entered. This information is essential to prevent payment of benefits to ineligible people or denial of benefits to eligible employees. Costly oversights can occur if people who have retired, resigned, or died are not removed from the health insurance plan. In addition, a company could become liable to pay for health care expenses if it fails to provide insurance coverage to an eligible employee or the employee's dependent.

A reassessment of active participants should be conducted annually. Employees' marital and family status change frequently, and when employees go on leave, confusion over benefit coverage can result. In most cases, even employees on unpaid leave for child-rearing and elder or other relative care should continue to receive

Exhibit 5-7 Cafeteria Plans (Section 125 of the Internal Revenue Code)

General Premise: Cafeteria plans must meet the requirements of Section 125 of the Internal Revenue Code, or the amount of cash available in lieu of benefits will be assumed to be received by all employees, and all employees will be taxed on that amount of cash even if they selected benefits instead.

1. The recommended bargaining language for such plans is as follows:

   The school district shall establish the plan described in Article _____ in a manner consistent with and to meet all requirements of Section 125 of the Internal Revenue Code, as amended.

2. If you have already bargained cafeteria plans which do not meet Section 125 requirements and the employer is under reporting income on employee W-2's, consider the following:

   a. Evaluate each CBA and employer on a case-by-case basis.

   b. Review the CBA and identify those elements of a Section 125 plan that are missing.

   c. Find out how long the cafeteria plan has existed.

   d. If you don't deal with the problem and the employer is caught by the IRS, it will have to issue amended W-2's and the employees will have to file amended tax returns.

   e. The employer could suffer substantial penalties for under-reporting income. The longer the practice, the higher the penalties.

   f. If you amend the plan to include Section 125 requirements, then the employer can continue its practice of simply reporting salaries in W-2's, thus it is to everyone's benefit to amend the cafeteria plan.

   g. The amendments can be done in the CBA or in a separate written plan.

   h. Consider your timing: Is the CBA about to expire and will the health insurance plan change in bargaining? Is the employer ready to issue W-2's, (meaning that if you draw this to the employer's attention, it will include the constructive receipt of cash in everyone's W-2)?

   i. Help is available from Headquarters if you have any questions.

Source: Pennsylvania State Education Association, Harrisburg, PA (Dec. 12, 1990).

coverage. Many states now mandate family leaves of two months to one year and require employers to continue payment of fringe benefits during this period.[5] Congress also has initiated similar legislation that would require employers with more than 50 employees to provide up to 12 weeks unpaid family leave.[6] Additions and deletions of dependents also should be reviewed annually or even semi-annually to ensure that everyone has proper coverage and that the company is not paying premiums for ineligible individuals.

Subrogation of Benefits

Subrogation of benefits is a method that provides for reimbursement to the primary health insurance plan if another payer (besides a secondary plan) provides coverage. This situation can occur when a third party is liable for the illness or injury requiring medical treatment, as is often the case of automobile accidents.

To illustrate how this provision works, consider a situation where an automobile accident that was someone else's fault caused injury to an employee. Whether the other individual's car insurance or a no-fault claim is responsible for coverage, the employer or the health plan can obtain reimbursement from the responsible party for any accident-related claims paid by another insurance plan. In effect, subrogation of benefits prevents double recovery, since the employee otherwise might collect twice for the same injury.

While these cases occur infrequently, claims collected through subrogation often are quite large. As a result, all insurance contracts should have a clause specifying the nature of the subrogation. The following example illustrates the typical wording of such clauses:

> The company shall have full rights of subrogation in any legal proceeding involving an employee in which the employee claims, or receives as part of a court judgment or out-of-court settlement, reimbursement for lost salary or wages covering period during which the employee received full or partial payments by the company. In instances where subrogation rights of the company are successfully exercised, no deduction from an employee's accumulated sick leave shall be made for days on which the employee was absent and for which the company receives reimbursement under this section.

Medicaid and Medicare Requirements

Third-party liability has become an important cost-control issue in the health care field, particularly with respect to Medicaid and Medicare. In 1985, Medicaid alone paid between $500 million and $1 billion in claims that should have been paid by other insurers.[7] Third parties which are legally responsible for paying medical claims of Medicaid recipients before Medicaid pays include such sources as private health insurance, employer-provided health insurance, medical support from noncustodial parents, auto insurance, court judgments or settlements, state workers' compensation, first-party probate, and some federal programs.

A new initiative related to third-party liability focuses on recovering claims paid first under Medicare from the private insurance companies of active employees.[8] For individuals over age 65 who are still actively employed and covered by health insurance, the employer's plan should be the primary payer. The Health Care Financing Administration has written over 800,000 employers requesting information on whether or not they offer group health plans. Employers offering insurance will receive a questionnaire seeking detailed information about the coverage of specific employees and their spouses who are Medicare beneficiaries. Through these efforts, the HCFA hopes to recover between $600 million to $1 billion from employer health plans.

Alternative Insurance Carriers

A frequent assumption among insurance purchasers is that comparison shopping will produce a less expensive alternative. This assumption may or may not hold true. In general, prices among carriers will not vary by more than 15 percent for the same product.[9] What does vary significantly, however, are the quality of services, especially claims processing, and the types of underwriting, particularly as to the amounts of reimbursement and coverages provided.

Comparing Carriers

In switching companies, differences in claims processing can pose the most difficult problem. Under a plan that has participating physicians and hospitals (such as Blue Cross/Blue Shield plans, HMOs, PPOs, and other point-of-service networks), no claims filing or prepayment of fees is necessary. Under plans without participating providers, the patient must pay first and then file a claim for reimbursement, which usually takes two to six weeks.

Numerous variations in coverage among insurers also complicate any attempt at comparison shopping. No two companies seem to write their insurance policies exactly the same way, which largely reflects the myriad possibilities and complex nature of medical care. In addition, few carriers can replicate the Blue Cross/Blue Shield policy of providing full reimbursement when participating physicians and hospitals are used. Other insurance companies usually do not have the same type of discount leverage. Even if the non-Blues reimburse more dollars per service, that sum may not cover the complete charge or make up for the interest the patient loses during the six weeks or so of waiting for reimbursement.

During labor-management negotiations over health care, these differences among insurers can have important implications. Language in the contract may or may not specify the carrier. Coverage, however, is usually considered a mandatory subject of bargaining, as is the exact type of benefits to be offered. In general, the more explicit the language is in detailing the nature of the insurance coverage, the fewer problems in interpretation will result. In addition, specifying as precisely as possible the provider of coverage should help resolve any disputes or grievances over benefits that may arise. Examples of language concerning these specifications appear in Exhibit 5-8, while Exhibit 5-9 illustrates contract clauses governing a change of carriers.

When to Switch Carriers

Whenever price hikes would necessitate a change in benefits under the original plan, then coverage differences from the original carrier no longer matter and comparison shopping can prove valuable. In one case, the negotiating team of a small union found that premiums had risen to more than $10,000 for family coverage in a first-dollar plan, and were slated to increase another 25 percent if the contract were renewed. The team found that changing to an alternative carrier offering similar coverage would save more than $100,000 on current premiums, and even more on future premiums, considering the proposed rate hike.

To ensure union members accepted the plan, the union distributed a summary analysis of major variations between the two plans, along with the message that winning a large wage increase would depend on making some concessions in health care. Appen-

Exhibit 5-8 Example of Contract Language Specifying Coverages

BENEFIT PROGRAMS FOR LANDMARK EMPLOYEES
20.1 *Medical-Hospital:* The employer will continue to cover all full-time employees and regular part-time employees whose regular schedules are at least 20 hours per week, who elect such coverage under Blue Cross semi-private, 365 Day Plan and Blue Shield Plan 100 with Major Medical coverage of $250,000. The employee monthly contributions are noted in the Memorandum of Understanding covering the cafeteria plan.
20.2 *Alternative Health Care Plans:* The employer will continue to cover employees entitled to the coverage provided in paragraph 20.1 on an options basis, under Rhode Island Group Health Association (RIGHA), Health Maintenance Organization of Rhode Island (HMO-RI), Ocean State Physicians Health Plan (OSPHP), or alternative health care plans, and employee monthly contributions are noted in the Memo of Understanding covering the cafeteria plan.

MEMO OF UNDERSTANDING FOR THE CAFETERIA PLAN
The parties agree to the Flexible Benefit Plan Proposals of 9/8/88 and 5/26/88 with the following modifications:
(1) The monthly copayment rates for Blue Cross will be: full-time individual, $6.00;
                                                     part-time individual, $8.00;
                                                     full-time family, $14.00;
                                                     part-time family, $17.00.
(2) The monthly copayment rates for Healthmate will be the same as those in (1) above.
(3) The monthly copayment rates for Delta Dental IV will be: $2, $3, $5, and $6 respectively.
(4) The monthly copayment rates for HMO-RI will be $0, $1.43, $2.64, and $5.64 respectively.
(5) The monthly copayment rates for OSPHP will be $2.88, $4.88, $11.98, and $14.98 respectively.
(6) The monthly copayment rates for RIGHA will be $14.05, $16.05, $37.72, and $40.72 respectively.
(7) It is understood that Vision Care is subject to enough employees signing up to satisfy the carrier.
(8) The plan will be implemented no later than March 1, 1989. In the meantime, copayments will be as specified in the current contract (10/1/86–9/30/88), but will not be paid with after-tax dollars.

Source: Article X, Oct. 1, 1988—Sept. 30, 1990 contract between Landmark Medical Center and Landmark Federation of Nurses and Health Professionals, Local 5067 AFT-AFL-CIO.

dix 6 presents the comparative data compiled by the union to illustrate differences between the two plans.

Plan Redesign or Alternative Types of Insurance

When negotiations with insurance providers or the medical community do not provide enough savings, plan redesign may offer the only recourse to avoid additional costs. The structural changes in plan redesign, however, necessitate some basic philosophical changes in the attitudes of management and labor. For labor, acceptance of plan changes often depends on recognition that keeping the status quo will mean either accepting less in salary or sharing in the costs of rising premiums.

Regardless of the actual elements affected by plan redesign, management and labor should jointly investigate the options and develop an employee education strategy to communicate the rationale behind the change. This cooperation demands a departure from current practice. While labor unions ultimately might agree to changes, they often balk at prenegotiation studies of the issue. Management, on the other hand, often is unwilling to work on such studies when labor suggests them. A cooperative committee to address these issues will help shift the focus from labor-management conflicts to the brokers, carrier, and medical providers.

Switching to a Different Type of Insurance

The most obvious way for a company to save money through plan redesign is to substitute a comprehensive plan for an indemnity

Exhibit 5-9 Samples of Contract Language Governing a Change of Carriers

A. That Guarantees Equal Coverage

In the event the employer seeks to provide insurance coverage equal to or better than that specified in the current contract, s/he will consult with the President of the Union and gain written clearance from the Executive Board of the Union before proceeding.

B. Including Dispute Remedy

The employer shall have the right to change insurance carriers and/or to self-insure in whole or in part in order to provide the insurance coverage set forth above, provided that there shall be no reduction or diminution in those coverages and no increase in expense to any employee, and provided further that coverages which result from change in carriers and/or self-insurance are at least equal to the coverages described above in terms of coverage, benefits, and administration.

The union president shall be notified in writing within 30 days of any need to change carriers and/or to self-insure and shall have reasonable opportunity to review the proposed changes. Should the union and the employer disagree that the changes proposed will provide coverages at least equal to the coverages, benefits, and administration presently in force and at no increased cost to the employee, the disagreement(s) shall be subject to impartial arbitration before an arbitrator experienced in insurance matter under the rules of the American Arbitration Association and, if possible, under the expedited rules of the AAA. No change in the insurance policy shall be made until the arbitrator has rendered his/her award. The status quo shall be maintained during the above proceedings.

plan offering first-dollar coverage. While this switch creates higher costs for employees, they will continue to receive full protection against large medical costs. The use of deductibles, coinsurance, and copayment arrangements in a comprehensive plan can lower costs even further. Indeed, some consultants argue that instituting these options will prove more cost-effective than paying incentives for employees to opt out of the program.

Raising Deductibles and Coinsurance Requirements

In moving from first-dollar coverage to a comprehensive plan, other variations are possible. The revised plan could limit first-dollar cover to specific services, such as diagnostic X-rays, mammograms, laboratory procedures, and other preventative types of care. For other types of treatment, the plan could establish a $200 deductible and a $1,000 out-of-pocket maximum exposure in coinsurance.

For plans that already have a deductible, one alternative is to vary deductibles and out-of-pocket expenses by indexing these requirements to either the Consumer Price Index or actual salary adjustments. A comparison of the effect of inflation on fixed-dollar deductibles helps to illustrate the possible savings from instituting this option. As shown in Exhibit 5-10, Middletown Paper Company was told that to maintain savings equivalent to those provided by a $100 deductible in 1980, the deductible in 1990 would have to increase to $172, using a simple Consumer Price Index (CPI) adjustment. If medical inflation, which runs double the CPI rate, were taken into account, the deductible would have to increase to $226. Add on other general trend factors, and the company could justify raising the deductible to $631.

Altering Particular Benefit Riders

Besides deductibles, other facets of an indemnity program also can increase at rates higher than the value returned. The same consultant explained to Middletown Paper Company that the cost for the home and office rider of its policy exceeded the money available for this benefit. The policy provided a maximum annual benefit of $270 per person for unrestricted visits to a physician, but the cost to the employer totalled $282 per person. For a family, the cost was $1,048 for a benefit that could not exceed $710. In addition, premiums for the plan's prescription drug benefit, which covered

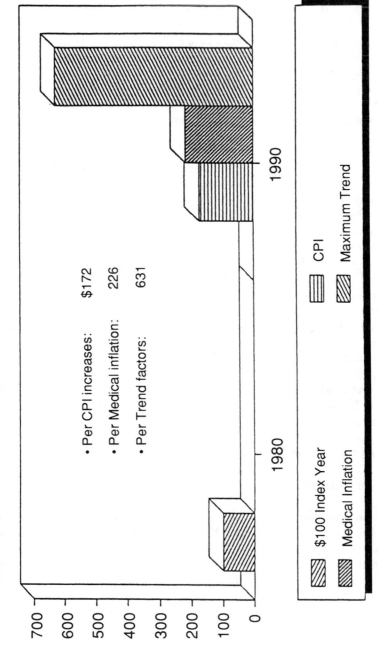

Exhibit 5-10 Effect of Inflation Factors on Fixed Dollar Deductible

• Per CPI increases: $172

• Per Medical inflation: 226

• Per Trend factors: 631

Legend:
- $100 Index Year
- Medical Inflation
- CPI
- Maximum Trend

Source: The Lindberg & Ripple Company.

up to $500 per person in expenses for medicine, cost the company almost half the benefit provided, or $233 per person.

These findings prompted Middletown Paper to consider more cost-efficient alternatives, including:

- Integrating the home and office coverage into the basic medical coverage;
- Funding the home and office rider directly through a self-insured administrative agreement;
- Funding the rider as an optional benefit in a flexible benefit account.

Instituting Flexible Benefits

Implementation of flexible benefits is one method of reducing the costs of current coverage. As mentioned in Chapter 3, the primary advantage to management is that a flexible benefit plan fixes the employer's contribution and shifts the risk for covering cost increases onto employees. The offsetting asset for employees is that a flexible benefit plan can be designed to suit individual needs. The tax advantages available under section 125 of the Internal Revenue Code also have boosted the popularity of flexible benefit plans relative to other cost-containment measures.

One example of the use of flexible benefits as a cost-control strategy occurred in a 1990 contract dispute in Mona Shores, MI.[10] The school board and union's proposals regarding salaries and health insurance were miles apart, prompting threats of a strike. Just one day before the walkout date, teachers agreed to pay $2,000 toward the annual cost of insurance, with two caveats: (1) teachers' salaries would have to be increased by $2,000, and (2) a section 125 salary reduction plan would have to be implemented so that teachers could make their premium payments in pretax dollars.

These caveats ensured that subsequent salary increases would be determined on a higher base, so the teachers actually came out ahead. Based upon anticipated salary increases, the union calculated that teachers would recoup the $2,000 paid out for premiums within seven years. As a final demand, however, the union had also insisted that teachers' pensions be based on a $4,000 annual increase. Even though teachers paid five percent of the tax-free $2,000 premium contribution to the state for their pensions, the net result was an overall increase in their salary benefits, a future increase in their pensions, and an increase in the dollars available to spend on health insurance through elimination of any federal tax bite.

As described in Chapter 3, a variety of adaptations of flexible benefit programs exists, which increases the possibility that some aspect of a program will prove beneficial to all parties. One of the most prudent decisions would be to offer a core program with some selected add-ons. In this way, all employees are protected against substantial loss and have the option of choosing which extras they are willing to purchase. The Landmark example in Appendix 2 provides a good illustration of a well-communicated flexible benefit program.

Notes

1. A. Foster Higgins, Inc., *Health Care Benefits Survey* (1987): 17.
2. Ibid., 1990.
3. "Can't Afford to Get Sick," *Time* (Aug. 2, 1989): 43.
4. Employee Benefits Research Institute, *Employee Benefit Notes* 10, no. 12 (December 1989): 1–4.
5. Employee Benefit Research Institute, *Employee Benefit Notes* 11, no. 10 (October 1990): 1–3. This issue summarizes state legislation requiring family leaves, which may or may not be paid or require the continuation of employer-paid health insurance. Effective July 1, 1992, Connecticut, for example, will require payment of health benefits for up to 24 weeks for state employees and for up to 12 weeks for private-sector workers employed by a company with more than 76 employees. States with similar requirements include Washington, Wisconsin, Pennsylvania, Vermont, Oregon, and Minnesota, as well as the District of Columbia.
6. HR 2 and SB 5 were passed in November 1991, and a Senate/House conference to develop a compromise bill is expected in early 1992. See "Family Leave," *WEB Network* 2, no. 7 (January 1992): 12, and Employee Benefits Research Institute, *EBRI Notes* 12, no. 11 (November 1991): 7.
7. National Conference of State Legislators, *The Fiscal Newsletter* no. 5 (September/October 1988): 8.
8. Bureau of National Affairs, Inc., "Medicare: HCFA Sends 800,000 Employers Letters to Find Wrongly Paid Medicare Benefits," *Daily Report for Executives* no. 64 (April 3, 1991): A–9.
9. Bureau of National Affairs, Inc., "Develop Small Firm Buying Strategy by Imitating Big Firms, Consultant Says," *Benefits Today* 8, no. 4 (Feb. 2, 1991): 62. This article discusses comments by Mark J. Meade and concludes that any carrier more than 15 percent out of the average price range has probably made an error.
10. Stan Burnell, 913 Uniserv Director of the Michigan Education Association, speech at the National Education Association's Health and Benefits Forum, Hollywood, FL, April 28, 1990.

Chapter 6

Bargaining to Contain Costs

In contrast to cost-shifting strategies that can pit labor against management, finding ways to contain costs will prove useful to both sides. Major cost-containment methods involve decreasing utilization and finding less expensive care. During the last decade, several of these approaches have resulted in lowering costs by 5 to 15 percent. For example, the AFL-CIO Department of Occupational Safety, Health, and Social Security published a pamphlet in the late 1980s with a chapter that analyzed nine cost-containment options that produced savings ranging from 8.1 percent for precertification of hospital admissions to 9.6 percent for coordination of benefits.[1] Management too published a study suggesting similar cost-containment measures. Called *National Health Care Strategy* and published by the National Chamber of Commerce, one chapter analyzed the effects of hospital utilization review, second surgical opinions, preadmission testing, ambulatory surgery, and home health care, among others.[2]

Many of these options have become so integrated into most health plans that their cost-saving effects are no longer visible. Without them, however, health insurance would be even more expensive. What is needed at this stage are strategies that target major users of health care. According to AFL-CIO estimates fewer than 5 percent of all health care users in any given year account for more than 90 percent of total health care costs.[3] Others in the field agree that up to 20 percent of the users may contribute to the large majority of the costs. These users are the people who tend to suffer from serious injuries, illnesses, or diseases. According to the AFL-CIO, once heavy users are eliminated, approximately one-third of the remaining 95 percent of plan users have no medical expenses at all, and many more incur only minimal medical care costs.

The union uses this argument to point out that cost shifting will not work for those who use the medical system little or not at all.

Cost-containment strategies, however, can target the five to twenty percent who are the big users. A discussion of some of the conventional cost-containment issues follows. For detailed examples of contract language specifying cost-containment measures, see Appendix 7.

Case Review or Managed Care

Case review should not only prevent unnecessary treatment but also should increase awareness of alternatives among both plan participants and providers. Insurers often provide specific case review programs that can be bought as add-ons to a standard insurance policy. These programs are often called "managed care" or "managed benefits." Thus the term "managed care," when used in relation to cost containment, refers to a form of case management and intervention, and not to a health maintenance organization or a preferred provider network.

Managed Care Policies

Whatever they are called, such programs generally provide three major components: (1) preadmission certification or authorization for elective hospital admissions, (2) a second surgical opinion, and (3) some type of review process, along with discharge planning and individual benefits management. For this service, the charges can average anywhere from $2.00 a month per person upwards. Each of these components is described further below.

Preadmission Certification

Preadmission certification or authorization often is combined with continued stay review (PAC/CSR) for hospital admissions. These plan features require a participant to have a provider certify the appropriateness of the hospital care. For elective procedures, the certification must occur prior to admission, and for emergency situations, some notice and approval must occur within a prescribed time limit, usually 24 to 48 hours. If authorization is not sought, then when it comes time for reimbursement, some type of financial penalty will be imposed. The nature of the penalty is often negotiable and may be modest or large. Of course, the larger the penalty, the less expensive the policy.

Mandatory Second Opinions

Mandatory second opinions are usually required before various types of surgery can be performed. In general, surgeries subject to second opinion requirements include upwards of 16 different procedures thought to be performed more often than necessary. The insurer pays for the cost of the second opinion and often for a third opinion. Patients, however, do not have to forgo the surgery, even if the second and third opinions find it unnecessary. Nonetheless, in most cases, the result of this requirement is at least less surgery.

If a second opinion is not obtained, a penalty is imposed at the time of reimbursement. Once again, the policy should clearly specify the size of the penalty. It may be a flat dollar amount or a percent of the allowable reimbursement, which often amounts to a 25 to 30 percent reduction in what would normally be reimbursed. Explanatory brochures often do not reveal the amount of the penalty to be assessed if the requisite procedures are not followed. Thus employees often are not aware of the magnitude of the penalty. As a safeguard, the policy should include an appeal process for remission of unfairly imposed penalties.

Typical savings from requirements according to insurers' quotes, amount to five percent of total plan costs. Some insurers will guarantee a specific percentage savings and will reduce the total premium by that amount. Actual savings, however, are difficult to measure, given the need to establish two identical or similar control groups, one covered by a plan with the feature and one without, and to monitor costs over a significant time span. Some experts argue that delaying surgery may only lead to more significant and costly problems later. Yet much evidence is available in the medical literature to prove that many operations are performed needlessly. Exhibit 6–1 contains a list of the surgical procedures most likely to be subject to possible abuse, and therefore, candidates for mandatory second surgical opinions.

Case Management

Case management through utilization review or concurrent review and discharge planning is another approach to containing utilization of medical services. In the past, less expensive alternative

Exhibit 6-1 Some Surgical Procedures which may be Subject to Requirement for Mandatory Second Surgical Opinion

Bunionectomy—removal of bunions
Hysterectomy—full or partial removal of ovaries and/or uterous
Carpel Tunnel Syndrome—surgery of hand or wrist
Coronary bypass surgery—replacement of heart arteries
Tonsillectomy with or without adenoidectomy—removal of tonsils and/or adenoids
Hemorrhoidectomy—removal of hemorrhoids
Varicose vein ligation with stripping—removal and tying of varicose veins
Cordotomy—operation on section of vocal cord
Coccygectomy—excision of coccyxk, "tail bone"
Hernia repair—treatment of hernias
Cholecystectomy—removal of gall bladder
Repeat Disc Surgery
Eyelid Ptosis surgery—treatment of droopy eyelid
Fenestration of semicircular canal—creation of new opening in ear
Foot Surgery
Knee Surgery
Laminectomy—removal of part of vertebrae in back
Lipectomy—removal of fat tissue
Lumbar fusions—fusion of back bones
Mastectomy—removal of breast or removal of breast tissue
Phrenicotomy—surgical division of phrenic nerve
Prognathism—correction of protusion of jaw
Prostatectomy—removal of prostrate
Spinal fusion—surgical welding of spine segments
Septorhinoplasty—nose surgery for functional improvement, usually for a deviated septum

treatments were sought only for the more severe types of illnesses. Now, as insurance companies seek to discourage utilization, almost all treatment procedures undergo case monitoring. Case management reviews can either monitor an ongoing treatment to determine if less-expensive measures exist, review the charges of treatments already received, or examine the appropriateness of some suggested care before it is implemented. In the latter case, case management is a form of prereview that may even make recommendations for forms of treatment.

Case management is not always mandatory, and some policies simply offer utilization review as a voluntary option. Others, however, mandate utilization review by imposing a penalty if a review is not sought prior to treatment and/or if the advice resulting from the review is not followed.

The phrases used to describe the advantages of case review programs are often unclear, and misunderstandings arise. For example, assurances may be given that case management is completely voluntary and cannot be forced on a plan participant. Yet plan members may not understand that even if they agree to go through the process, they are not obligated to accept the recommendation.

Although this program produces a savings to the employer, there is also an out-of-pocket charge to use the services of the program. While the fee is not proportionally large, the expense still could offset the savings.

Case management can involve three types of reviews: prospective, concurrent, and retrospective.

Prospective Review. Prospective review involves preadmission screening to check that health care providers are doing only what is medically necessary and that the condition warrants hospitalization. If not, outpatient treatments will be recommended. This practice has become so successful that many hospitals have empty beds while the costs for outpatient treatment have been soaring. After instituting policies to encourage outpatient surgery, Ryder Corp., for example, saw a 35 percent reduction in emergency room cases and a 50 percent drop in benefits paid for these cases between 1983 and 1988.[4] More prescreening for ambulatory surgery may have to occur to evaluate the necessity of some of the surgery that is taking place on an outpatient basis. One of the most likely candidates for this type of screening would be cataract surgery, a procedure sometimes thought of as being done more often than needed.

Concurrent Review. Concurrent review evaluates the appropriateness of the recommended treatment. Insofar as it can lead to a shortened hospital stay, cost savings will be realized. The interest in concurrent review has been increasing and many insurance companies have departments dedicated to this aspect of managed care.

The suitability of treatment programs typically is measured against standards set by the Foundations for Medical Care (FMC) and by the federally mandated Professional Standards Review Organization (PSRO). Both have come into being primarily as a result of the use of DRGs (diagnosis-related groups) in the Medicare and Medicaid programs. The review program is designed to ensure both quality of care and efficient economies. The cost of this service varies between $5 and $15 or higher per admission.

Another aspect of concurrent review involves discharge planning, which seeks alternatives to acute care facilities. In some cases, continuing care in a skilled nursing facility or at home would be preferable to hospital care, but the benefit package may not provide reimbursement for that type of treatment. Through the intercession of case reviewers with the insurer, the patient can utilize these alternative arrangements that are likely to be less expensive and more humane.

Alternative types of care are plan exceptions and must be justified as medical necessities; simply having an expensive or serious illness does not mean that optional treatment centers may be available or feasible. Alternative care arrangements are usually most effective in the treatment of traumatic injuries, severe nervous disorders, and alcohol and substance abuse. One other situation where alternative care can be provided is in the case of terminal patients, where referral to a hospice might prove more suitable and usually cost less.

Retrospective Review. Retrospective review is a formal audit of the billing and treatment received. This review can occur in two ways: (1) as a claims review where all physician decisions are evaluated before reimbursement is made, or (2) by providing cash incentives to employees for reviewing their bills for overcharges or errors.

In addition to examining individual claims, retrospective reviews can involve an analysis of the types of care used annually. Such an analysis could show trends and suggest areas where action may be taken to reduce costs. For example, Blue Cross/Blue Shield has developed a "Joint Profile System" that can identify norms, unusual utilization patterns, and long-term trends. The United Mine Workers of America's Health and Retirement Fund also has developed an automated claims review system that profiles costs, utilization, and quality of care received. Appendix 5 provides an example of a Blue Cross/Blue Shield analysis. Other insurance companies can and do provide even more comprehensive data analysis of the usage of medical services.

Legal Issues

Given the restrictions they place on medical care, managed-care policies have the potential to adversely affect a patient's health, possibly with life-threatening consequences. As a result, managed-care programs raise some liability concerns. In addition, a number of states have established regulations governing the operation of these programs.

Liability

More expensive than the cost for the review procedure is the potential liability that could result to the employer when the managed care recommendations lead to mistakes. In such an event, liable parties could include the organization or physicians making the recommendation, as well as the insurer and the holder of the policy.

In the *Wickline* case in California,[5] the court in dicta stated that the particular cost containment program, which required advance approval of treatment, put undue pressure on patients and care providers to comply with the procedures.[6] For that reason, some consultants in the field feel wary about the potential for cost containment measures to corrupt medical opinion on appropriate treatment.

Insurers and third-party payers have also been found liable for damages, as in the *Total Health Care* case in Missouri.[7] In this case, the court applied a theory of corporate negligence when an HMO had limited subscriber access to only its doctors and prevented selection of any others. The court stated that the HMO could not deny its common-law duty to investigate the competence and reputation of the doctors it selected so as not to put a subscriber at risk of harm.

The issue of employer liability may become more critical in the future, particularly when cost-containment strategies are adopted with a clear goal of stopping the flow of funds from the plan and the employer. One case, currently on appeal, has asserted that under ERISA, a corporate negligence theory is not necessary for liability, since the employer has fiduciary responsibility for the selection, monitoring, and if necessary, removal of service providers. In this case, a Pennsylvania court ruled against Bethlehem Steel Co. for penalizing plan members who failed to obtain precertification for treatment that was later found to be medically necessary.[8] Judge William W. Caldwell found this practice violated public policy because the penalties were arbitrary and capricious and not in compliance with the fiduciary duties that ERISA imposes on plan administrators. In other words, case control is fine if it does not conflict with the employer's fiduciary responsibility.

To avoid liability, the following principles of risk management should be initiated before hiring a firm to implement a managed care program:

- Do a thorough search for qualified companies using a detailed request for proposal form (RFP) to document efforts to make an informed choice.
- Be sure the utilization review firm is independent and not in any way affiliated with your organization.
- Have the utilization review firm sign a hold-harmless agreement so it will be responsible for any liability that arises.
- Be sure the utilization review firm has liability insurance.

State Laws

Many states currently are adopting legislation that oversees the process of utilization review. In most cases, this legislation either establishes strict requirements for licensing utilization review firms, thus empowering the state to regulate the profession, or imposes certain restrictions and requirements on the process and participants. For example, Maryland, one of the first states to enact such legislation in 1988, mandates licensure of utilization review consultants through a procedure that requires applicants to detail

(1) review standards and procedures,
(2) reviewers' qualifications,
(3) procedures for protecting the confidentiality of Medical records,
(4) process for ensuring accessibility to review agents during business hours, and
(5) appeals procedures.

Similar laws currently exist in Arkansas, South Carolina, Virginia, West Virginia, and Georgia. Legislation to regulate managed care or utilization review firms is also pending in Florida, Mississippi, Kentucky, and Connecticut.

Effectiveness of Managed Care

Determining the exact savings from managed care is difficult due to a variety of considerations. For example, shortened hospital stays might result not from intervention procedures but from other factors, such as variations in age, sex, and general physical well-being. In addition, the discharged employee may face some expenses related to ambulatory care, such as discontinuance of disability payments or the cost of getting to the ambulatory care, that will not be reimbursed if he/she is at home. Finally, if it takes longer for the employee to get better at home, then the employee may have to use up more sick time or lose pay.

In short, alternative care is not always less expensive for the employee. Hospitals also are ingenious in compensating for this lost revenue by increasing their rates or assessment of charges for other services. Cost savings seeming to result from utilization review may also be due to less appropriate care, as well as from the failure to provide necessary care.

Very little research has investigated the actual cost savings of utilization review. A study by the Institute of Medicine has found that for some employers, utilization review had reduced total hospital days and admissions and proved cost-effective for employers who had above-average plan usage. Offsetting any savings, however, is the cost of the services provided by the utilization review firms themselves. These fees may vary from 50 cents to $5.00 or more per employee and range from $80 to $265 per hour or more for case management. In general, cost-containment efforts only work for long-term care.[9]

Even if direct cost savings do not result, some benefits can be clearly attributed to utilization review. These benefits include the following:

- decreased length of hospitalization,
- higher quality of care,
- identification of specific areas of need to be corrected through education, and
- increased cost-consciousness on the part of physicians and facilities.

Bargaining With Providers

Negotiating directly with care providers is another means of cost control. When physicians are provided with data indicating how their utilization patterns correlate with other doctors, those who are out of sync with the norm often will reform.[10] Even the U.S.

Chamber of Commerce has urged business to become involved in community health planning activities by bringing their concerns and suggestions for reform to hospital and physician boards.[11]

Bargaining directly with doctors and other providers over fees for elective surgery can be another effective technique to keep down costs. Such a strategy has been implemented by Dr. Eugene G. McCarthy, director of the Health Benefits Research Center at Cornell University Medical College.[12] Under this program, the third-party contractor and doctors consult prior to non-emergency surgeries to set fees. In four out of five cases, the patient is able to stay with his/her regular doctor for no more expense than if the published list of panel doctors had been used. This outcome reflects the willingness of most surgeons to negotiate their fees. The program covers about 650,000 people in the New York, New Jersey, and Washington D.C. areas.

Wellness and Employee Assistance Programs

General wellness and employee assistance programs are another answer to cost containment. Wellness programs focus mainly on improving employees' physical health, while employee assistance programs (EAPs) target areas more related to mental health and quality of life. The potential health improvements, and cost-savings resulting from these programs are discussed below.

Wellness Programs

Prevention is the mainstay of such programs, which usually include prediagnostic screening or a plan profile analysis. If heart disease, diabetes, emphysema, bronchitis, or even cancer are present among the employee population in numbers larger than expected, then some types of remedial wellness program may produce a benefit. Wellness programs may be offered by an insurance company, but local hospitals or clinics most often are better suited to set up the program.

Smoking cessation and weight loss programs are popular wellness projects, but a prescreening program should be conducted to verify the necessity of such programs. In one case, prescreening revealed that out of 120 employees, only four were smokers. While a smoke cessation program for those four people would still be helpful, the employer would not need to host such a program on site.

Prescreening programs can be done for about $7.00 per individual and may be completely voluntary. The first part of the program, sometimes called a health risk appraisal, is to screen for cholesterol levels, weight, alcohol addiction (if possible), blood pressure, diabetes, eye sight, hearing deficiencies, and stress levels, among other key symptoms. Depending on results, positive programs for weight loss, exercise, smoke cessation, substance abuse, and other general nutrition programs may be offered. Sometimes management even offers to subsidize participation in health spas or community programs for their employees rather than design a separate on the job program.

Cost Savings

The effect of improved health in reducing health care utilization cannot be determined definitely, but if even one heart attack is prevented then the program is worth the expense. In addition, some insurers will provide financial incentives for purchasing these programs. The incentives include waiving deductibles and/or copayments for employees who control their weight and blood pressure, don't smoke or drink, wear seat belts, have periodic physical exams, and so on. Some insurance programs are designed to provide specific preventative recommendations as a result of a health appraisal. If these recommendations are not followed, then the insurance company reduces the amount of payment allowed for subsequent medical expenses incurred. In some rare cases, insurers will even reduce premiums to employees if wellness programs are instituted.

In the opposite vein, an employer can charge a higher percentage of the premium sharing to those employees who are smokers or overweight by a certain amount. Or a company can use a positive incentive and reward employees who do not use the medical program by remitting any premium-sharing payments made during the year in which insurance was not used.

One recent analysis of the clinical and research literature has found that worksite wellness programs which are well-designed and effectively implemented will work.[13] Several variables found in this analysis to impact the program's cost-effectiveness are shown in Exhibit 6–2.

Three key characteristics of an effective wellness program include appropriate design, competent implementation, and effec-

Exhibit 6-2 Features of Effective Wellness Programs

The stronger top management's support	➩ The lower employee turnover rates
The lower the ratio of dependents per employee	➩ The greater the risk of occupational injury, and thus The greater the need for preventive measures
The older the work force	➩ The higher employee trust in the program
The more aggressive the outreach and follow-up	➩ The wider the usage and the stronger the incentive to use the program
The greater the emphasis on self-care and education	The better the program's effectiveness
The fewer the number of work sites	➩ The easier the program's control & implementation
The larger the work force	➩ The more effective the program
The higher the level of employee absenteeism	➩ The greater the program's success in correcting absenteeism
The lower the capital investment in programming	➩ The better the program's cost-effectiveness
The better the continuity and follow-through on programming	➩ The more the program's return on the dollar
The higher the prevalence of life-style health risks	➩ The more the program's return on investment
The more menu-driven and choice-oriented the program	➩ The higher the program's usage and cost-effectiveness
The greater the linkage with other employee benefits	➩ The higher the program's usage and cost-effectiveness
The greater the degree of defined contribution pension structure	➩ The more employee participation in company affairs, and in the wellness program
The more adequate the funding	➩ The better the program and the higher its usage

Source: Larry S. Chapman, *Proof Positive: An Analysis of the Cost-Effectiveness of Wellness* (Seattle, WA: Corporate Health Designs, 1990).

tive integration into the workplace or life-style of the employee. External factors, such as labor strikes, marked loss of market share, failed tax initiatives, geographic re-location, and bankruptcy, can also impact the effectiveness of wellness programs.

Given a sound program design, competent people to implement the program, and no unforeseen external catastrophes, then the wellness program should prove effective. For examples of effective wellness programs, see Appendix 8, which illustrates a Charlottesville, VA program in existence since 1985.

Employee Assistance Programs

An employee assistance program (EAP) is another type of a wellness program but one for mental health. Management's motivation for installing an EAP often is not just to improve mental health but also to assist with alternatives to punitive discipline. Indeed, some EAPs may be used primarily as a disciplinary alternative rather than as a health benefit for the employee.

The confidentiality of an employee assistance program is a frequent concern of employees. Management may opt for an EAP so they can insist that a difficult employee go to the EAP for counseling or be terminated. In such cases, the EAP program often contacts management to report on the employee's cooperation, but without revealing the nature of the treatment. Alcoholism, drug dependency, and mental illness also can be treated in these programs, but only if the employee is willing to undertake the treatment. Protection of members' privacy rights should be built into any negotiated agreement, and participation should be voluntary, not mandatory.

EAPs also can assist with family problems that relate to serious illnesses of family members, such as cancer, and may also help with problems of marital discord, troubled teenagers, and ailing parents. Counseling services offered by EAPs usually provide two to four free visits and will include advice on the least expensive methods of more prolonged assistance. When the employee's major medical policy provides for treatment only in a full-time mental health facility, an EAP counselor often can intervene and get the insurer to pay for non-institutionalized treatment on an outpatient basis.

The cost of an EAP program averages about $10 to $75 or more per employee, with family members usually covered for no additional cost. Before instituting an EAP, most companies hold extensive orientation sessions with the supervisors, employees, and sometimes with union representatives to explain the nature of the program.

Sample contract language regarding an EAP might read as follows:

> The employer will provide professional assessment, counseling, and referral services for employees experiencing personal problems through special arrangements with the Employee Services Clinic.

This service is extended to all members of the employee's immediate family. Further treatment beyond the basic coverage will be at the employee's expense or may be covered by other insurance benefits. Principles concerning use of the program will be worked out by a committee made up of equal representation from management and the union and finalized in a memorandum of agreement prior to a specific date and incorporated into the new contract.

The use of EAPs as a cost containment measure has not been proven. While used most frequently as ways to avoid disciplinary actions, EAPs are most helpful is assisting with alcohol and substance abuse. EAPs no doubt can assist with improving mental health, but the effect and scope of any resulting cost savings in health insurance has yet to be measured. Additional information on EAPs can be found in various texts; several sources are noted in the Resource Section.

Discounted Medical Services and Alternative Delivery Systems

This trend usually involves HMOs, PPOs, or other types of networks with doctors and hospitals which offer discounts to users. Providing incentives to use a specified group of providers also can produce greater savings than those attributable to the simple use of an HMO. Southwestern Bell and Allied-Signal are two companies which have customized health care plans, known in the trade as point-of-service plans, through which services provided in a designated network or site are charged at a discounted rate. Numerous other discount arrangements are possible, and some examples of these programs follow.

Case Illustrations

Southwestern Bell and Prudential Insurance Company of America developed a point-of-service health plan, called Custom Care, which uses a PPO network in major cities. The plan, initiated in 1987, has a risk-sharing feature specifying that if costs exceed certain limits, then the insurer and the company will split these extra expenses.

On the other hand, the Allied Signal plan contains additional written guarantees. The plan is administered by CIGNA Corporation and is self-funded based on a national network of CIGNA physicians. The only risk-sharing present is that CIGNA guarantees the rate of the company's expenditure increases for three years. Employees pay deductibles equal to one percent of annual base pay for individuals and three percent for families. Those who use non-network providers make a 20 percent co-payment, with a maximum out-of-pocket expense equal to 12 percent of the annual base pay. Coverage for vision, hearing, and preventive care is available only to network users. CIGNA reported that after 18 months, average costs for network participants were $2,450, while non-network users had $3,200 in expenses.[14]

AT&T has negotiated with three firms to set up a large health care system for 100,000 union employees and 250,000 dependents. Representing an unusual labor-management effort to address the increasing costs of health insurance, this program could influence labor negotiations in a variety of industries.[15] Despite AT&T's recent expenditures of $3 million a day on health insurance for its employees, the company's cost increases had been more reasonable than those faced by many other employers. Nonetheless, the new program is expected to reduce cost increases from 10 percent a year since 1984 to single digit rates. The program began in October 1990 and was fully implemented in 1991.

Selected from 20 companies to administer AT&T's plan were the Prudential Insurance Company of Newark, NJ; Travelers Corporation of Hartford, CT; and Empire Blue Cross/Blue Shield of New York. The evaluation and choice of administrators were determined by a joint committee of management and representatives from the two unions, Communications Workers of America and the International Brotherhood of Electrical Workers. According to the plan, which resulted from a protracted labor dispute and strike in the summer and fall of 1989, employees will pay a $150 deductible and up to 10 percent of non-hospital medical procedures. Hospitalization will be 100 percent covered. Those who see physicians outside the plan will have a $200 deductible and pay 20 percent of all care up to an annual maximum of $1,000.

AT&T's plan also sets targets for overall costs. If the insurers' experience is at the targeted level or less, then the carrier will share in the savings; if the experience is excessive, then the insurer will share the additional costs. AT&T feels that this plan will shift costs to the providers, rather than to the employees. Because it is less stringent than the terms of the Allied Signal plan, rates are not guaranteed.

Despite high hopes for cost savings, the burden is on labor and management to persuade AT&T employees to use the discounted system. Both sides know that if savings do not materialize, they will face more headaches in the 1992 negotiations. Some protective concessions won by labor in this agreement include the following: Any employee who currently has a chronic or long-term illness, such

Exhibit 6-3 Sample of a PPO Savings Analysis Summary

CHARGE TYPE	CURRENT PLAN	DISCOUNTED PLAN	SAVINGS	PERCENTAGE
Hospital	$2,449,718	$1,615,136	$ 834,582	34.1%
Physicians	1,337,315	1,046,450	290,865	21.7%
X-Ray/Lab	482,888	400,797	82,091	17.0%
Other	340,375	306,377	34,039	10.0%
TOTALS	$4,610,296	$3,368,720	$1,241,576	26.0%

BILLED VERSUS PAID ESTIMATES ANALYSIS		
Estimated Billed		$3,368,720
Estimated Not Covered	$336,872	
Estimated Deductibles	235,810	
Estimated Coinsurance*	518,783	
Total Reductions		− 1,091,465
ESTIMATED PAID		$2,277,255
Current Paid		$3,115,082
Estimated Paid		2,277,255
ESTIMATED SAVINGS Less Access Fee		$ 837,827 230,515
NET SAVINGS**		$607,312
PERCENT SAVINGS ON CURRENT PAID		19.5%

 * Based on lesser of billed or allowed
** Does not include $194,457 savings to members

Source: Reprinted with permission from Martin E. Segal Company, Phoenix office.

as cancer, will not have to change doctors for coverage. In addition, employees may nominate doctors to be network participants.

One other example is that of a joint team of United Auto Workers and General Motors benefit specialists who have begun a pilot project at two plants: C-P-C Assembly in Arlington, TX and Service Parts Operations in Fort Worth, TX. Early results of the project, which addressed delivery of mental-health care and use of substance-abuse benefits, show significant reduction in expenses and improved quality of care through a revised delivery system. The program also established a closed panel of medical providers and coordinated care through a common, local diagnostic and referral agency in the Dallas/Fort Worth area. Under the 1990 national contract, the UAW and GM plan to expand the central diagnostic and referral system to other plants.[16]

As these examples indicate, only through joint labor-management cooperation can the struggle to obtain less costly quality insurance be won. Both sides need to realize that cooperation need not mean co-optation. One other unusual solution recently adopted in some labor agreements has established a pool of dollars, with so much per employee designated over the life of the contract, to pay for increased premiums if necessary. If the premiums are less than the reserve, the employees share in the savings and may have an insurance rebate. This arrangement certainly provides an incentive for employees to use whatever cost-containment measures are included in their plan.

Savings from the use of a discounted network are represented in Exhibit 6-3. For employers interested in establishing such a system, Appendix 4 contains an example of a request for proposals for a physician and hospital network.

Notes

1. Karen Ignagni, Jeff MacDonald, and Meredith Miller, *Health Care Cost Containment Crisis, Bargaining for Improved Health Care Benefits* (Washington, DC: AFL-CIO Department of Occupational Safety, Health, and Social Security, Labor Institute of Public Affairs, George Meany Center for Labor Studies, undated). See especially Chapter 5.
2. National Chamber Foundation, *National Health Care Strategy* (Washington, DC: U.S. Chamber of Commerce, undated). See especially Chapter 4.
3. Ignagni *et al.*, *Health Care Cost Containment Crisis*, 7.
4. Jeffrey D. Mamorsky, ed., *Health Care Handbook*. Warren, Gorham, & Lamont, Inc., Boston, Mass. & N.Y. 1991 p 22–4.

5. *Wickline v. State of California*, 192 Cal. App. 3d 1630, 239 Cal. Rptr. 810 (Ct. App.), *cert. granted*, 231 Cal. Rptr. 560, 727 F.2d 753 (1986), *review dismissed*, 239 Cal. Rptr. 805 741 F.2d 613 (1987).
6. Cindy Combe, extracts from speech reported in *Working in Employee Benefits* (Sept. 1989): 4.
7. *Harrell v. Total Health Care, Inc.*, West Law 39311 (Mo. App. April 25, 1989), aff'd 781 S.W. 2d 58 (1989). This case involved a claim against open panel HMO for corporate negligence. See also *Employee Benefits Law System E* (Washington, DC: BNA Books, forthcoming).
8. Michael Schachner, "Ruling May Jeopardize Utilization Review," *Business Insurance* (June 24, 1991): 1, 76. This case is currently on appeal to the 3rd U.S. Circuit Court of Appeals in Philadelphia.
9. Michelle Hart, health services consultant for Martin E. Segal Company, "Utilization Review—Appropriate Features and Analysis," speech before the National Education Association's Health and Benefits Forum, Hollywood, FL, May 1, 1990.
10. James B. Kenney, "Responsible Cost Management: Assuring Quality in Your Health Care Plan," speech before National Education Association's Health and Benefits Forum, Hollywood, FL, May 2, 1990.
11. National Chamber Foundation, *National Health Care Strategy*, 13.
12. Glenn Kramon, "Business and Health, Bargaining on Fee with a Surgeon," *The New York Times* (April 19, 1988): D-2.
13. Larry S. Chapman, *Proof Positive: An Analysis of the Cost-effectiveness of Wellness*. Seattle, WA: Corporate Health Designs, 1990.
14. "BLS Percentage of Participants by Medical Care Delivery System," *EBRI Issues Brief* (March 1990): 9.
15. Ron Winslow, "AT&T's Plan on Health Costs May Set Pattern," *Wall Street Journal* (July 19, 1990): B-1.
16. Human Resource Center, "Quality Health Care and Cost Is Joint Concern," *UAW-GM People* (Winter 1991): 7.

Chapter 7

Negotiating With Providers and Maintaining Contract Benefits

Once management and the union have decided to provide a particular kind of insurance, then a plan offering that coverage must be bought. To ensure the kind of insurance coverage desired actually exists, both sides should understand what is available, under what conditions and at what price before reaching a final agreement. What was available yesterday may no longer be on the market. In addition, subtle changes in terms can result in a product that is not what either labor or management expected to buy. For example, many of the requirements described in the previous chapter are rapidly changing the coverage offered in plans today. New policies often include second surgical opinions, pre-admission review, utilization review, and managed care programs.

Purchaser Strategies

The simplistic policies of prior years now include more variations, restrictions, and penalties for failure to follow proper procedures. Even traditional indemnity policies, HMOs, PPOs, and other network programs change frequently. This section will focus on potential changes and other considerations to take into account before negotiating a final agreement.

Preliminary Considerations

The first step prior to purchasing a new insurance product is to gather data to determine if the present product meets current needs in a cost-efficient manner. A review of the current health plan documentation, such as appears in Appendix 5, is vital. The profile analysis should document the type of plan usage and membership demographics, along with comparing the costs with the benefits provided. This data is essential whether dealing with utilization review firms, insurance companies in general, HMOs, or PPOs, as well as in direct negotiations with hospitals, pharmacists, or other health-related suppliers. New providers will demand this information in any case so as to forecast their risk exposure. In addition, some providers require a guarantee of minimum or maximum enrollment in the plan.

Another point to check concerns the providers' liability and the conditions under which the provider may terminate the agreement. Know how an employee who is undergoing treatment can obtain benefits if the contract is terminated. Employers should also determine what happens if an employee opts out of the plan and subsequently wishes to return. The policy for re-insuring such individuals may exclude pre-existing conditions or it may require the employee to undergo a physical. Even if reinstatement is allowed, the policy may contain an additional cost factor connected to the restoration of benefits. (See Chapters 4 and 5 for a more detailed discussion of these considerations.)

When reviewing a proposal, check services to be provided. Be certain to verify what is included, as well as what has been excluded since the last policy purchase. For example, the policy may reimburse purchase of generic drugs only unless the prescribing physician offers sufficient substantive reasons to justify the particular brand. These types of simple changes often are not adequately publicized.

Besides examining the services covered, understand the particular restrictions of the plan. For example, an insurance policy may state that if more than one surgery is performed at the same time, such as removal of an appendix and a gallbladder, then only half of the usual allowance is paid for the second surgical procedure or may be that only one surgeon's fees will be covered. Such insurance industry attempts at restricting allowable costs, however, are often derailed by medical practitioners who find costly alternatives. In the case of two surgeons, for example, many hospitals list the second doctor as an assistant to ensure the full fee is paid. Indeed, care provider industry publications, such as the magazine *Hospitals*, include articles on the most profitable services a hospital can offer, as well as others on negotiation strategies for the medical practitioner.

Data Collection

A common theme in all these pointers concerns the need to have data. Most consultants suggest obtaining data on utilization, costs, demographics of the membership, and local providers. Vendors obviously have this data, yet employers often have difficulty securing this information.

Information on the provider community may have to be extracted from professional organizations and/or consultants' data bases, or collected by a consortium put together for that very purpose. In Rhode Island, for example, a group of nonunion businesses banded together to share their data and then had it analyzed professionally.[1] Similar consortiums are possible, although not always successful. Most of the other data is available from the vendor, but sometimes insurance companies are reluctant to provide aggregate data, particularly when they feel the employer is comparison shopping. With enough insistence, however, it can be obtained. A reasonable explanation of the yearly quote and method used to project the next year's rate can prove even more difficult to obtain. Indeed, this information is often aggregated in such a way as to be purposely obscure. The example produced by Wyatt Company as shown in Exhibit 4-1 in Chapter 4 demonstrated an abbreviated method of summarizing comparisons of future premiums.

Union Access to Information

Beyond these general problems of obtaining understandable information, many unions have difficulty obtaining any data at all unilaterally from the insurance company or management. Unless the union is the provider, as is the case with multi-employer unions such as (Service Employees International, the Teamsters, or Independent Electrical Workers), unions often cannot receive information directly from the insurance company without some form of company-provided authorization.

Recent administrative decisions, however, have offered some interesting insight into what information a company may have to provide a labor union. While management usually must provide essential information that would affect a union's ability to bargain, the NLRB recently ruled that Warner Press, Inc., did not have to provide the data on costs of providing health insurance benefits desired by the union (Graphic Communications Union Local 17) under the company's current insurance coverage.[2] The decision was not unanimous, but the majority found that "what is of help to the union in framing its demands does not define the company's obligation to do the union's research." In this case, however, the union failed to present evidence that it could not obtain the data independently. The minority opinion did not agree and felt the company had a responsibility to assist the union in determining if the counterproposal would be feasible.

On the other hand, a decision by the Connecticut State Labor Board found that the request by the police union for information on health insurance as it related to wages was "presumptively relevant" and should be supplied through appropriate means. The board held that information on health insurance, life insurance, and pension benefits are forms of economic remuneration and a union is entitled to this data.[3]

Utilizing the Information

Once the data is available, especially the profile of usage, then the company can determine what types of services are in the greatest demand. Depending on the services needed and the size of the employer, direct negotiations with providers may generate a discount arrangement. For smaller employers, forming coalitions to negotiate cost-saving arrangements with providers is another option.

Discount Negotiations

If outpatient treatment is the largest single expenditure, an alternative might be to negotiate with a center to allow some discount if a certain number of employees used this facility. Of course, this alternative will require additional research to determine member satisfaction with that facility and whether one facility is used much more than any other. If members live in two or three different states or are spread over the country, then effecting this type of cost-saving arrangement becomes more difficult, although the point-of-service plans described in chapter 6 offer one option.

If a discount arrangement should prove feasible, consider bargaining with providers for a percentage discount for billed charges when usage is extensive, or for some per diem arrangements, per case arrangements or specified DRG (diagnosis-related group) related schedule of payments. UCR (usual, customary, and reasonable) payment schedules are not a good idea since they tend to encourage providers to increase their fees. An ideal would be to move toward a relative value scale, based on the resources used to provide the service, such as the amount of training required, the time and intensity of effort the procedure took, and the costs involved for the providers. With health care, however, frequently performed procedures, not only will be charged less per unit but also may cost less in terms of the surgeon's fee and recovery periods. Doctors who perform a surgical procedure infrequently often may charge more, and the result may not be of as high a quality as would be possible if done by someone who specializes in that particular procedure.

When management and labor join forces to seek quality health care at the most reasonable price, the result can only be profitable for both. Such efforts, however, often lead to disputes over who will make the decisions. If the decisions are made with an employer-dominated board, the choices may be based more on cost than quality. A good example of how management and labor worked together over the years to become true partners is illustrated by the efforts of the Virginia Education Association and the Fairfax, VA Board of Education. More on this appears in Appendix 10.

Cooperative Ventures

Forming coalitions or creating large districtwide groups to negotiate with providers and insurers is an option for smaller employers. This strategy initially produces savings due to the economies of size. Yet, after time, this advantage seems to dissipate as costs continue to increase. Nonetheless, when an insurer has to deal with thousands of members, it tends to listen and to bargain more reasonably than it would if the group size numbered in the hundreds or less. School districts have successfully implemented this tactic on a statewide basis in Maine, Vermont, Michigan, New Jersey, Virginia, and Wisconsin, among others.[4] A newer trend has developed in which diverse industries band together to increase their purchasing power.

Such coalitions can prove valuable even when formed for informational, rather than joint purchasing, purposes. Sharing of information on the types of care available and the costs for this care can only bring about better and less expensive care. One such cooperative effort is illustrated by the Rhode Island coalition described earlier. Employers in West Coast, Midwest, and Southern states find cooperation comes more easily than it does for those in the East and Northeast, where much of labor is organized and employers therefore may be more reluctant to share and coordinate their efforts. The Rhode Island venture did not involve unions, but it does set a precedent for what could happen if unions would cooperate. If implemented under the umbrella of AFL-CIO, AFSCME, or NEA unions, cooperative ventures could insure territorial rights while effecting large economies of scale.

An interesting example involves the United Food and Commercial Workers Union, which implemented a cost-containment program in the Northeast and St. Louis areas, only to find that it worked well in the Northeast but not in St. Louis. The program consisted of a bonus system of rewards for savings from members' bill audits, restrictions on weekend admissions to hospitals, and second surgical opinions, among other strategies. While the first two tactics produced cost-savings, the second surgical opinion requirement was not as cost-effective and generated opposition among workers in the St. Louis area. The 75,000 New England food workers, however, were cooperative and accepted the cost-saving device.[5]

Other unions also have begun to consider large-scale cooperative ventures. At a recent conference of the National Education Association, for example, a proposal to use the clout of the NEA's two million members to negotiate with health care providers received attention.[6] One practical difficulty, however, is that NEA members are spread over 1,000 separate school districts, in 50 states and several territories, which are not closely knit.

Dispute Resolution and Contract Maintenance

When purchasing health insurance, employers should attempt to maintain the benefits that have been negotiated with labor and to which the employees are entitled. Unions vigorously protect their members' entitlement to what has been negotiated, and if management does the same, it will avoid costly litigation or liability for errors in administration of the plan.

Case Illustration

Several of the following examples illustrate the need for careful surveillance on the part of both management and labor in implementing the health insurance contract.

New Hires

The first example, which concerns a recent hire, demonstrates the importance of ascertaining that the insurance policy complies with the labor contract.[7] An employee hired on November 28, 1991 became ill on December 2, 1991. She required emergency surgery and was hospitalized for five days. Upon returning to work, she was denied medical insurance coverage for the emergency. Fine print on the form she had signed when she selected medical insurance indicated that the employer's insurance policy did not provide coverage until the first day of the second month after her date of hire. As a result, the employee's insurance would not become effective until January 1, 1992.

The union took the case to arbitration, arguing that the employer had violated the terms of the labor contract in selecting this policy. At arbitration, the insurance booklet was introduced as evidence to indicate that coverage became effective the first day of the second month after hire. The insurance carrier, however, testified that three-quarters of all subscribers were not subject to a two-month waiting period, that several thousand subscribers had no waiting period at all, and that the carrier could provide first-day coverage.

In supportive testimony, the union showed that it had previously warned the employer that the policy might not fulfill the labor contract's requirement that insurance coverage be effective as of an employee's date of hire. The union also demonstrated that it had notified the employer that the employer would be liable for coverage during any waiting period the insurer imposed, and introduced correspondence to prove its point. The union had invited the employer to discuss the matter further if the employer disagreed with the union's warning, but the employer had declined.

After considering the evidence, the arbitrator found that the contract language obligated the employer to provide insurance for all employees from their date of hire and ordered the employer to pay for the medical claims of the employee.

For employers, the lesson from this case is that management must ensure that the policy bought fulfills the labor contract and take corrective action if an oversight occurs. For unions, the lesson is that they should verify and review the actual policies purchased to determine if they do in fact comply with the specifications of the contract. The arbitrator's decision implied that unions must notify an employer about inconsistencies and petition that the employer conform to the terms of the contract for the employer to have sole liability for improper coverage in future litigation.

Return From a Leave of Absence

Another dispute over denial of coverage involved an employee who was returning to work from a leave of absence.[8] The employee, who had been out on child-rearing leave for six months, had kept her basic insurance by paying the premiums through her employer. She had, however, opted not to continue the dental insurance. Upon her return to work in January 1991, she asked to be reinstated in the dental plan. In mid-January, she visited the dentist but found that the charges for fillings and cleaning would not be paid. The carrier had imposed a standard two-month waiting period before the insurance coverage would become effective, and she had been in the plan for only two weeks. According to the contract, the effective date of coverage should have been the beginning of the calendar year. Once again, an employer had not purchased the proper coverage. Fortunately for the union, the employer paid the employee's expenses and adjusted the policy's effective date with the insurer to comply with the contract. The problem was resolved without benefit of costly arbitration.

Adding Coverage for Family Members

Adding on additional family members can also create problems for an employee, management, and the union. An example of these problems concerns the denial of coverage to an employee who sought to add his wife and her children (his step-children) to his policy after having single coverage for several years.[9] The major medical insurer requested that the children and spouse undergo physicals before being added to the husband's policy. They complied, but only the children were deemed fit enough to be added. The wife was told she was overweight by 40 pounds, and coverage was denied. When the decision was appealed to the employer, the employer did not know what to do. The contract specified payment for spouse's insurance but did not say what to do if the spouse was ineligible for coverage.

The family purchased, at its own expense, generally available major medical insurance at a higher rate, while struggling to effect compliance with the contract through the union's intervention. Management refused to pay the expenses for the alternative insurance. Finally, after consulting directly with the insurance company, the union representative learned that if a job loss had prompted the attempt to add the wife on to the insurance policy, she could be covered as though her husband were a new hire. For new hires, the policy placed no conditions on inclusion of family members in the plan. The insurance company also stated that if the wife had received comparable coverage with her former company, she could be included in this company's insurance plan without benefit of passing a physical. Both criteria applied and the wife was added onto the policy without losing the 40 pounds.

The liberalness of this particular insurance company in waiving its procedures excluding pre-existing conditions or requiring a physical when the potential enrollees had previous coverage is not always the case. Therefore, employers may want to alert employees that if family members are not included when an employee accepts coverage, obtaining coverage for relatives later on may prove difficult. Unions too should also inform their members of this potential problem.

Newborns and Adoptions

In the case of newborns or newly adopted children, employees also should provide prompt notice to the employer that additional coverage is desired. In one case, six months after their baby was born, a couple learned that since the carrier had not been notified to add their son to the policy, coverage would not be provided for a minor surgical procedure of $150.[10] The carrier would have provided coverage had the employer paid the higher premiums from the time of the birth, but the added premium cost would have exceeded the $150 medical bill. Since the employer, if notified, would have allowed the parents to pay the premium increase, it would not sustain the $150 expense as management's.

Given the small sum involved, the union did not take the case to arbitration and the employee paid the $150 out of pocket. As a result, who would have prevailed if the case had gone to arbitration remains uncertain. Nonetheless, unions should instruct employees who marry, have children, or make some other change to their medical insurance coverage to notify the employer in writing of the changes as soon as possible. Employers also should establish, and publicize to employees, a procedure for adding on dependents. A bi-yearly canvas of eligible members, as described in Chapter 6, also can prevent this type of coverage dispute.

Finding a Remedy in Arbitration

One of the most difficult problems in health insurance arbitration cases is fashioning an appropriate remedy. This problem becomes particularly acute when the dispute involves a change in carriers and the need for equal, equivalent, or similar coverage at no increased cost. The many variations and nuances in insurance policies make it hard to find a way to "make whole" participants whose carrier and insurance coverage has changed unless the arbitration takes place prior to the change. As a result, a health care contract with labor should contain language providing that arbitrations be held before any change in coverage occurs. Several of the following cases demonstrate the problems that arise when an insurance change has taken place and the results are clearly not equal coverage.

When the Carrier Is Named in the Contract

The first example deals with two cases that are similar, except that the same arbitration allowed a change of carriers in one but not the other. In the first case, the dispute involved a change from Blue Cross/Blue Shield's premium-based program to a self-insured program also managed by Blue Cross/Blue Shield. The arbitrator allowed this switch because the programs were extremely similar, and were administered by the insurance carrier named in the contract. [11] In the second case, the employer was precluded from changing from Blue Cross/Blue Shield to a self-funded trust administered by an independent company, since this third-party administrator could not deliver the same quality of services as had been provided by Blue Cross/Blue Shield. The critical difference, according to the arbitrator, was that "So long as identified carriers continue to be specified in the contract, the employer is precluded from meeting the goal of reducing premiums by the method of changing carriers". [12]

The lesson here is that when the union contract specifies the exact program desired, the carrier, and the type of management program to be implemented, management will find it very difficult to change carriers, if the union opposes the change.

When the Carrier Is Not Named

When the labor contract does not name the carrier, a change in carriers becomes easier, although problems still can arise. In January 1986, the East Haven, CT. school board notified its employees that the major medical carrier had been changed from Eagle Co. (a pseudonym) to Blue Cross/Blue Shield, but no change in benefits would result from this action.[13] Less then two months after the change, an employee's son had a tonsillectomy and the employee filed for payment of excess doctors' charges under the major medical plan. The new carrier, however, would not cover most of the excess charges because only the Blue Cross/Blue Shield ratings for usual and customary charges were allowed. Since the physician did not participate in the Blue Cross/Blue Shield system with its negotiated ceiling on fees, extra charges resulted in the filing for additional reimbursement under the major medical policy.

The following illustrative table compares the reimbursement that would have been provided under the Eagle plan with what the reimbursement was under Blue Cross/Blue Shield carrier. In this example, the cost of the tonsillectomy was $890 and the allowable expenses are those shown in line 1. The surgeons's fee in both cases exceeded the allowable amount (the UCR rate), so the remainder was subjected to the major medical insurance under the indemnity program.

	Old Plan	New Plan
Usual, customary, and reasonable allowance	$220	$225
Amount subject to major medical coverage	$670	$270
Line 2 less $100 deductible	$570	$170
80% of line 3	$456	$136
Reimbursable expenses (line 1 + line 4)	$676	$361

The two plans clearly differed: The new carrier's reimbursement was $315 less than what the previous carrier would have provided. As a result, the union filed a grievance claiming that the employer had made a unilateral change in the negotiated contract coverage. Since the labor contract had not named a carrier, the employer believed it had the right to reduce its costs by changing carriers. In addition, the new insurance company had promised to supply coverage identical to that of the previous company, which specified a million-dollar major medical policy with a $100 per person deductible. But the language in the master trust agreements differed. The master trust agreement of Eagle referred to a particular rate sheet for usage in allowable major medical claims, without specifying the actual limits of coverage. The Blue Cross/Blue Shield rates are often less than other companies due to their custom of discounts, and the language in the new carrier's master trust agreement proved so vague as to be incomprehensible, and unenforceable. The employer had relied instead on the insurance company's assurances that identical coverage would be provided.

As a result, the arbitrator ruled that the school board was liable to pay the additional charges that were incurred by the employee. The main problem with this remedy, however, was that the actual differences could not be determined due to the vagueness of the master trust agreement. In addition, by the time the case was resolved, the Blue Cross/Blue Shield policy language had been changed to match coverage under the old carrier.

In a different case, the employer had no choice but to change carriers because the current carrier was no longer interested in providing major medical insurance.[14] The labor contract, however, contained strong language which only allowed a change in carrier "provided that there shall be no reduction or diminution in the above coverage and no increase in expense to any bargaining unit members, and provided further that coverages which result from change in carriers are at least equal to the coverages described above, in terms of coverage, benefits, and administration." The contract also provided that any dispute over interpretation of this language would be adjudicated according to the grievance procedure in the contract and before an impartial arbitrator who had experience in insurance matters. While coverage appeared not to be equal under the new carrier this particular case was settled before arbitration and changes were made in the new policy to comply with the requirement for equal coverage.

Many other similar disputes, however, are not so fortunate to have such strong contract language. Even when the parties agree that change in carriers has resulted in less than equal coverage, fashioning a suitable remedy satisfactory to both parties can prove difficult. In another arbitration case, both sides agreed that when the incumbent insurance company withdrew from the market and ceased to provide coverage, the replacement of this insurance with Blue Cross/Blue Shield did not provide equal coverage.[15] Once again, Blue Cross did not reimburse claims at the same dollar amount as the previous carrier had. Yet finding a remedy proved problematic, as no carrier offered precisely duplicate coverage. As a result, negotiations had to be instituted to reach an agreement as to what would be an acceptable substitute. Ultimately, both parties agreed to abide by whatever solution was recommended by a consultant agreeable to both union and management.

Other Types of Problems

Foresight also can help prevent some other types of problems which may not always be subject to arbitration. Two more case studies will serve to illustrate the age-old saying "caveat emptor."

Understanding Coverage Conditions

The first case involved a union's interest in buying additional benefits: a prescription drug plan and a vision rider.[16] The employer offered to pay the full cost of additional benefits for employees, but only if the employees would pay 75 percent of the cost for family and spouse, coverage. The union accepted this offer and negotiated specific terms. Employees would be eligible for some $500 a year per person in reimbursements for the cost of medical prescriptions. They would also be eligible for a plan that would pay for eye exams and provide a partial allowance for the costs of required eyeglasses.

Just prior to ratification, the union and management learned that in order for the plan to be purchased, 100 percent of the membership must agree to participate in the plan. Since the current contract contained an opt-out provision which paid employees 50 percent of the cost of the individual premium not to take the insurance, including the additional benefits, some employees would inevitably opt out. Moreover, the plan already provided similar dental benefits—at no cost to individuals and at only 25 percent of the cost to employees for dependents—without requiring 100 percent participation.

Union members obviously were not going to be happy about having to pay for something they might not want. The additional benefits would entail out-of-pocket costs for spousal and family coverage amounting to about $180 a year for the vision plan and another $250 for the prescription drug plan. The 100 percent participation requirement could not be changed. Although the agreement was subsequently ratified, the vote was not unanimous and the union experienced some grumbling from its members about having another $430 deducted from their paychecks.

The lesson here is to be certain to understand prior to purchasing a plan what requirements are going to be imposed by the insurer. An insurance carrier may not clearly communicate these conditions, so a thorough checking of the fine print is necessary. The assistance of a reputable insurance consultant, agent, or broker also can help alert an employer and the union to these potential problems.

Following Through With Employee Briefings

The second case concerns a special review panel for appeals instituted in the state of Connecticut's plan for its employees who have had penalties imposed for failure to use pre-certification, second surgical opinions, and managed care or utilization review programs.[17] Connecticut state employees had negotiated a provision that management would hold on-site orientation meetings to explain these policy requirements to all members. The main reason that the union won 95 percent of its appeals in the plan's first year was management's failure to conduct these on-site information sessions. While appeals in later years may not be as successful, this example demonstrates the importance of explaining as fully as possible to every employee the penalty for failing to follow the new procedures of utilization review. As mentioned in Chapter 6, penalties for not using the required cost-saving reviews can vary, and the literature provided members often does not specify the exact penalty they will incur. It would behoove both labor and management to have such requirements clearly explained in a conspicuous work location and in the summary plan descriptions.

While many of these managed care programs are marketed as packages, employers do not have to buy the entire plan and can negotiate numerous modifications with the provider. Since managed care can directly impact the patient's medical care, both unions and management should be careful to avoid liability due to issuance of incorrect medical advice or failure to provide sufficient explanation about the plan.

Summary

While negotiations with the provider can facilitate effective contract maintenance, the basic negotiations are still between labor and management. As insurance gets more complex and innovative, dispute resolution of contract language concerning insurance provisions is becoming an arbitration specialty. Using available resources, educational tools, and consultants can help bring about satisfactory resolutions during the negotiations process. Understanding the ramifications of governmental regulations on the state and national scene also can prevent unnecessary pitfalls. These regulatory issues are discussed in the next two chapters.

Notes

1. For more information on this consortium, contact the Rhode Island Business Group on Health, Inc., 222 Richmond St., Suite 305, Providence, RI 02903.
2. Warner Press, Inc., 301 NLRB no. 146, Feb. 28, 1991. See also Bureau of National Affairs, Inc., *Daily Labor Report*, no. 52 (March 18, 1991): A1-2, for mention of the ruling by NLRB members Mary Miller Cracraft and Clifford R. Oviatt Jr., with dissenting opinion by Dennis M. Devaney.
3. City of Stamford and Stamford Police Association, Connecticut State Board of Labor Relations, nos. MPP-9625 and MPP-10, 752, decision no. 2623, March 11, 1988.
4. Glenn Darr, "Executive Analysis of NEA State Affiliates Health Insurance Activiti s," Fort Myers, FL: Glenn Darr Consulting, 1991.
5. Louis Spetrini, president of the United Food and Commercial Workers Local 328, speech at the second annual Rhode Island Conference on Labor Management Relations, Quidnesset, RI, Oct. 7, 1987.
6. Cynthia Hosay, "Negotiating with Health Care Providers," speech at the National Education Association's Health Care Benefits Forum, Miami, FL, May 2, 1989.
7. Arvid Anderson, Bridgeport Education Association and the Bridgeport Board of Education, AAA case no. 12 39 0175 84 (Dec. 21, 1984). (Dates in example have been altered for illustrative purposes.)
8. Case illustration derived from author's personal experience.
9. *Ibid.*
10. *Ibid.*
11. Larry J. Foy, New Haven Board of Education and New Haven Federation of Teachers, AAA case no. 12 39 0301 83 (May 7, 1984).
12. Larry J. Foy, Putnam Education Association and Putnam Board of Education, direct selection (August 27, 1984).
13. M. Jackson Webber, East Haven Education Association and East Haven Board of Education, AAA case no. 12 39 0523-87 (June 20, 1988). (Some editorial license has been taken to change dollar figures and names of companies for illustrative purposes.)
14. Case illustration derived from author's personal experience.
15. *Ibid.*
16. *Ibid.*
17. *Ibid.*

Chapter 8

Obtaining and Providing Information

Unions and management need to educate both workers and managers about the various kinds of health care available and the ways in which insurance policies work. Users of health care must understand how expensive the benefit has become and that usage increases the cost. Unlike life, casualty, or auto insurance, the costs and profits of a health insurance policy are determined within each individual group. In property and casualty insurance, the risk is shared among all the purchasers of the policies, and each user's risk exposure may be taken into account in setting individual rates at renewal time. In contrast, higher usage and inefficient use of health insurance generally are charged directly to each group without any cushion against one individual's bad experience, although very small groups can gain some cushion by pooling together.

Explaining to employees what constitutes effective, quality health care and where it can be obtained in the most reasonable fashion is one major way to control costs. Previous chapters have emphasized this point without specifying the resources available to inform employees about health care. The following discussion provides a general overview of the types of different resources available; a detailed list appears in the Resources section.

Employee Education

Sources of general information include newsletters and magazines that stress healthier living, guides to hospitals, lists of national treatment centers that provide information on certain diseases, referrals to resources on particular health problems through such programs as Tel-Med,[1] and guides to mental health care and substance abuse treatment. Additional information is often available from public libraries, which have begun to screen books and provide recommended "nutritional cookbooks," "effective exercise and life-style books," and sensible diet books, among other resources.

In addition to general information on healthy living and health care resources, employees also need specific information on benefits available under the company's particular plan and how to utilize these benefits in the most effective fashion. A number of the efforts described below can enhance education in this area.

On-Site Specialists

One method which the company or union can use to provide on-site assistance is to hire specialists to counsel employees about the intricacies of their health plan and to inform them where to go for additional help. In addition, these health ombudspersons could listen and determine the nature of the employee's problem, which could supply useful information for the company. Provided confidentiality is maintained, a compilation of information regarding employees' health care needs would form a meaningful data base on which to make more informed decisions about purchasing health care plans.

Informational Meetings

The most important and beneficial type of information dissemination is an explanation of the insurance program to each employee. Periodic meetings of employees with insurance company representatives who can review and explain the current benefits are a good idea. Scheduled sessions with insurance representatives can also provide an opportunity for employees to ask questions and resolve claim disputes.

This program could take place through a series of "brown bag" lunches, during coffee breaks, or on some time off provided by the employer. The lost work-time is worth the investment, since more informed employees will save the plan money in the long run.

Written Materials

In addition to informational meetings, employees should have access to summary plan descriptions in an easy-to-read format. These summaries should describe the major feature of the basic hospital and physician plan, as well as any other ancillary benefits. Additional benefits, such as the major medical policy, the dental plan, the prescription drug benefit, and the vision plan, are often best explained in separate booklets.

A good booklet is explicit and describes the specific operations to be covered and where an employee can find information on what will be paid. Penalties for not following certain procedures also should be outlined explicitly. The booklet should contain helpful charts, diagrams, and phone numbers to call for additional assistance. If the booklet provided by the insurance company lacks useful information, the union or management should provide additional summaries.

Individualized Services

If neither booklets nor informational meetings are sufficient, employees may need access to someone who can answer their particular questions. If both the employer and the union insist, the primary insurance carrier may provide a toll-free dedicated phone line, staffed by a company representative, to answer employees' questions. This service should supplement, not replace, the provision of on-site company and union specialists who can answer employees' questions.

New employees should receive extra counseling as they enroll in the various plans and choose options. Individual counseling also should be provided to employees who are leaving and to the families of employees who have died, given the myriad of complicated rights granted to terminated employees and their families by Congress and state legislatures. These rights receive detailed discussion in Chapter 9, but to give an example, the Consolidated Omnibus Budget and Reconciliation Act provides an extension of health insurance coverage, at the departing employee's expense, for up to 78 or 156 weeks, depending on the particular circumstances for the termination.

While federal legislation applies this requirement to companies of 20 or more employees, some similar state statutes may apply to companies with fewer employees. In Connecticut, for example, the continuation of coverage law applies to all companies regardless of size and to all employees, no matter what the cause of the termination. New York, on the other hand, requires that all employees receive notice, within five days of termination, of their rights to continue in the insurance at their own expense and to have the former employer remit their premiums to the insurer. [Note: At the time of this writing, a ruling on whether these continuation of coverage requirements should be considered under the federal Employee Retirement Income Security Act (ERISA) instead of state statutes was pending.[2]]

Program Surveillance

Another strategy for protecting and improving access to benefits is to have management and labor work cooperatively to monitor the delivery of benefits, the adequacy of claims servicing, as well as the general nature of the benefits provided. The form and methodology of these cooperative efforts can vary greatly and the following discussion outlines only a few strategies. What counts is that some formal system should be set up to ensure quality control reviews.

Labor-Management Committees

A joint labor-management committee could study and monitor the basic insurance program, as well as review alternative programs. When working cooperatively to study the problems, unions and management should strive to be equally well-informed about new developments in the health insurance field. An excellent publication on this type of cooperation is the *Labor-Management Guide to Health Care Cost Containment*.[3] The U.S. Chamber of Commerce, in its *National Health Care Strategy*, also suggests labor-management cooperation.[4]

At times, a union may offer to share the expenses involved in hiring consultants and working with management. In some cases, the labor contract even states the union and management will jointly share in a study for the purpose of cost containment and/or specifies a dollar amount for the union's monetary contribution (see Appendix 7 for examples of such contract language). In other cases, the union may agree to pay for a portion of the costs of implementing and administering a new benefit that has been negotiated. Both types of cost sharing can make the union feel as though it has as many rights as management to police the policy and formulate solutions.

Membership Surveys

Surveys of members' satisfaction and knowledge are often instrumental in ascertaining what information is not getting to employees. When done by a union, these surveys not only provide important feedback but also serve to inform the membership about the nature and cost of their benefits. Since members frequently do not have any idea about the actual cost of their insurance benefits, a survey is a useful public relations tool. Once members understand and appreciate the value of these benefits, their support of cost-containment measures designed to discourage unnecessary usage can become a reality. In addition, data from the survey provide a good basis for negotiating benefit improvements with management.

Outside Assistance

Some companies or unions may not feel informed enough to undertake these information dissemination or monitoring efforts without the assistance of some outside expertise. In such instances, a variety of firms are available to help. Insurance companies themselves are probably the first and most logical place to turn. The carrier's advice and counsel, however, may not be as extensive or as rapidly forthcoming as desired. More objective assistance may come from agents, brokers, and third-party administrators, whose services were discussed earlier in Chapter 3. Other outside resources for assistance are described below.

Consultants

The most objective consultants are employed by employee benefit consulting firms whose employees do not act as brokers/agents or earn revenue from commissions. Several national firms with numerous regional offices offer these services; some even specialize in performing various research studies on particular topics. Although too many excellent companies exist to list in this chapter, the following examples illustrate some of the types of counsulting firms and services available:

A. Foster Higgins and Company. Since 1989, this company has published an annual survey of health care benefits, which includes reports on managed care plans, indemnity plans, flexible

benefit program, retiree health care, and mental health and substance abuse benefits.[5]

Martin E. Segal Company. This company maintains a large
research office in New York City and specializes in studies of public
employees. Its annual study of state employee health benefit plans is
especially popular.[6]

The Wyatt Company. Wyatt maintains an extensive research
office in Washington, D.C., with regional offices in many states. It
also publishes an annual newsletter called *The Compensation and
Benefits File*.[7]

Coopers and Lybrand. This accounting firm's employee benefit division publishes news advisories, including *Actuarial Benefits
and Compensation Information Releases* or *Notes*.[8] Besides
Coopers and Lybrand, other national, state, and regional actuarial
firms have diversified from pensions into employee benefits and
regularly deal with health insurance. Many also publish their own
proprietary newsletters.

Along with offering research and reports, an impartial consultant can provide any number of services, including the following:

- Perform ongoing surveillance of the uses and costs of the
  insurance.
- Review the fit between the type of insurance provided and
  the employer's needs.
- Make annual contact with the carrier and renegotiate fees.
- Prepare a request for proposals (RFP) to shop among various
  carriers and analyze the responses for conformity, similarity,
  and value.
- Suggest and implement cost-containment features.
- Assist with the communication of the benefit package to
  employees.
- Review the delivery of services by the insurance provider.

Nonprofit Firms

Outside the realm of for-hire consultants are special nonprofit
firms that also conduct research in this area. One of the most notable
is the Employee Benefits Research Institute (EBRI) in Washington,
D.C. This organization's monthly newsletters and periodic studies
are among the most comprehensive in the field. EBRI also sponsors
special studies, hosts seminars, and publishes significant texts in the
area of employee benefits. It is, however, considered to have more

of a management than a union perspective since most of its funding comes from business. Nevertheless, EBRI has assisted non-management groups; for example, it provided the National Education Association with editorial help on a text concerning employee benefits.[9]

Another organization offering research and publications on employee benefits is the International Foundation for Employee Benefits in Brookfield, WI.[10] It not only holds numerous conferences but also publishes extensively, provides training, and sponsors the certified employee benefits specialist (CEBS) program. This organization has a mixed board of directors, reflecting both management and union perspectives, and seeks to maintain this balance of viewpoints in its training sessions and conferences. The foundation also offers a data base to any group which wishes to subscribe and it will do comparisons of individual plans against its national data base. The data base represents 1.5 million people, two-thirds of whom are in trust funds, with a heavy concentration on the West Coast.

Working in Employee Benefits (WEB) is a national network whose membership is employed in the field of employee benefits, including many from the health insurance area.[11] This organization originally started as Women in Employee Benefits but soon became so influential that it attracted professionals of both sexes.

Federal and State Governments

One of the most overlooked sources of information on employee benefits is Congress. Its legislative committees responsible for overseeing insurance and public health compile much data and hold hearings on new legislation to regulate and protect the public safety. The Subcommittee on Labor-Management Relations of the House Committee on Education and Labor has spearheaded much recent activity, including a report summarizing its extensive hearings on national health care reform proposals.[12] The Congressional Research Office also issued a report on the health care crisis in the spring of 1990, while the Pepper Commission (more formally known as the U.S. Bipartisan Commission on Comprehensive Health Care) released its findings that summer.[13]

Federal government agencies also can provide helpful data, as the following descriptions illustrate:

The National Center for Health Statistics. This agency publishes a variety of data on hospitals and physicians. NCHS surveys hospitals to obtain information on trends in surgery, admissions, and stays. It also surveys physicians to determine trends in the use of their services.

The Health Care Financing Administration. Charged with administering the national Medicare program for Social Security retirees, this agency collects detailed information from hospitals, doctors, and insurance companies to determine typical physician fees for services.

The Bureau of Labor Statistics of the Department of Labor also collects information on national and regional trends in employee benefits and their costs, as well as hospital and physician cost trends.

The Department of Labor compiles the forms which employers are required to file for each health and pension plan. While management is supposed to supply copies of these forms upon request by employees or unions, copies also can be obtained directly from this federal agency.

At the state level, legislatures have various regulatory committees on public health and safety. In addition, each state has an insurance department or commission that collects data; a full listing of these agencies appears in the Resources section.

Other Sources

Various organizations of unions, public officials, and legislators sponsor groups and conferences that promote education about health care and insurance. The U.S. Chamber of Commerce, for example, hosts conferences and publishes on the topic. The Conference Board in New York City has held annual conferences on employee benefits for more than a decade.[14] The National Conference of State Legislatures used to have a special committee devoted to pension and health insurance, but it now focuses on these concerns as part of its continuing agenda at all conferences and in its national publications.[15] The National Association of Insurance Commissioners also offers a wide array of publications.[16]

Magazines in the health care field are numerous. All the various practitioners—doctors, pharmacists, hospitals, hospital administrators—have their own organizations and professional societies that issue publications, hold forums, and sponsor annual conferences. The Resources section of this text lists some of these groups and their publications, but the list is by no means an exhaustive index to what is available.

Several studies currently underway may offer some help in the future. The New England Medical Center in Boston is developing a standardized survey to measure how well a patient functions after a medical procedure, while the American Medical Association, in conjunction with the Rand Corporation, is planning a study to format guidelines to assist physicians in determining the appropriateness of diagnostic tests and surgical procedures.[17] Standards of patient care are under study by the Joint Commission on Accreditation of Healthcare Organizations.[18]

If sorting through all these sources of information seems overwhelming, seeking help from an impartial consultant, while seeming to be expensive at the outset, may actually save time and money in the long run.

Notes

1. Tel-Med is a public health information service, accessible by telephone that is maintained by local hospitals.
2. Rosalyn Retkwa, "Consultant Requests ERISA Preemption," *Pension World* (April 1990): 8.
3. *Labor-Management Guide to Health Care Cost Containment*, published through a grant from the Federal Mediation and Conciliation Service (Washington, DC: The U.S. Conference of Mayors, the American Federation of State, County, and Municipal Employees, the AFL-CIO, and the National Public Employer Labor Relations Association, no date).
4. National Chamber Foundation, *National Health Care Strategy*, (Washington, DC: U.S. Chamber of Commerce, undated).
5. A. Foster Higgins and Company, *Health Care Benefits Survey* (Princeton, NJ: Foster Higgins Survey and Research Services, 1989, 1990).
6. Martin E. Segal Company, *State Employee Health Plan Costs Rise Twenty Percent: A Summary of Findings* (New York: Martin E. Segal Company, 1989).
7. Wyatt Company, *The Compensation and Benefits File* (Washington, DC: Wyatt, various years and months).
8. See, for example, Coopers and Lybrand, "NAA Study—Retiree Health Benefits: How to Cope with the Accounting, Actuarial, and Management Issues," *Actuarial Benefits and Compensation Information Release* 91/2 (Jan. 23, 1991) or "Health Management: A Survey of Company-Sponsored Wellness Programs, 1990."
9. Employee Benefits Research Institute, *Fundamentals of Employee Benefit Programs for Education Employees* (Washington, DC: EBRI, 1987).
10. For more information, contact International Foundation of Employee Benefits, P.O. Box 69, Brookfield, WI 53008-0069.
11. For more information, contact Working in Employee Benefits, 1629 Eye St. NW, Suite 220, Washington, DC 20006.
12. Subcommittee on Labor-Management Relations of the House Committee on Education and Labor, *Growing Crisis in Health Care: The Basic Health Benefits for All Americans Act (HR 1845) and Other National Health Care*

Policy Options (hearings held Oct. 11 and 12, 1989), serial no. 191-64 (Washington, DC: U.S. Government Printing Office, 1990).

13. U.S. Congress, Bipartisan Commission on Comprehensive Health Care, *Access to Health Care and Long-Term Care for All Americans* (Washington, D.C.: U.S. Government Printing Office, 1990).

14. For more information, contact The Conference Board, 845 Third Ave., New York, NY 10022.

15. For more information, contact The National Conference of State Legislatures, 444 North Capitol St. NW, Washington, DC 20001. For information on its publication *The Fiscal Letter*, write the organization at 1050 17th St., Suite 2100, Denver, CO 80365.

16. For a list of publications, write the National Association of Insurance Commissioners, NAIC Publications, P.O. Box 419038, Department 43, Kansas City, MO 64183-0042.

17. Based on author's research.

18. *Ibid.*

Chapter 9

Government Regulations

Numerous state and federal agencies oversee the regulation of employer-sponsored health care plans. Fifty state insurance departments and dozens of federal regulatory bodies have some jurisdictional role. In general, the federal government's oversight of the marketplace has much less significant impact than that of state insurance agencies. This chapter, while not a comprehensive examination of all relevant laws, regulations, and government rules, will provide an introduction to some of the major regulatory themes and initiatives affecting employer-provided health care plans. The regulation of employee benefit plans is very complex and while the following discussion summarizes some of the regulatory requirements, readers should rely on legal counsel for guidance on compliance.

State Regulations

State regulation of employee health care plans occurs through the traditional role of the states in regulating insurance products and insurance companies. In 1945, Congress passed the McCarran-Ferguson Act, which essentially prevented federal law from regulating the insurance business to the extent it was regulated by the states.[1] Consumer groups have recently attacked the act on grounds that it reduces competition and results in higher insurance costs. Nonetheless, while numerous proposals for reform are pending in Congress, no major changes in the act have been made to date.

Regulations promulgated by state insurance commissions and departments control insurance companies, agents, and policies (see the Resources section for a listing of state insurance commissions and departments). Virtually all states have laws and regulations directly related to group insurance. Health care plans are regulated through state commissions' oversight of the insurance policies used to provide the benefits. Indeed, most states require insurance companies to file their insurance policies for state review before issuing the policy for sale.

The thrust of state laws has primarily targeted two areas of insurance activity: mandated benefits and "provider recognition" statutes.

Mandated Benefits

Mandated benefits generally refer to state-imposed minimum levels of benefits which must be provided in an insurance policy. Some examples would include a requirement for coverage of at least 60 outpatient psychiatric treatment visits, mandatory coverage of certain scheduled immunizations and vaccinations for newborns, or a requirement, such as exists in Rhode Island, that in-vitro fertilization must be a covered expense. A detailed state-by-state listing of such mandated benefits appears in Appendix A at the end of this chapter.

Controversy surrounds these state-mandated benefits. Some critics charge that such legislation has contributed to the escalation of health care costs. Others believe that broader insurance coverage ultimately lowers health care costs, since in the absence of coverage, individuals might have delayed treatment, which ultimately would result in greater medical costs. A further discussion of this debate is contained in transcripts of congressional hearings on national health care options.[2]

Provider Recognition Statutes

The second major area of state regulation of insurance policies concerns provider recognition statutes. These laws require insurance companies to recognize, for purposes of reimbursement, various types of medical care providers in addition to physicians. Examples of provider recognition laws would include statutes that require reimbursement to psychologists, podiatrists, chiropractors, nurse-midwives, and other nonphysicians. Many state laws prohibit distinguishing among health care providers if the practitioner is licensed and operating within the scope of that license. Appendix A at the end of this chapter displays a state-by-state breakdown of these provider recognition mandates.

The following excerpt from Connecticut's provider-recognition statute typifies this type of regulatory requirement:[3]

> (b) Every individual or group hospital or medical expense insurance policy or individual or group hospital or medical service plan contract, delivered, issued for delivery or renewed in this state on or after October 2, 1984 shall provide coverage for the services of certified nurse practitioners, certified psychiatric mental health clinical nurse specialists and certified nurse-midwives, if such services are within the individual's area of professional competencies as established by education and certification and are currently reimbursed when rendered by any other licensed health care provider.

Multi-State Employers

The state regulatory framework can cause difficulty for multi-state employers and employees. For example, an employer that is headquartered in New Jersey but has manufacturing operations in Maine, California, and Texas might very well have to maintain different health care plans in each state to meet each jurisdiction's specific rules. In general, however, employers need only comply with the regulations of the state in which the master policy is issued, provided other states' laws are not "extraterritorial" (extending beyond the state's borders).

Most states' insurance regulations, however, are not extraterritorial in scope. Thus, if a policy is issued out of state but covers workers in the state, the local law typically does not apply. This jurisdictional issue explains why many multi-employer trusts choose to be domiciled in those states that have less burdensome regulations.

States have tried to address the problem of interstate differences through the activity of the National Association of Insurance Commissioners.[4] This organization attempts to standardize legislation, reporting forms, and operating procedures among the states. It also develops model bills and procedures and keeps various data files. However, NAIC is a purely voluntary body, with no control over state legislatures or individual members. Participation in the organization does not even compel members to utilize any of the model legislation or to follow suggested policies and procedures.

Mandatory Universal Health Care or Insurance

State-mandated universal health care is a topic of growing interest. To date, only three states—Massachusetts, Oregon, and

Hawaii—have legislated some stringent forms of mandated health care. While this topic receives detailed discussion in Chapter 10, a brief description of these states' laws deserves mention here.

Massachusetts passed a law that would broaden coverage of many uninsured residents, but by 1992 economic problems caused the legislation to be only partially implemented. Highlights of the act along with a summary of what has been implemented appear in Appendix 9.

Oregon is another state trying to reform its Medicaid program by implementing a system of priorities as to what kind of medical care will be provided to whom. Full debate of this system appears in Chapter 10, but mention is made here to illustrate state involvement in regulating medical care.

The last state, Hawaii, is also discussed in Chapter 10, but merits discussion here because some of Hawaii's health care regulations predate even enactment of the federal Employee Retirement Income Security Act (ERISA) in 1974. Since then, the state has continued to reform and improve its statewide program. For Hawaii to regulate insurance on a statewide, rather than regional, basis is not unusual, since statewide regulation is often the norm. For example, school funding and teachers' salaries are determined completely by the state and not local school boards.[5]

Federal Regulations

Although the federal government plays a less intrusive role than the state government does, its influence is growing. The first federal legislation to affect employer-sponsored health care plans came about through the Taft-Hartley Act in 1947.[6] About a decade later, Congress passed the Welfare and Pension Plan Disclosure Act to guard against fraudulent activity with benefit plan assets.[7]

Most regulatory activity, however, has occurred following the 1974 enactment of ERISA.[8] Since its passage, ERISA has been continually amended and its effect on employers has expanded. Besides ERISA, additional federal laws affecting employer-sponsored health care plans came into being during the 1980s, partly in response to the huge federal deficit and the growing number of uninsured Americans. In general, these laws accomplished one or more of the following goals:

- Reduction of federal expenditures through shifting costs of federal programs (primarily Medicare and Medicaid) to employer-sponsored plans.
- Increase in federal revenue through restricting the tax-free nature of employer-provided benefits.
- Expansion of coverage to some uninsured individuals by requiring continuation of the employer's group coverage.
- Extension of employees' rights with regard to nondiscrimination as well as reporting and disclosure.
- Liberalization of federal regulations on HMOs.

Highlights of these laws, as well as of other federal regulations, are discussed in the following sections.

ERISA

This act is jointly enforced by the Department of Labor and the Internal Revenue Service of the Department of Treasury. Title I of ERISA contains broad disclosure, reporting, and fiduciary requirements that affect not only pensions, but also health care plans. ERISA also contains a section providing for limited preemption of state regulations in the employee benefits area.

Reporting and Disclosure Provisions

ERISA requires employers to provide plan participants with summary plan descriptions of benefits in "easy to read" language. Employees also must have access to financial information about the plan. Section 102 of ERISA requires employers to file with the Department of Labor an annual report, which, depending on the employer's size, must be entered on a particular form (5500), complete with accompanying schedules. Employers also are required to file any changes in the plan on a "Summary of Material Modifications" form. Employees, upon request, can obtain these and other related documents from their employers and also from the Department of Labor.

Fiduciary Requirements

Employers, trustees, co-fiduciaries, and advisors who have authority over purchase and sale of plan securities all are subject to ERISA's "prudent person" standard. This standard, which requires

that the plan be operated exclusively for the benefit of plan participants, is designed to minimize the risk of loss to plan participants
and the plan's beneficiaries. Under the "prudent person" requirement, anyone who manages the plan's assets must do so with the
reasonable degree of prudence expected of any responsible person
in the same position of trust and avoid any conflict of interest with
the needs of those served by the plan.

To this end, any investment or additional business transacted
between the plan and the fiduciaries or other interested entities is
prohibited by ERISA. Any fraudulent mismanagement, misuse of
funds, or other indiscretion by the fiduciary may render the fiduciary personally liable. In the case of self-insured plans, this protection could have more than minor relevance to employers.

ERISA and State Laws

Section 514 of ERISA provides a limited preemption of state
laws covering employee benefits plans, although the states still may
regulate the insurance policies used to fund benefit plans. In most
states, self-insurance plans are technically not viewed as insurance,
since no policies are in force. As a result, employers with "uninsured" plans can avoid some state regulations, particularly state-
mandated benefits. As state regulations and mandates increase,
greater numbers of employers choose to self-insure their programs
rather than pay the increased costs for broader coverage mandated
by state regulations. These plans are, however, still subject to
federal regulation under section 514 of ERISA.

Medicare Cost Shifting

In 1981, the Omnibus Budget Reconciliation Act (OBRA)
required employers to cover Medicare-eligible employees suffering
from end-stage renal disease during their first year of Medicare
eligibility. This requirement thus reduced the federal government's
expenditures under Medicare, particularly given the high medical
expense related to kidney failure.

The Tax Equity and Fiscal Responsibility Act of 1982 further
shifted the costs of Medicare onto employers. TEFRA required
most employers to offer continued participation in the group plan to
employees or their working spouses between the ages of 65 and 70
who would ordinarily have been eligible for Medicare. Medicare

then became the secondary payer of medical expenses for these employees and their spouses.

These requirements were extended again in 1984, with passage of the Deficit Reduction Act. DEFRA made Medicare the secondary payer for individuals ages 65 to 70 whose working spouse was under age 65 and covered by an employer-sponsored insurance plan. In 1985, the Consolidated Omnibus Budget Reconciliation Act removed the age 70 cap and required that active employees' health plans be the primary payer regardless of age. COBRA further required all employers to offer all spouses over age 65 the same insurance policies available to those under age 65.

In 1986, OBRA prohibited large group health plans from excluding a disabled active employee or spouse from coverage, even if this individual was receiving Medicare disability benefits. OBRA '86 also required most employers to provide primary health care coverage to an employee's disabled dependent upon the dependent's attainment of Medicare eligibility due to the disability. If the employer's plan did not conform to these requirements, the employer could be subject to a 25 percent excise tax on all the large group health insurance plans provided by the company.

By 1989, these rules were further clarified to ensure that Medicare was the secondary payer for active insured employees. In 1990, OBRA extended the secondary status of Medicare for disabled employees and their spouses to Oct. 1, 1995, while lengthening the employer's obligation to cover employees eligible for Medicare due to end-stage renal disease (kidney failure) from 12 to 18 months. Employers were prohibited from offering incentives to older employees to opt out of the insurance plan, unless such incentives were offered to younger employees as well.

Taxation of Benefits

TEFRA 1982 initiated some tax advantages and disadvantages with respect to allowable deductions for medical insurance paid by individuals. It eliminated the previously allowed deduction of up to one-half the money contributed to the insurance premium ($150 maximum) and increased the minimum expenditure from 3 percent of adjusted gross income to 5 percent. In 1986, TEFRA increased the threshold on medical expense deductions from 5 percent up to 7.5 percent of adjusted gross income. It also allowed the self-employed to take a 25 percent deduction from their gross income for the amounts they paid for health insurance.

In addition to these general tax laws, a number of specific laws govern the taxation of cafeteria plans and dependent care benefits.

Cafeteria Plans

The Revenue Act of 1978 established the Internal Revenue Code section 125 cafeteria plan. Before this bill, employees covered by cafeteria plans were taxed on even those optional benefits which they did not take. The theory behind this tax requirement posited that since these optional benefits were available, they constituted a form of constructive receipt. In general, after the Revenue Act, those employees who chose only nontaxable benefits no longer had to pay taxes on other benefits that they could have taken but did not.

In 1984, DEFRA modified the rules for cafeteria plans to permit employees a choice of either mandated benefits or cash. Other modifications also were made at that time, including a requirement that a joint report on the effect of cafeteria plans on health care costs be completed. In 1986, TEFRA expanded the scope of choices available under a cafeteria plan, but limited choices to only qualified benefits, that is, those non-cash benefits considered eligible for inclusion in a cafeteria plan. However, in 1989, the Technical and Miscellaneous Revenue Act (TAMRA) clarified that participants should be able to choose among two or more benefits that might be either cash or benefits.

Regulations pertaining to cafeteria plans are very complex, and ongoing modifications by the Internal Revenue Service make it essential to review these requirements each plan year. Along with the tax and nondiscrimination regulations outlined in this chapter, employers should review the additional considerations presented in Chapter 3's discussion of cafeteria plans.

Dependent Care

Families with dependents have received some federal assistance in regard to health care costs, mostly with respect to the amount that is deductible from income taxes. For example, the Economic Recovery Tax Act of 1981 (ERTA) provided dependent care assistance program under section 129 of the Internal Revenue Code. This provision allowed amounts paid by an employer for dependent care, whether health-related or not, to be exempted from the employee's gross income for tax purposes. In 1986, TEFRA limited this income tax deduction to $5,000 a year for a family and $2,500 for a head of household or married person filing separately.

Additional restrictions on child care tax breaks came about through passage of the Family Support Act of 1988. This act limited the child care credit to children under age 13, not age 15 as was previously allowed. The limit on expenses eligible for the child care credit also was reduced by the amount excludable from income under an IRC section 129 dependent care assistance program. This exclusion prevents double income tax advantages by ensuring parents do not receive deductions both on their taxes and from their income for the same child care expenses.

Continuation of Coverage

One of the most significant changes of all recent federal laws came about through a very complicated provision contained in the Consolidated Omnibus Budget Reconciliation Act (COBRA). This provision required employers to temporarily offer continued plan participation to certain persons upon loss of job, death of a spouse, divorce, and similar "qualifying events." If an employee or dependent (qualified beneficiary) would lose coverage as a result of one of these events, the employer must allow that person to continue in the group benefit plan for 18, 19, or 36 months, depending on the nature of the event (see Exhibit 9-1).

Exhibit 9-1 Federal Continuation of Coverage Requirements

	LENGTH OF TIME FOR CONTINUATION	
REASON FOR LEAVING	EMPLOYEE	SPOUSE/DEPENDENT
Quit, retired, fired	18 months	18 months
Reduced job hours, no longer eligible for full-time plan	18 months	18 months
Employee's death	Not Applicable	36 months
Divorce from employee	Not Applicable	36 months
Employee eligible for Medicare, spouse not	Not Applicable	36 months
Dependent ceases to be eligible under terms of health plan	Not Applicable	36 months

Under COBRA, an employer may require the qualified beneficiary to pay up to 102 percent of the average cost for the insurance. Although the law contains many complicated notification and election rules, it provides mandatory continued coverage in almost all cases, except when an employee is fired for gross misconduct. In some instances, state laws may be even stronger and require continued coverage even of persons fired for gross misconduct, as does Connecticut.[9]

COBRA notification requirements specify that the employee or spouse must be told at the time of job termination that they have at least 60 days in which to decide whether to continue the coverage. The employee can choose to limit the extension only to the core coverage provided other employees and need not take any optional programs, such as dental insurance.

Continuation in the group plan may be permitted until one of the following conditions is satisfied:[10]

- The employee and/or family become covered under another health insurance plan.
- The employee and/or family stops paying premiums in a timely fashion, which is usually interpreted to be within 30 days of the due date.
- The time limits on continuation of coverage contained in the law expire.

One modification currently under consideration by Congress is to allow spouses ages 50 or 55 to continue coverage until they reach age 65.

Penalties for failing to offer the continued coverage are fairly rigorous. In such cases, the employer is prohibited from deducting benefit costs as allowable business expenses. In addition, highly paid employees may be required to pay income taxes on the value of their health insurance benefits. Under these COBRA penalties, a highly paid employee, that is, one who earns more than $50,000, would have to pay taxes on any employer-paid health plan worth more than $2,500.

An unanticipated effect of COBRA is that employers have learned that the true cost of continued coverage often exceeds the 102 percent allowable charge. This shortfall reflects the principle of "adverse selection," since those most likely to need and use the insurance protection are the ones who continue it. However, employers cannot base COBRA premiums on the exclusive claim experience of the COBRA population, which may be higher than that of the general population.

As a result, some employers have argued that the allowable premium charge is insufficient to cover their risk. To date, no suggestions for increased charges have been seriously considered as legislative reform. Interpretation of the law and its application, however, continues to evolve as various challenges are brought through the courts. An informed legal consultant can provide the best advice on how to avoid costly litigation regarding compliance with COBRA.

Nondiscrimination Requirements

The Tax Reform Act of 1986 added a new section (section 89) to the Internal Revenue Code to prevent discrimination in employee benefits. In its efforts, however, to prevent unequal treatment among high- and low-paid workers, the IRS developed regulations so complex and almost unfathomable that many employers were very confused. For three years, employers, employees, and consultants devised elaborate tests for complying with IRC section 89 and conducted numerous studies to verify the results, without much success. Millions of dollars later, Congress finally got the message that IRC section 89 was not working and on Nov. 8, 1989, President George Bush signed a law repealing this section of TRA 1986.[11]

While these particular nondiscrimination rules are gone, the regulatory environment is still unclear since a plethora of other disparate, vague, and often contradictory IRS rules and regulations remain. Each type of plan may end up under different rules. Expert consultant advice is essential, and even then, the result is often subject to court decisions on individual cases.

In general, however, regulations remaining in effect after repeal of IRC section 89 hold that a plan will be found to be nondiscriminatory if it passes one of the following eligibility tests:[12]

- The plan benefits at least 70 percent of employees.
- At least 85 percent of plan participants are not key employees.
- The plan benefits a class of employees judged not to discriminate in favor of key employees.
- For a cafeteria plan, it must meet the requirements of IRC section 125.

In addition to these requirements with regard to employees' salaries, other nondiscrimination regulations regarding age have recently become a prominent topic for litigation. The Age Discrimination in Employment Act (ADEA), which was passed in 1967 and amended in 1975, 1979, and 1986, contains complex rules with respect to age-sensitive benefits and rates. In general, an employer must be prepared to produce actuarial evidence that age-related benefits or contributions are not a subterfuge to evade ADEA's requirements. The famous *Betts* case,[13] decided by the Supreme Court in the late 1980s, prompted Congress to enact new legislation in October 1990 to prohibit discrimination against older workers.[14]

Reporting and Disclosure Requirements

In addition to ERISA's stringent reporting and disclosure requirements, TEFRA 1986 amended sections 60391 and 6093D of the Internal Revenue Code to extend the reporting and disclosure requirements to all accident and health, group term life insurance, and dependent care plans. Thus, these plans must be accountable to the public and to employees, just as pension plans must provide financial information and summary plan documents to participants.[15] TEFRA 1986 also expanded the scope of information that must be reported for all highly paid compensated employees. In 1988, TAMRA amended this section again to mandate that multi-employer plans provide required information held by the plan.

HMO Act Amendments

As discussed earlier in Chapter 3, several changes have relaxed the regulations originally contained in the HMO Act of 1973.[16] The 1988 amendments have altered the HMO Act to accomplish the following:

- Provide greater flexibility in setting employer's contributions.
- Loosen rules regarding the operation and organization of HMOs.
- Liberalize the use of nonaffiliated physicians by HMOs.
- Give HMOs discretionary authority as to whether to offer coverage to any organ transplants other than those for which coverage had been required April 15, 1985.

- Allow HMOs to fix premium rates for families and individuals in specific groups of enrollees, based on the revenue requirements for providing services to the group's members. For example, HMOs now could rate shipyard workers separately from others in the community.
- Repeal the dual-choice requirements.

Other Federal Laws

Many other laws and agencies—including the Department of Labor, the U.S. Civil Rights Commission, the Equal Employment Opportunity Commission, and the Securities and Exchange Commission—affect the design and operation of employer-sponsored health-care plans. Laws affecting the federal Medicare program also are of interest, since much of the federal government's activity in this area is replicated by commercial carriers and/or impacts on costs to private and public industry.

At present, Congress is considering further alterations to Medicare, including a change in the method of payment to hospitals for capital expenditures. In the past, the government had reimbursed hospitals for capital expenses as they occurred by paying 85 percent of the hospitals' reasonable costs. Current law requires the Secretary of Health and Human Services to implement regulations for reimbursement that would charge for capital expenditures over a prospective time period, thus delaying hospitals' receipt of funds. Hospital administrators are concerned that this reimbursement method will not cover their "mortgage" payments at the beginning of this obligation.[17]

Another proposal that is nearing implementation establishes a totally different method of Medicare reimbursement to physicians. A national physician fee schedule is to be in place by January 1, 1992, although a four-year transition period is allowed for the system to become fully operative.[18] Development of a similar fee schedule for hospital outpatient care was proposed in September 1991 by the Secretary of Health and Human Services.[19] Various other Medicare reforms are under consideration, including the development of Medicare "safe harbor" regulations and challenges to the Medicaid reimbursement rates set by states.

Whatever happens in the area of Medicare will impact on the overall costs of health care, since, in 1989, this federal program accounted for 40 percent of all hospital revenues.[20] Since federal allowances can make or break a hospital, future changes to the

Medicare rates will affect everyone else in the industry. While the percentage of income doctors derive from Medicare is unknown, many doctors also will receive less under the new fee scale, although others will receive more. Those states which have undertaken similar programs to effect cost controls on practitioners have realized some savings.[21]

Notes

1. In the McCarran-Ferguson Act, which was passed March 9, 1945 and known as Public Law 15, Congress reaffirmed the right of the federal government to regulate insurance, but agrees that it would not exercise this right as long as the industry was adequately regulated by the states. Bills to repeal or modify the act have been introduced since 1977. Among these proposals is a bill introduced by Sen. Howard Metzenbaum (D-OH) to repeal the act and restructure insurance regulations.
2. U.S. Congress, *Hearings on the Growing Crisis in Health Care; The Basic Health Benefits for All Americans Act (H.R. 1845) and Other National Health Care Policy Options*, serial no. 101-65 (Washington, DC: U.S. Government Printing Office, 1990).
3. Connecticut General Statutes, section 38-174v, "Mandatory Coverage for Services of Certain Nurse Practitioners."
4. National Association of Insurance Commissioners, P.O. Box 419038, Kansas City, MO 64183-0042.
5. National Conference of State Legislatures, "Hawaii's Universal Health Care Program: Bridging the Gap," *The Fiscal Letter* 12, no. 1 (Jan./Feb. 1990): 7.
6. The Taft-Hartley Act of 1946 was an amendment to the National Labor Relations Act of 1935.
7. The Welfare and Pension Disclosure Act of 1958, 29 U.S.C. 301-309. 1962 Amendments P.L 87-420, 76 Stat. 35.
8. For an overview of ERISA standards, see Barbara J. Coleman, *Primer on ERISA* (Washington, DC: BNA Books, 1989).
9. Connecticut General Statutes, section 38-262d provides that if an employee become ineligible for continued participation in any group health insurance plan for any reason, s/he is entitled to extend coverage under the same basic terms as required by COBRA.
10. Service Employees International Union, AFL-CIO CLC, *Healthcare Benefits Bargaining Manual.* (Washington, DC: SEIU, no date): 12. B-9.
11. The Debt Limit Extension Act of 1989 repealed the nondiscrimination requirements of IRC section 89 but reinstated the nondiscrimination rules and qualification requirements governing cafeteria plans that had existed prior to implementation of IRC section 89. Pamela Sande, Applied Research Services, the Alexander Consulting Group Inc., "Welfare Plans: Major Federal Legislation," analysis for *Pension Reporter* 18, no. 3 (Jan. 21, 1991): 94–123.
12. John D. Reynolds and Robin N. Bischoff, *Health Insurance Answer Book*, 3rd ed. (New York: Panel Publishers, 1991).
13. *Public Employees Retirement System of Ohio v. Betts*, 492 U.S. 158 (1989). In this case, the Supreme Court held that the only way that an employer could

violate section 4(f)(2) of ADEA (the exemption for bona fide employee benefit plans that are not a subterfuge to evade the purposes of the law) was to discriminate as well in some other non-fringe benefit aspect of the employment relationship. In addition, the court reversed the decisions of every appellate court that had ruled on the issue and required employees to bear the burden of proving that the benefit plan was a subterfuge to evade the ADEA.

14. House Select Committee on Aging and the Employment Opportunities and Labor-Management Relations subcommittees of the House Committee on Education and Labor, *Hearings on Age Discrimination in Employee Benefit Plans: The Impact of the Betts Decision* (Sept. 21, 1989), House Committee on Aging Pub. No. 101-744, House Committee on Education and Labor Pub. No. 101-60 (Washington, DC: U.S. Government Printing Office, 1990).

15. For more information on Government Accounting Standards Board (GASB) statement No. 12 of the Requirement for Disclosure by Public Employer of Non-Pension Post-Employment Benefits, see Charles D. Spencer and Associates, Inc., *Spencer's Research Reports*, no. 308.3.13 (Feb. 22, 1991): 1–2.

16. Ibid., 110.

17. Bureau of National Affairs, Inc., "Health Care: Reform, Capital Payments, Budget Initiatives, Key Issues for 1991," special report S33, order no. 0148-8155/91. (Washington, DC: BNA, 1991): S32–S38.

18. Ibid., S34–S35.

19. Ibid.

20. Service Employees International, *Healthcare Bargaining*, p. 11.F-12.

21. Ibid., p. 11.F-13.

Appendix A

State Mandated Benefits and Providers

BENEFITS	AL	AK	AZ	AR	CA	CO	CT	DC	DE	FL	GA	HI	ID	IL	IN	IA	KS	KY	LA	ME	MD	MA	MI	MN	MS	MO	MT
Alcoholism Treatment	●	●		●	●	●	●	●		●	●	●		●			●	●	●	●	●	●	●	●	●	●	●
Ambulance Transportation							●			●									●						●		
Ambulatory Surgery			●	●						●		●						●					●			●	
Anti-Abortion		●	●		●								●					●									
Breast Reconstruction										●				●						●			●				
Cleft Palate					●	●							●		●						●	●					
Diabetic Education																●											
Drug Abuse Treatment	●	●		●	●		●	●		●	●	●					●		●	●	●		●	●		●	●
Home Health Care			●		●	●	●			●										●	●						●
Hospice Care						●	●											●			●		●					
Invitro Fertilization				●								●	●	●								●					
Long Term Care																		●									
Mammography Screening		●		●	●	●	●	●		●	●	●		●	●	●		●	●	●	●	●		●		●	●
Maternity					●	●					●	●				●	●			●	●			●		●	●
Mental Health Care				●	●	●	●	●		●	●	●		●			●	●	●	●	●	●	●	●	●	●	●
Orthotic/Prosthetic Care					●		●			●											●		●				

Notes: Mandated offerings are shaded. Mandates that do not apply to BCBSA are asterisked.

Source: Adapted and reprinted from "Issue Review," W.R. 8-92, Feb. 1992, Blue Cross And Blue Shield Association, Office of Government Relations, Washington, D.C.

157

	AL	AK	AZ	AR	CA	CO	CT	DC	DE	FL	GA	HI	ID	IL	IN	IA	KS	KY	LA	ME	MD	MA	MI	MN	MS	MO	MT
BENEFITS																											
Prescription Drugs																				●							
Rehabilitation Services							●												●	●		●					
Second Surgical Opinion																					●						
TMJ Disorders																		●						●	●		
Well-Child Care				●	●		●			●		●					●					●		●		●	●
PROVIDERS																											
Acupuncturists		●	●		●	●	●		*	●	●			●	●	●	●	●	●	●	●	●	●	●	●	●	*
Chiropractors	●	●	●	●	●	●	●	*		●				●	●	●	●			●	●	●		●	●	●	*
Dentists			●	●	●					●		●									●						●
Licensed Health Professions				●										●	●						●						
Nurses (RNs)						●										●											
Nurse Midwives (CNMs)		●	●		●	●	●		●	●									●		●	●	●	●	●		●
Nurse Anesthetists (CRNAs)			●			●	●			●											●			●	●		●
Nurse Practitioners		●	●		●	●	●		●	●							●				●			●	●		●
Nurse, Psychiatric					●	●	●			●											●	●		●			
Occupational Therapists	●	●	●		●				*										●		●			●			
Optometrists		●								●	●			●	●	●	●			●	●	●		●	●	●	
Oral Surgeons										●				●									●				
Osteopaths		●	●	●										●							●						
Physical Therapists		●	●				●														●			●			

	AL	AK	AZ	AR	CA	CO	CT	DC	DE	FL	GA	HI	ID	IL	IN	IA	KS	KY	LA	ME	MD	MA	MI	MN	MS	MO	MT
PROVIDERS																											
Podiatrists	●		●	●	●					●				●	●		●				●	●		●		●	
Professional Counselors				●	●					●											●						●
Psychologists	●		●	●	●	●	●			●	●	●		●	●		●		●	●	●	●		●	●	●	●
Public & Other Facilities				●	●		●			●			●		●		●			●	●		●	●	●		●
Social Workers				●	●	●	●			●				●						●	●	●	●				●
Speech/Hearing Therapists				●	●			*											●		●					●	
PERSONS COVERED																											
Adopted Children		●	●				●			●	●	●		●	●		●				●	●		●			●
Continuation/Dependents			●	●	●	●	●				●			●		●	●	●	●		●			●		●	●
Continuation/Employees			●	●	●	●				●		●	●	●	●	●	●	●	●	●	●	●	●	●		●	●
Conversion to Non-Group				●	●	●					●										●			●			
Dependent Students							●				●							●	●								
Handicapped Dependents			●		●		●			●	●	●	●	●	●		●	●	●		●	●	●	●	●	●	●
Newborns	●	●	●		●		●			●							●		●	●		●		●	●	●	●
Non-Custodial Children							●													●							

State Mandated Benefits and Providers

BENEFITS	NE	NV	NH	NJ	NM	NY	NC	ND	OH	OK	OR	PA	RI	SC	SD	TN	TX	UT	VT	VA	WA	WV	WI	WY
Alcoholism Treatment	●	●	●	●	●	●	●	●	●		●	●	●		●	●	●	●	●	●	●	●	●	
Ambulance Transportation		●								●														
Ambulatory Surgery										●														
Anti-Abortion								●				●												
Breast Reconstruction		●		●		●															●			
Cleft Palate							●																	
Diabetic Education											●												●	
Drug Abuse Treatment		●				●	●	●	●		●	●	●			●	●	●	●	●	●		●	
Home Health Care					●	●							*				●		●		●		●	
Hospice Care		●				●							●											
Invitro Fertilization											●						●							
Long Term Care		●	●	●	●	●	●	●	●	●	●	●	●		●	●	●		●	●	●	●	●	
Mammography Screening		●	●			●		●	●	●	●					●	●			●			●	
Maternity						●		●		●						●	●		●	●	●		●	
Mental Health Care			●			●				●	●		●			●	●		●	●	●			
Orthotic/Prosthetic Care																								
Prescription Drugs								●																
Rehabilitation Services																						●		
Second Surgical Opinion				●		●							*				●							
TMJ Disorders		●			●			●										●			●	●		
Well-Child Care						●							●					●		●			●	

PROVIDERS	NE	NV	NH	NJ	NM	NY	NC	ND	OH	OK	OR	PA	RI	SC	SD	TN	TX	UT	VT	VA	WA	WV	WI	WY
Acupuncturists		●									●													
Chiropractors	●	●		●	●	●	●	●	●	●	●	●	●			●	●	●		●	●		●	
Dentists	●	●		●	*	●	●		●	●	●	●				●	●						●	
Licensed Health Professions			●												●									●
Nurses (RNs)	●	●		●		●	●	●				●		●				●			●			
Nurse Midwives (CNMs)		●			●			●	●	●		●	●		●			●			●	●		
Nurse Anesthetists (CRNAs)								●				●	●		●									
Nurse Practitioners								●			●	●	●		●						●			
Nurse, Psychiatric		●						●				●								●		●		
Occupational Therapists																								
Optometrists	●	●		●	*	●	●	●	●	●	●	●	●	●	●	●	●	●		●			●	
Oral Surgeons			●												●									
Osteopaths	●	●			*				●	●		●					●			●				
Physical Therapists		●		●	●	●	●		●	●		●		●	●	●	●	●		●	●		●	●
Podiatrists	●	●		●	●		●			●		●					●	●		●				
Professional Counselors					*						●									●				
Psychologists	●	●	●		*	●	●	●	●	●	●					●	●	●		●	●		●	●
Public & Other Facilities	●		●			●	●	●			●				●					●			●	●
Social Workers		●														●	●			●				
Speech/Hearing Therapists																●	●			●				

PERSONS COVERED	NE	NV	NH	NJ	NM	NY	NC	ND	OH	OK	OR	PA	RI	SC	SD	TN	TX	UT	VT	VA	WA	WV	WI	WY
Adopted Children		●			●		●	●		●	●				●			●		●	●			●
Continuation/Dependents	●	●	●		●	●	●	●		●	●		●	●	●	●	●	●	●	●	●	●	●	
Continuation/Employees	●	●	●			●		●		●	●					●	●	●	●	●	●	●	●	
Conversion to Non-Group	●	●			●	●	●	●	●		●	*	●	●	●	●	●	●	●	●	●		●	●
Dependent Students	●							●																
Handicapped Dependents			●	●	●	●	●	●	●			●		●	●	●	●	●	●	●	●		●	●
Newborns		●	●	●			●	●	●	●	●	●		●	●	●	●	●	●	●		●	●	●
Non-Custodial Children								●			●							●						

Additional Benefit Requirements as of February 1992

AK	Naturopaths (87)	**MD**	Blood Products (75) Catastrophic (78+) Dieticians (85) Nutritionists (85) Alzheimers (86+) Physician Assistants (86) Partial psychiatric Hospitalization (88)	**NC**	Pap tests (91)
AZ	Maternity benefits for the natural mother of an adopted child on adoptive parents' policy (86)			**OH**	Outpatient dialysis (72)
				PA	Birthing Centers (82) Chemotherapy (89)
CA	Sterilization (70) Prenatal care (79+) Treatment of infertility, except IVF (89) Blood lead level screening for covered children (91+)	**MA**	Pap Tests (87) Enteral formula (87) Lead Screening (88) Early intervention to age three (89)	**RI**	Pap tests (88) Newborn metabolic and sickle cell testing (88) Blood lead level screening for children under 6 (91)
		MI	Physician Assistants (91)	**TN**	School psychologists (82)
CT	Tumor/Leukemia (79) Home Health Aides under Medigap policies (86)	**MN**	PKU (85) Areata (87)	**TX**	Complications of Pregnancy (77) OP psychiatric centers (83+) Dieticians (87) Alt. Mental Health Centers (87+) Alzheimers (89) PKU (89)
		MS	Pre-existing conditions (82)		
DE	Pap tests (88)	**MT**	Denturists (85) PKU (89) Physician Assistants (89)		
DC	Pap tests (90)			**VA**	Chiropodist (77) Opticians (77) Pregnancy from rape or incest (81)
ID	Complications of pregnancy (76)	**MO**	Pharmacists (78)		
		NV	Pap tests (89)	**WA**	Removal of rider (87) Nutrition for PKU children (88) Neurodevelopment therapy (89)
IL	Rape or sexual assault (82) Liver transplants in HMOs (84) Pharmacists (89)	**NJ**	Chiropodists (53) Diag. X-rays by Chiropractors (76) Wilm's tumor (90)		
KY	Newborn nursery care (80)	**NM**	Lay midwives (85)	**WI**	Kidney disease (74) Tuberculosis in SNFs (75) Insulin infusion pumps (81) Diabetic outpatient (82)
		NY	Pre-admission testing (76) Ambulatory cancer treatment (82)		
LA	Non-group to age 65 (74) Pap tests (91)			**WY**	Dieticians (91+)

Note: + Mandated offering only
Source: Blue Cross and Blue Shield Association, 1992

Chapter 10

Emerging Health Care Reforms

Reform of health care in America is underway. Debate remains whether to replace the current system with one similar to that of Canada or whether to modify the system only within its existing parameters. Nonetheless, the general trend of government activity over the last decade has become more regulatory. In the past, public plans have been exempted from regulation, but recent changes in the Internal Revenue Code have impacted on both private- and public-sector plans. Many Washington observers believe the deficit is driving Congress to scrutinize the employee benefit area for some ingenious ideas to raise additional revenue. Estimates of the amount of excluded revenues in 1990 amounted to about $49 billion in the pension area and about $43 billion in the health benefits area. In short, a total of $82 billion was not collected in order to encourage voluntary benefits for employees.[1]

Until recently, no single lobbying group worked to secure legislative protection of employee benefits. This situation is beginning to change, however, as unions and other groups form more coalitions. The absence of readily mobilized interest groups to respond to threats of more taxation may be supplanted with new coalitions who think "enough is enough" in health-care costs.

Several federal studies have explored and analyzed the health-care problem. The foremost among these studies is the Pepper Commission report, which concluded that the millions of uninsured individuals are increasing the expenses of the insured as uncovered medical costs are passed on to those with coverage.[2] Thus the report's main thrust was to recommend mandatory insurance coverage. In general, other legislative studies focus on a similar rationale for providing health care for all at less expense.

Specific reform proposals vary, and new ones seem to come out every week. While a comprehensive listing of each proposed reform is impossible, most of these initiatives are variations of a few broad models for health-care reform. This chapter describes a few of the proposals that best illustrate these broader models.

National Reform Proposals

As least two opposite solutions have been proposed: One reform, built on the current system, would provide a type of mandatory insurance; the other proposal would establish a universal health care system like that in Canada. Other solutions advocated by various groups are some kind of cross between these two programs.

Model One

The Pepper report proposed the prototype of the first type of reform: mandatory insurance for employed workers, a wraparound program for those not covered, and provision of a subsidy to the poor. In general, the Pepper report would require private health insurance for all employees and their unemployed dependents or, in lieu of an employer-sponsored coverage, payment into a public plan. Employers opting to pay into a public plan would have to contribute at least 80 percent of the premiums for full-time workers and a proportional amount for part-time workers. An employer-provided plan would have to provide benefits at least equal to those of the public plan available. This plan would include benefits for basic and preventive services with $250 deductibles, and maximum out-of-pocket expenses of $3,000. Individuals enrolled in the public plan would pay a premium based on either their wages or, if not working, on their ability to pay. Subsidies would assist those unable to pay the full premiums. Access to insurance would be guaranteed with no exclusions allowed for pre-existing conditions.

All these requirements would apply to employers with 100 or more workers, for smaller groups and the self-employed, other protective measures would be initiated. The report also contained extensive long-term care recommendations to be financed and subsidized by the government. The tab for this program, which would be phased in over five years, would cost $23.4 billion for health care and $42.8 billion for long-term care in 1990 dollars.

Model Two

Instead of mandatory insurance coverage, other advocates suggest adoption of a true national health care system similar to the Canadian one. Canada has a single-payer system with total freedom of choice for consumers. Individuals receive a uniform benefit, and the government handles reimbursement, systemwide budgeting, and effective hospital administration. Each hospital is annually allocated a set amount of money, based on its last year's budget adjusted by the Consumer Price Index. Hospitals are prohibited from billing over and above these charges to recoup any losses. The same payment method is used for doctors, where a set fee schedule is determined and no extra billing is permitted.

A prominent supporter of this concept is Dr. David U. Himmelstein of Cambridge Hospital at Harvard Medical School and coordinator of Physicians for a National Health Program, a group representing some 2,400 physicians. He believes that inadequate access to health care and the resultant poor health status of many U.S. citizens compels the nation to consider such a plan. Over the last 25 years, the Canadian program has provided coverage for virtually all medical care, with health costs running only about 8.5 percent of the GNP, in contrast to the 12 percent in the United States. In the U.S., 24 percent of health care costs are for administration, while in Canada, only 8 to 11 percent goes toward administration. Eliminating the money wasted on billing and administration under the current system would produce a savings of over $100 billion, enough money to pay for all the uninsured, according to Himmelstein.[3] In Canada, 50 percent of the lower rates is attributable to savings on billing, 25 percent to lower physician incomes, and 25 percent to less spending for technology services, according to Himmelstein.[4]

Extending access without these other basic reforms will cause large increases in costs of care, according to Himmelstein. Insurance companies will continue to charge 12 percent of revenues for "overhead," in contrast to the 2.5 percent paid in Canada, as well as waste some 11 percent of revenues on billing. With fewer cost savings, improving access will not reduce costs but may increase them. Providing the equivalent of high-option Blue Cross coverage for all Americans, without reform in billing and administrative practices, would cost more than $52 billion each year above current health spending, Himmelstein has estimated. He believes that a national health plan can eliminate most bureaucratic waste if Congress is willing to confront powerful interests such as the insurance industry.

The program advocated by Himmelstein, Dr. Carolyn Clancy, and the Physicians for a National Health Program would do the following:[4]

- Extend coverage to include standard medical care, as well as care for mental health, long-term illness, dental services, occupational health services, prescription drugs, and equipment.
- Allow patients to receive a national health program card entitling them to care at any doctor's office or hospital. They would not be billed for approved medical care and would not pay deductibles, co-payments, or out-of-pocket costs.
- Allow hospitals and nursing homes to remain privately owned and operated, receiving an annual "global" sum from the government to cover all operating costs.
- Distribute capital expansion funds separately by regional boards on the basis of health planning goals.
- Permit private doctors to continue to practice on a fee-for-service basis with fee levels set by the government.
- Allow HMOs to receive a yearly lump sum from the government for each patient.
- Eliminate private insurance which duplicates government coverage, saving an estimated $15 billion annually in industry profits and overhead.
- Remove the complex and redundant insurance bureaucracy by simplifying paperwork now required of doctors and hospitals.

Other Federal Initiatives

Besides these two major proposals, other ideas for health-care reform have caught the attention of Congress. The following discussion highlights some of these proposals and the debate surrounding them.

The Basic Care for All Americans Act

At the hearings held in the fall of 1989 by the U.S. House of Representatives, Rep. William L. Clay (D-MO-1) advocated passage of HR 1845, The Basic Care for All Americans Act.[5] This legislation, according to Clay, would take a first step toward solving the growing crisis of uninsured Americans and the resulting high costs of those who do buy health insurance. As Clay expressed:[6]

> In a frantic effort to limit financial exposure, employers are either abandoning their health plans entirely or shifting more costs to employees. America's health care delivery system is in crisis. Costs are out of control. Consumers are incapable of making rational market choices because they lack basic information necessary to assess the quality of health care that is available. It is appalling that millions of citizens must face the possibility of going without medical treatment because they cannot afford to pay for it. We must begin to address the health care crisis through innovative and far-reaching legislation. HR 1845 is designed to assure that by the year 2000 all Americans will enjoy access to health insurance either through an employer-sponsored group health plan or a government-sponsored public program. The time has come for Congress to abandon its piecemeal approach to health care issues and develop a comprehensive, integrated plan to achieve the goals of universal coverage, affordable costs and quality care.

The two days of hearings generated both opposition and support for HR 1845 and its concepts of universal health care subsidized by the government. Opponents of the bill included the National Association of Manufacturers,[7] the American Medical Association,[8] the U.S. Chamber of Commerce,[9] the Health Insurance Association of America, the American Council of Life Insurance,[10] policy analysts for the Heritage Foundation, and Blue Cross/Blue Shield. Supporters of national intervention were the AFL-CIO,[11] The Physicians National Health Program,[12] and the Coordinating Council of Multi Employer Plans.[13] Other proponents not present at the hearings included the American College of Physicians, which represents some 68,000 doctors who support national health insurance,[14] and the Service Employees International Union, which has a nationwide campaign underway for national health insurance. Some unions are so intent on supporting national health insurance they have even suggested putting language into their contracts that states the union will actively lobby and support national health care plans in exchange for maintenance of current benefits (see Appendix 7 for an example of contract language). In the case of Gulf Western, this proposal was put forward by the union in order to maintain the employees' premium contribution at 90 percent.

Spring 1991 Hearings and Proposals

In April 1991, additional hearings before the House Ways and Means Committee and the Senate Finance Committee explored suggestions for health care reform. Rep. Dan Rostenkowski (D-IL-8), chairman of the House Ways and Means Committee, noted "Nothing is going to be done without the president's leadership."[15] This comment came in response to the statements by Louis W. Sullivan, Secretary of the Department of Health and Human Services, who stated that the Bush administration wants to educate the public prior to any reform. According to Sullivan, public education is necessary to avoid a repeat of the situation where the Social Security tax to provide long-term health care had to be repealed. Sullivan also indicated that the Bush administration wanted time to review the results of two new studies: one by the National Governors' Association and the other by the Quadrennial Commission on Social Security.

In response to additional congressional criticism, Sullivan said that the Bush administration was preparing a proposal that would have Medicare enrollees whose incomes exceed $125,000 pay more for taxpayer-subsidized benefits. The resulting savings would be invested to provide access to health care for the underprivileged. Other measures under consideration by the Bush administration included a proposal for malpractice insurance reform.

During the House hearings, Sullivan would not comment on when a comprehensive reform plan might be ready, although Richard Darman, director of the Office of Management and Budget, did tell the Senate Finance Committee that a comprehensive reform proposal would be ready in 18 months, or in fall of 1992.[16] The proposal was actually released earlier on Feb. 6, 1992. The plan offers new tax credits and deductions to reduce health care costs for the middle income while providing some basic coverage for the poor and unemployed. Also included are some rearrangement of Medicare and Medicaid, as well as reforms of insurance regulations and malpractice insurance. In general, the program tries to stay within the current system and is no major systemic change.[17]

Two representatives, Pete Stark (D-CA-9) and Marty Russo (D-IL-3) have introduced other proposals for national health insurance plans (HR 650 and HR 1300, the Universal Health Care Act of 1991). This legislation would reduce high administrative costs by instituting a plan with a uniform payment system applicable to all payers nationwide. This concept, also suggested by Charles A. Bowsher, comptroller general of General Accounting Office,[18] received the endorsement of the Bush administration and major health groups. Efforts are currently underway to implement such a system by the late 1990s.[19]

Another Democratic proposal, advanced by the Senate Labor and Human Resources Subcommittee, would provide access to health care for every U.S. citizen through revamping the Medicaid program to provide coverage for the uninsured. The plan also features a so-called "play or pay" provision that would require employers to provide a minimum standard of benefits, with subsidies for individuals whose incomes are below the poverty level. Further aspects of the program include having insurers guarantee issue and renewability of policies, limits on premium increases, as well as funding to research outcomes and develop physician practice guidelines. Initial costs estimates prepared by the Congressional Budget Office range from start-up costs of $10 billion to $30 billion annually after phase-in of the program.[20]

A Spring 1991 report issued by the Congressional Budget Office, *Rising Health Care Costs: Causes, Implications, and Strategies,*[21] concluded that reducing health care costs will require major restructuring of the current health care system. Among the report's suggestions are the following:

- elimination of plans providing first-dollar coverage;
- uniform utilization monitoring and review, applied to all physicians rather than to individual patients and specific procedures;
- uniform payment levels for all payers, plus a prohibition against billing patients for any additional amounts;
- health planning that establishes capital and technology targets relative to the population at national and regional levels; and
- effective national and regional budgets for overall spending.

The report also suggested that to effect reform, some givebacks from health care consumers might be necessary. These sacrifices might include less spending on research and development; longer waiting times for use of new medical technologies; and limitations on choices of providers and health-care coverage. As for other cost-control strategies, the study found nothing positive to report with respect to five common strategies: consumer cost-sharing, managed care techniques, price controls, efforts to increase competition among insurers and providers, and regulation of the health services' market.

Grassroots Efforts

A citizens' alliance for health insurance reform, the Committee for National Health Insurance, has proposed a plan called "Health

Security Partnership: An Equitable and Universal National Health Plan."[22] This proposal combines the two major solutions discussed at the outset of this chapter. It would allow freedom of choice among providers and encourage each state to develop and organize programs suitable to the needs of its residents. Funding would be shared by the federal and state governments, with some contributions from the private insurance industry and consumer payments. Beyond the broad outlines, however, comprehensive details for implementation of this plan have not been worked out yet.

These proposals represent only a portion of the union and management effort that is being channeled to lobby the federal government for change. Even the American Medical Association, long an advocate of the status quo, has come out in support of reform. In 1991, more than 70 articles appeared in *JAMA* and related journals that described how bad conditions are for the uninsured and called for the government to require employers to provide basic health insurance for all their workers.

State Reforms

In addition to the national efforts described above, much activity is taking place at the state level as well. Indeed, change may occur in the states before national health care reform becomes a reality. The following discussion summarizes some of the more significant initiatives underway at the state level.

The Washington State Experiment

At the 1989 congressional hearings, Rep. James McDermott (D-WA-7) explained how four areas of Washington state had implemented some insurance for the working poor. He also advocated a grassroots movement at the state level to develop plans that would address the two basic issues of access and cost containment.[23] Toward that goal, McDermott introduced HR 2996, which would provide planning grants for states to develop their own programs for the uninsured.

The Washington insurance program called the "Basic Health Plan," exists in Seattle, Tacoma, Spokane, and one rural county, Clallam. In 1989, some 7,000 people under age 65 with incomes less than 200 percent of the poverty level were enrolled in the system.

Monthly charges for coverage ranged from $7.50 for an individual to $274 for a large family at 200 percent of the poverty level. The average monthly charge per person was $35, or the amount set for persons whose incomes fell at the poverty line. For a family of four, the poverty line was $11,000 in 1989.

Private-sector providers, organized as managed health-care systems, deliver health services under contracts with the basic health plan in each service area. Most of these systems are existing health maintenance organizations, but two counties are served by local Blue Shield organizations. In the largest county, enrollees have a choice of two managed care systems, and similar choice among provider organizations is planned for other project areas.

The plan collects premiums from enrollees and pays around $75 to $85 per month per enrollee to the managed care system covering the area. The state provides a subsidy to make up the difference between the premium the enrollee can afford to pay and the amount the plan has contracted to pay. The cost of these subsidies means that enrollment is "lidded," that is, the numbers of enrollees is limited based on available funding. Enrollment is on a first-come, first-served basis.

In evaluating whether to expand the program, the state found several problems:

- The state will have to find a new revenue source to expand the plan to cover all the uninsured people, whose numbers exceed 600,000. The cost of increasing enrollment to 25,000 in 1990 and 1991 was estimated at about $38 million.
- The plan in effect provides a subsidy to employers who do not supply their employees with insurance, since workers pay the costs of insurance. As a result, the state's plan could become a substitute for employer-purchased health insurance, which is not the intent of the current legislation.
- The plan is "basic" and has limitations on coverage. It currently requires a one-year waiting period for preexisting conditions other than pregnancy, and provides no dental, mental health, or a variety of other coverages.

In commenting on the development of the Washington plan, McDermott noted that during the plans initial four-year implementation opposition came from doctors and hospitals. In the end, however, everyone participated in the final implementation of the legislation. Those initially opposed ultimately realized they would not lose much business, because the state's market niche totaled a very small share of the existing business, McDermott said. Opponents also realized the state, rather than providers, was actually subsidizing the cost of the program at some $38 million.

The Oregon Plan

The question of how much care can be provided for the insurance dollar is also facing Oregon's new experiment with statewide health insurance for the uninsured. In 1991, Oregon attempted to expand its Medicaid program to cover all the non-elderly living on incomes at or below the poverty line. The state previously had offered Medicaid coverage only to single-parent families with incomes at or below 58 percent of the poverty line.

As a result, the number of people entitled to benefits has dramatically increased. In order to balance its budget, Oregon is choosing to ration the amount of care, and these rationing efforts are being watched with interest by the entire country.[24] The state intends to limit coverage to services that are the most cost-effective in promoting, maintaining, and restoring good long-term health. Coverage for some of the costliest programs, such as experimental organ transplants, will most likely be denied to some individuals, such as those over a certain age or whose quality of life would only be marginally affected. These experiments will no doubt influence other states and the nation.

The initial study to set health-care priorities analyzed results from 50 statewide meetings of some 1,048 residents. By May 1991, the Oregon Health Services Committee had developed some 709 health services that should constitute a standard benefit package. The state legislature controls the determination as to what procedures will be funded, which citizens will receive care, at what stage of illness or debilitation will help be provided, and how much money can be appropriated from what sources to support the program.

Providing all 709 services to all those below the poverty level would cause a 30 percent increase in the state's Medicaid funding. As a result, the Health Services Committee recommended that the state fund only 640 of these services, which would represent a $36 million annual expenditure, seven percent less than the funds needed for all 709 services. To fund only 475 services would cost $21 million, but the program would cover only about half of all "medically necessary" expenses. The 1991 legislature finally agreed to allocate $33 million to fund 587 services. Before Oregon's program can be implemented, the HFCA would have to waive the Medicaid requirement that states must fund all medically necessary expenses. As of January 1992, the HFCA's decision on this waiver was still pending.

Oregon's ability to support the program will be a severe test in the depression of the early 1990s. Oregon is a test case in the laboratory of making hard choices to ration health care. What happens there may be a guidepost for other states and the nation.

Other Programs

Other demonstration programs exist in some cities and states across the country. Many resemble Washington state's program, but are not as broad-based in their expected future implementation. In the 1989 congressional hearings, mention was made of plans in Tulsa, OK and Memphis, TN, which were begun with grants from the Robert Wood Johnson Foundation. These plans, as well as some Blue Cross/Blue Shield initiatives and state legislative proposals, are summarized in the following discussion.

The Tulsa, OK Plan

The Tulsa plan, created for large and small businesses alike, allows a choice of an HMO or a PPO. With some 34,000 enrollees in 1989, the program had the largest participation rate among businesses with 10 or fewer employees, although it also featured a product specifically for firms with 16 to 49 employees. Single-coverage costs ranged from $55 to $75 per month, with a net savings of $7 million to the insured firms. The Tulsa program is now being considered for statewide implementation.

The Memphis, TN Program

In Memphis, a small med-trust trust formed by the Tennessee Primary Care Association negotiated a voluntary discount from three local hospitals to obtain lower insurance rates for small businesses. Primary care, case management, and referral services are through an HMO, with monthly individual costs of $40 and family premiums of $75 to $100 in 1989. Participating employers made monthly contributions of $30 per employee. Firms with fewer than 10 employees were required to have 100 percent participation, while large companies had to have only 80 percent participation.

Between April and October 1989, some 117 groups with 334 individuals had enrolled in the program.

Blue Cross/Blue Shield Initiatives

Blue Cross/Blue Shield companies have also undertaken some initiatives. In Rochester, NY, a "ValueMed" plan was designed for uninsured persons under age 65 whose incomes are below 175 percent of the federal poverty level. The plan subsidizes administrative and other costs, which kept monthly premiums in 1989 at $39 for single coverage and at $70 for couples with an additional $10 per child. In Iowa, a similar plan called BasiCare is available for $50 a month per individual. The plan covers inpatient hospitalization, outpatient surgery, as well as emergency and accident care, and is paid directly through employers. In Tennessee, IMPACT is available to the self-employed, employers with four or fewer employees, students, and others without access to health care under a group plan. The plan incorporates some cost-containment features such as second surgical opinions, concurrent care review, and preadmission certification and testing. Premiums amount to $28.13 for persons under age 29, with a 10 percent discount for nonsmokers.

Another Blue Cross/Blue Shield program is called the Caring Program for Children. Developed in 1985 in western Pennsylvania, the program provides free preventive and emergency health-care service coverage to low-income families who are not eligible for Medicaid. As of September 1989, nine other Blue Cross and Blue Shield plans had established this program in Alabama, Iowa, Maryland, Missouri, North Dakota, North Carolina, Ohio, Syracuse, New York, and Kansas, with more in the planning stages.

In South Carolina, the Blues and the state are cooperating to institute an insurance program that assesses premiums on the basis of health behaviors. Most similar programs have been limited to companies that self-insure, so the Blues' effort to develop a statewide plan is unusual. The program will offer discounted rates for those who comply with health promotion goals and who use preferred providers. Risk rates would be determined by having employees undergo a health risk assessment, as well as by rating the employer's claims profile and other relevant information, such as absenteeism and productivity data. Employees would then be assigned to patient advocates, and those in high-risk categories would have case managers who ensure they receive appropriate levels of assistance.

Along with risk rates, charges would be assessed in proportion to an enrollee's cooperation with the program. For example, charges would be covered at the 90 percent level if the individual uses preferred providers and follows the advice of the health advocates. Penalties would be assessed or lesser percentages would be reimbursed if preferred providers were not used or advice was not followed.

A recent CBS commentary found this type of insurance was prevalent among employers, but despite cost savings, such plans also produce some angry employees who claim that their civil liberties are being restricted.[25] Thus, creating a healthier America may not be the answer to containing costs if Americans don't want to be healthy. The South Carolina plan is not yet fully implemented and if the administrative costs become too excessive, it may never get tested.[26]

Pending State Initiatives

In 1991, the New Hampshire House of Representatives passed Resolution 9, which urges Congress to enact a national health care program based on the principles of universal access, comprehensive benefits, financing based on the ability to pay, cost containment, and fair payment to providers.

The Iowa Universal Health Plan calls for a single-payer system of health care throughout the state and has been the subject of statewide hearings during 1991. Maine likewise has legislation pending on the provision of universal access through a state-run health care plan. New York's recently released report from its Senate Majority Task Force on Aging in the 21st Century also calls for major changes in the provision of health care.[27]

Summary

An ambitious nationwide program of radical change is not likely to occur in the very near future, although some legislative changes will probably take place. As of this writing in early 1992, the issue of health care reform is second only to the nation's economy in Congress and the presidential race. Major health-care reform, however, will likely occur slowly and happen on the state and local levels before a major national effort gets underway. A time lag of five to

10 years is probable before radical changes will occur. In the meantime, companies and unions bear the burden of negotiating for change in contracts with each other and with insurance providers. Increases in the medical CPI may have begun to slow, but the rate is still almost double the overall rate of inflation. In 1990, 43 of 86 negotiated contracts resulted in increased premium costs to employees, while 21 resulted in increased deductibles.[28] Despite this trend, employers face considerable costs. To illustrate, one of the most outstanding and comprehensive health care plans in American industry has been the one offered by General Motors to its union employees. GM projects that while $622 of the cost of each car sold in 1989 went toward health insurance, this figure will rise to $1,000 by 1993.[29] How long can American businesses compete at this rate?

As a final commentary on the need for reform, a Metropolitan Life Insurance Company poll, released in 1991, found five areas of agreement with regard to the health care problem:[30]

- The nation's health system is not well.
- The system of the future should continue to involve both public and private sectors.
- Health insurance for everyone is appropriate and likely, even if this means higher taxes.
- A majority of all groups surveyed except for state officials (and 50 percent of them) would favor, in principle, reallocating $50 billion currently spent on other goods and services to provide some kind of health insurance for those who are currently uninsured.
- To create a better health care system, compromise is perceived as necessary and acceptable by all stakeholder groups.

While only a small percentage of this sample, with the exception of union leaders, believed change should involve a national health insurance plan, major reforms of some type seem inevitable. Most of the rhetoric and testimony before both Congress and state legislatures has advocated health-care reform. Both labor and management are aware that they cannot afford the bill going up much more and are asking for help from Congress and the statehouse.

Notes

1. Phyllis Borzi, speech before the National Education Association Health and Benefits Forum, April 30, 1990, Hollywood, FL.

2. U.S. Bipartisan Commission on Comprehensive Healthcare, *The Pepper Commission Report*, (Washington, D.C.: U.S. Government Printing Office, 1990).

3. David Himmelstein, speech before the National Education Association Health and Benefits Forum, April 30, 1990, Hollywood, FL.

4. Himmelstein and Steffie Woolhandler, "The Deteriorating Administrative Efficiency of the U.S. Health Care System," *New England Journal of Medicine* 324(18) (May 2, 1991): pp 1253–58.

5. U.S. Congress, *The Growing Crisis in Health Care: The Basic Health Benefits for All Americans Act (H.R. 1845) and Other National Health Care Policy Options*, serial no. 101-64 (Washington, DC: U.S. Government Printing Office, 1990).

6. Ibid., 1–2.

7. Ibid., 21–35.

8. Ibid., 86–174.

9. Ibid., 144–153.

10. Ibid., 154–172.

11. Ibid., 10–19.

12. Ibid., 65–84.

13. Ibid., 228–242.

14. *Medical Briefs* (May 30, 1990): 3. Citation from *Annals of Internal Medicine*.

15. House Ways and Means Committee hearings, April 25, 1991, statement by Chairman Dan Rostenkowski (D-IL-8).

16. Ibid., testimony by Richard Darman, director of Office of Management and Budget.

17. The complete text of the Bush proposal is available in Special Supplement Report No. 26 2/7/92 BNA White Fact Sheet and White Paper on the "President's Comprehensive Health Reform Program" released 2/6/92. See also DLR No. 26, "Current Developments" (BNA), 2/7/92 pp. A-15–A-23. "Bush proposes $100 Billion Health Plan using Tax Benefits to Expand Access."

18. "Reform: Possible Solutions Discussed and Criticized House and Senate Hearings," *Benefits Today* 8, no. 10 (May 21, 1991): 157–158.

19. Rich S. 1991. "Uniform Billing System for Health Care Planned." *Washington Post* (Nov. 6): A–3.

20. "Current Developments," *Daily Labor Review* (May 22, 1991): 7–8.

21. Congressional Budget Office, *Rising Health Care Costs, Causes, Implications and Strategies*, (Washington, DC: Government Printing Office, 1991).

22. For a copy of "Health Security Partnership: An Equitable and Universal National Health Plan," write the Committee for National Health Insurance, 1727 N St., N.W., Washington, D.C. 20036.

23. U.S. Congress, *The Growing Crisis in Health Care*, 186–203.

24. For a fuller description of Oregon's plan, see Bureau of National Affairs, Inc. "State Seeks Waivers for Universal Health Insurance," *Pension Reporter* 18 (Dec. 2, 1991): 2190–2191, and John A. MacDonald, "Is Health Care Rationing a Cure for Soaring Costs?" *Current* (Dec. 12, 1991): A1, A16.

25. CBS Evening News, May 30, 1991.

26. "Blue Cross/Blue Shield of South Carolina Developing Risk Based Product," *Benefits Today* 8, no. 10, (May 21, 1991): 152.

27. Copies of "Toward a New Tomorrow: New York State's Aging Society in the 1990's and Beyond," can be obtained from the Senate Majority Task Force on

Aging in the 21st Century, Room 903, Legislative Office Building, Albany, NY, 12247.

28. Mike Davis of BNA, speech before the American Arbitation Association Regional Conference, July 1990, Newport, RI.

29. Human Resource Center, "Quality Health Care and Cost Is Joint Concern," *UAW-GM People* (Winter 1991): 7.

30. MetLife, "Tradeoffs and Choices: Health Policy Options for the 1990s," a national opinion research survey (New York: Louis Harris and Associates, 1990).

Resources

Federal Agencies

Alcohol, Drug Abuse, and Mental Health Administration, Parkway Building, 5600 Fishers Lane, Rockville, MD 20857.

Bureau of Labor Statistics, 441 G St., NW, Washington, DC 20210.

Centers for Disease Control, 1600 Clifton Road NE, Atlanta, GA 30333.

Department of Commerce, Main Commerce Building, 14th Street and Constitution Avenue NW, Washington, DC 20230.

Department of Health and Human Services, 330 Independence Ave. SW, Washington, DC 20201.

Department of Labor, 200 Constitution Ave. NW, Washington, DC 20210.

Government Printing Office, Superintendent of Documents, 941 N. Capitol St. NE, Washington, D.C. 20401.

Health Care Financing Administration, 6325 Security Blvd., Baltimore, MD 21207.

Health Resources and Services Administration, Parklawn Building, 5600 Fishers Lane, Rockville, MD 20857.

National Center for Health Services Research and Health Care Technology Assessment, Parklawn Building, 5600 Fishers Lane, Rockville, MD 20857.

National Center for Health Statistics, 3700 East-West Hwy., Hyattsville, MD 20782.

National Health Information Clearinghouse, PO Box 1133, Washington, DC 20013-1133.

National Institute of Health, 9000 Rockville Pike, Bethesda, MD 20892.

Pension and Welfare Benefits Administration, 200 Constitution Ave. NW, Washington, DC 20216.

Social Security Administration, 6401 Security Blvd., Baltimore, MD 21235.

Organizations

AFL-CIO, Occupational Safety, Health Employee Benefits Department, 815 16th St. NW, Washington, DC 20006.

American Association of Health Care Consultants, 11208 Waples Mill Road, Fairfax, VA 22030.

American Association of Preferred Provider Organizations, Suite 600, 111 E. Wacker Drive, Chicago, IL 60601.

American Cancer Society, 1599 Clifton Road SE, Atlanta, GA 30329.

American College of Health Care Administrators, 325 S. Patrick St., Alexandria, VA 22314.

American Health Care Association, 1201 L St. NW, Washington, DC 20005.

American Hospital Association, Office of Health Coalitions and Private Initiatives, 840 N. Lake Shore Drive, Chicago, IL 60611.

American Insurance Association, Suite 1000, 1130 Connecticut Ave. NW, Washington, DC 20036.

American Medical Association, 535 N. Dearborn St., Chicago, IL 60610-0946.

American Medical Care and Review Association (AMCRA), Suite 610, 1227 25th St. NW, Washington, DC 20037.

Blue Cross/Blue Shield Association, 676 North St. Clair, Chicago, IL 60611.

Employee Assistance Program Association, Suite 1001, 4601 N. Fairfax Drive, Fairfax, VA 22203.

Employee Benefits Research Institute (EBRI), Suite 600, 2121 K St. NW, Washington, DC 20037-2121.

Employers Council on Flexible Compensation, Suite 1000, 927 15th St. NW, Washington, DC 20005.

Group Health Association of America, Suite 700, Two Westbrook Corporate Center, Westchester, IL 60153. This organization maintains a national directory and description of HMOs and tracks their trends.

Health Research Institute, 49 Quail Court, Walnut Creek, CA 94596. This organization, whose director was quoted in this text, compiles annual information on health care costs and trends.

Health Insurance Association of America (HIAA), 1025 Connecticut Ave. NW, Washington, DC 20004-2599. An association of commercial insurance companies, its research provides data on physician fees and maintains a national data base listing the prices of more than 2,000 medical procedures that are used by many insurance companies for setting their usual, customary, and reasonable (UCR) charges.

Hewitt Associates, 2121 K St NW, Suite 620, Washington, DC 20037-2121. This international acturial consulting firm, which was mentioned in this text, prepares a number of national research reports.

International Foundation of Employee Benefit Plans (IFEBP), 18700 W. Bluemound Road, PO Box 69, Brookfield, WI 53008-0069.

National Association of Employers on Health Care Alternatives, 104 Crandon Blvd., Key Biscayne, FL 33149. This association hosts annual conferences and publishes newsletters on HMOs and PPOs.

National Association of Health Data Organizations, 254B N. Washington St., Falls Church, VA 22046.

National Center for Health Promotion, 3920 Varsity Drive, Ann Arbor, MI 48108.

National Coalition for Health Care Reform, 555 13th St. NW, Washington, DC 20004.

National Employee Benefits Institute, Suite 400, 2445 M St. NW, Washington, DC 20037.

National Health Council, 350 Fifth Ave., New York, NY 10118.

National Technical Information Service, 5285 Port Royal Road, Springfield, VA 22161.

National Wellness Institute, South Hall, 1219 Freemont St., Stevens Point, WI 54481.

Robert Wood Johnson Foundation, PO Box 2316, Princeton, NJ 08543. This group funds research on health care financing and organization, in addition to other related topics.

Self-Insurance Institute of America, PO Box 15466, Santa Ana, CA 92705.

U.S. Chamber of Commerce, Clearinghouse on Business Coalitions for Health Action, 1615 H St. NW, Washington, DC 20062.

Value Health Sciences, Inc., 2400 Broadway St., Suite 100, Santa Monica, CA 90404. This company is a source of information on the data used by insurers in advising physicians on reimbursement qualifications for diagnostic and surgical procedures.

Publications

Advisory Council on Social Security. *Commitment to Change: Foundations for Change.* Washington, DC: Advisory Council on Social Security.

AFL-CIO Department of Occupational Safety, Health, and Social Security, Labor Institute of Public Affairs, George Meany Center for Labor Studies. *Health Care Cost Containment Crisis,* pub. no. 175. Washington, DC: AFL-CIO, no date.

Blue Cross/Blue Shield. *State Mandated Coverages: Enacted Legislation.* Washington, DC 20005: Office of Government Relations, January 1990.

Bureau of National Affairs, Inc. *Benefits Today.* Washington, DC: BNA.

————. *BNA Policy and Practice Series, Compensation* binder. Washington, DC: BNA.

————. *BNA's Employee Relations Weekly.* Washington, DC: BNA.

————. *Employment Guide.* Washington, DC: BNA.

Chapman, Larry S. *Plan 2000: A Model Health Benefit Program. A Health Benefit Plan to Assure High-Quality Care at an Affordable Cost.* Seattle, WA: Corporate Health Designs, 1990.

Congressional Budget Office. *Universal Health Insurance Coverage Using Medicare's Payment Rates.* Washington, DC: CBO.

Coopers and Lybrand. *Actuarial Benefits and Compensation Releases* and *Notes* (various issues).

Cowan, Belita H. *Health Care Shopper's Guide.* Annapolis, MD: Consumer Protection Division of the Maryland Attorney General's Office, 1987.

Doran, Phyllis A., Kenneth D. MacBain, and William A. Reimert. *Measuring and Funding Corporate Liabilities for Retiree Health Benefits—An EBRI-ERF Policy Study.* Washington, DC: EBRI, 1987.

Employee Benefits Research Institute. *Issue Briefs* and *Notes* (various issues).

————. *Fundamentals of Employee Benefit Programs,* 3rd ed. Washington, DC: EBRI, 1987.

Foster Higgins. *Health Care Benefits Surveys 1987, 1988, 1989.* A Foster Higgins & Co, Inc., 212 Carnegie Center, CN 5323, Princeton, NJ 08543-5323.

Lehman, June M., ed. *Employee Benefit Plans, A Glossary of Terms*, 6th ed., Brookfield, WI: International Foundation of Employee Benefit Plans, 1987.

Martin E. Segal Co. *1989 Survey of State Employee Health Benefits Plans: A Summary of Findings*. New York, NY: Martin E. Segal Co., 1989.

McArdle, Frank B., ed. *The Changing Health Care Market*. Washington, DC: EBRI, 1987.

National Association of Insurance Commissioners. *PUBLICATIONS*. Kansas City, MO: NAIC Publication, annually.

National Education Association. *Health Insurance Consumer Guide*. Rockville, MD: NEA Special Services, December 1988.

————. *Employee Insurance Benefits: A Guide Book for Bargainers*. Rockville, MD: NEA Special Services, June 1988.

————. *Trends in Health Care Expenditure*, vol. 1. Washington, DC: NEA, 1988.

————. *Trends in Health Care Cost Management*, vol. 2. Washington, DC: NEA, 1988.

————. *Trends in Employee Benefit Design*, vol. 3. Washington, DC: NEA, 1988.

————, and the American Council of Life Insurance and Health Insurance Association of America. *A Report on Wellness: A Study of Employee Wellness Programs Sponsored by School Districts*. Washington, DC: NEA, April 1987.

Reynolds, John D., and Robin N. Bischoff. *Health Insurance Answer Book*, 2nd ed. Greenvale, NY: Panel Publishers.

Rosenbloom, Jerry, ed. *The Handbook of Employee Benefits*. Homewood, IL: Dow Jones-Irwin, 1988.

Service Employees International Union, AFL-CIO, CLC. *Healthcare Benefits Bargaining Manual*. Washington, DC: SEIU Research Department, 1989.

————. *Labor and Management on a Collision Course over Health Care: A Study*. Washington, DC: SEIU, AFL-CIO, CLC, February 1990.

————. *Health Care in the U.S.A.: A Crumbling System*. Washington, DC: SEIU, AFL-CIO, CLC, no date.

————. *Towards an American Healthcare Solution*. Washington, DC: SEIU, AFL-CIO, CLC, no date.

U.S. Chamber of Commerce. *How Business Interacts with the Health Care System*. Washington, DC: U.S. Chamber of Commerce, various years.

————. *How Business Can Use Specific Techniques to Control Health Care Costs.* Washington, DC: U.S. Chamber of Commerce, no date.

————. *How Business Can Stimulate a Competitive Health Care System.* Washington, DC: U.S. Chamber of Commerce, no date.

————. *How Business Can Promote Good Health for Employees and Their Families.* Washington, DC: U.S. Chamber of Commerce, no date.

————. *Employee Benefits,* various years.

U.S. Conference of Mayors, the American Federation of State, County, and Municipal Employees, the AFL-CIO, and the National Public Employer Labor Relations Association. *Labor Management Guide to Health Care Cost Containment.* Washington, DC: Federal Mediation and Conciliation Service, no date (circa 1988).

U.S. Congress, Bipartisan Commission on Comprehensive Health Care (Pepper Commission). *Access to Health Care and Long-Term Care for All Americans.* Washington, DC: Government Printing Office, 1990.

————, Subcommittee on Labor Management Relations of the House Committee on Education and Labor. *Hearings on the Growing Crisis in Health Care: The Basic Health Benefits for All Americans Act (HR 1845) and National Health Care Policy Options,* serial no. 101-64. Washington, DC: Government Printing Office, 1990.

U.S. Department of Labor, Bureau of Labor Statistics. *Employee Benefits in Medium and Large Firms.* Washington, DC: BLS.

Wyatt Co. *The Compensation and Benefits File* (various issues).

Working in Employee Benefits (WEB). *Network* (various issues).

State Insurance Departments

Alabama
Department of Insurance, Administrative Building, Montgomery, AL 36130

Alaska
Department of Commerce and Economic Development, Division of Insurance, 134 E. Third Ave., Anchorage, AK 99501.

Arizona
Department of Insurance, 1601 W. Jefferson St., Phoenix, AZ 85007.

Arkansas
Department of Insurance, 400 University Tower, 12th and University Streets, Little Rock, AR 72204.

California
Department of Insurance, 100 Van Hess Ave., San Francisco, CA 94102.

Colorado
Department of Regulatory Agencies, Division of Insurance, 5th Floor, W. Colfax Ave., Denver, CO 80204.

Connecticut
Insurance Department, State Office Building, 165 Capitol Ave., Hartford, CT 06106.

Deleware
Department of Insurance, 21 The Green, Dover, DE 19901.

District of Columbia
Department of Insurance, North Potomac Building, Suite 512, 614 H St. NW, Washington, DC 20001.

Florida
Bureau of Field Operations, J. Edwin Larson Building, Room 332, Tallahassee, FL 32301.

Georgia
Insurance Department, West Tower, Room 716, #2 Martin Luther King Jr. Drive, Atlanta, GA 30334.

Hawaii
Department of Commerce and Consumer Affairs, Insurance Division, PO Box 3614, Honolulu, HI 96811.

Idaho
Department of Insurance, 700 W. State St., Boise, ID 83720.

Illinois
Department of Insurance, 4th Floor, 320 W. Washington St., Springfield, IL 62767.

Iowa
Insurance Department, Luca Building, Des Moines, IA 50319.

Indiana
Department of Insurance, 509 State Office Building, Indianapolis, IN 46204.

Kansas
Insurance Department, 420 SW 9th St., Topeka, KS 66612.

Kentucky
Department of Insurance, 151 Elkhorn Court, Frankfort, KY 40601.

Louisiana
Office of Commissioner of Insurance, PO Box 94214, Baton Rouge, LA 70804.

Maine
Department of Business Regulation, Bureau of Insurance, State House, Station 34, Augusta, ME 04333.

Maryland
Department of Licensing and Regulation, Insurance Division, 7th Floor South, 501 St. Paul Place, Baltimore, MD 21202.

Massachusetts
Division of Insurance, 100 Cambridge St., Boston, MA 02202.

Michigan
Department of Licensing and Regulation, Insurance Bureau, 1048 Pierpont St., PO Box 30220, Lansing, MI 48909.

Minnesota
Department of Commerce, 5th Floor, 500 Metro Square Building, St. Paul, MN 55101.

Mississippi
Insurance Department, 1804 Walter Sillers Building, PO Box 79, Jackson, MS 39205.

Missouri
Department of Consumer Services, Division of Insurance, PO Box 690, Jefferson City, MO 65102.

Montana
Insurance Department, Mitchell Building, Room 213, 125 N. Sanders, PO Box 4009, Helena, MT 59601.

Nebraska
Department of Insurance, 301 Centennial Mall South, PO Box 94699, Lincoln, NE 68509.

Nevada
Department of Commerce, Insurance Division, 201 S. Fall St., Carson City, NV 80710.

New Hampshire
Insurance Department, 169 Manchester St., Concord NH 03301.

New Jersey
Department of Insurance, 210 E. State St., Trenton, NJ 08625.

New Mexico
Department of Insurance, PO Drawer 1269, Santa Fe, NM 87504.

New York
Insurance Department, 160 W. Broadway, New York, NY 10013.

North Carolina
Insurance Department, Dobbs Building, PO Box 26387, Raleigh, NC 27611.

North Dakota
Department of Insurance, 5th Floor, Capitol Building, Bismarck, ND 58505.

Ohio
Department of Insurance, 2100 Stella Court, Columbus, OH 43215.

Oklahoma
Office of Insurance Commissioner, Will Rogers Memorial Office Building, Oklahoma City, OK 73105.

Oregon
Department of Commerce, Insurance Division, Commerce Building, 158 12th St. NE, Salem, OR 97310.

Pennsylvania
Insurance Department, 13th Floor, Strawberry Square, Harrisburg, PA 17120.

Rhode Island
Department of Business Regulation, Insurance Division, 100 N. Main St., Providence, RI 02903.

South Carolina
Department of Insurance, 2711 Middleburg Drive, PO Box 4067, Columbia, SC 29204.

South Dakota
Division of Insurance, 320 N. Nicollet St., Pierre, SD 57501.

Tennessee
Department of Insurance, 114 State Office Building, Nashville, TN
37219.

Texas
State Board of Insurance, 1110 San Jacinto Blvd., Austin, TX 78786.

Utah
Insurance Department, 160 E. Third South, PO Box 45803, Salt
Lake City, UT 84145.

Vermont
Department of Banking and Insurance, 120 State St., Montpelier,
VT 05602.

Virginia
State Corporation Commission, Bureau of Insurance, 700 Jefferson
Building, PO Box 1157, Richmond, VA 23209.

Washington
Office of Insurance Commissioner, Insurance Building, AQ-21,
Olympia, WA 98504.

West Virginia
Insurance Department, 2100 Washington St. East, Charleston, WV
25305.

Wisconsin
Office of the Commissioner of Insurance, 123 W. Washington Ave.,
Madison, WS 53707.

Wyoming
Insurance Department, Herschler Building, 122 W. 25th St.,
Cheyenne, WY 82002.

Appendix 1

Summary of the HMO Act

Source: Reprinted from *Employment Guide*, The Bureau of National Affairs, Inc., 70:215.

Health Maintenance Organization Act

The Health Maintenance Organization Act is designed to encourage the development of health maintenance organizations as an alternative to traditional health care plans by requiring certain employers to offer a qualified HMO plan to their workers as an optional health care plan.

Coverage—The Act requires an employer to provide its workers with the option of participating in a qualified HMO if the employer has received a written request from an HMO operating in an area where at least 25 of the firm's workers reside and the employer: has 25 or more employees on a full or part-time basis; is required to pay a minimum wage in compliance with the Fair Labor Standards Act; and contributes to a health benefits plan for eligible employees.

Requirements—Under the Act, HMOs must provide the following basic health coverage: physician services and inpatient and outpatient hospital services; emergency health services and short-term outpatient evaluative and crisis mental health intervention services; treatment and referral services for drug and alcohol abuse; diagnostic laboratory and diagnostic and therapeutic radiological services and preventative health services, including immunizations, well-child care from birth, periodic health evaluations for adults, voluntary family planning services, infertility services, and children's eye and ear examinations.

If the HMO is a qualified plan under the law, it can make a formal written request to an employer, asking it to offer its workers an HMO option. Once an employer with 25 or more employees receives such a request, it must offer its employees the HMO option as well as a standard health plan. (However, effective October 1, 1995, this "dual choice" requirement is eliminated by the HMO Amendments of 1988.) After receiving the request, an employer also must:

▶Arrange for HMO payroll deductions if possible.

▶Allow the HMO access to eligible workers 30 days prior to and during group enrollment periods.

▶Provide for a group enrollment period of 10 days per calendar year.

▶Offer HMO coverage without waiting periods and limitations based upon health status.

▶Give employees the opportunity to select the HMO in writing the first time it is offered.

▶Offer HMO coverage on terms that do not "financially discriminate" against employees choosing the option, according to the HMO Amendments of 1988. Under the requirements, contribution terms are deemed not "financially discriminatory" if they are reasonable and designed to assure employees a fair choice among health benefit plans. This nondiscriminatory contribution rule replaces the provision under the previous law requiring employers to make a per-employee contribution toward an HMO that is at least equal to the contribution made to the employer's standard health benefits plan.

Employees must not be forced to lose any eligibility rights to "free-standing" coverage, such as dental and optical care, if they select an HMO that does not include such benefits. Employers are not required to pay more for HMO benefits than they would pay for other health care coverage. If the HMO premium is higher, employees can be required to pay the difference.

Enforcement and Sanctions—Any person, group, association, corporation, or other entity, including unions and HMOs, may file a complaint with the Department of Health and Human Services if an employer fails to comply with the Act. Employers that don't correct violations are subject to civil penalties of up to $10,000 for each 30-day period of noncompliance.

Appendix 2

Example of a Cafeteria Plan: Landmark Choices

Source: Reprinted with permission from Landmark Medical Center, 115 Cass Ave., Woonsocket, RI 02895.

Landmark Choices 1992

This is your 1992 *Landmark Choices* Workbook. It describes each of the benefit options available to you, explains some of the differences, addresses points to consider and will assist you in selecting the benefits that best meet your individual needs.

The *Landmark Choices* program was established because Landmark Medical Center knows that the needs of individual employees vary. This comprehensive benefits program gives you the opportunity to review and make benefit selections each year. This means that as your personal situation changes from year-to-year, you can formulate a benefit package to meet your changing needs.

Making your Choices

Each of us chooses how to spend our paychecks. You may prefer to buy a home, while others prefer to rent an apartment. Some may rather save for a vacation, and others, a new car. *Landmark Choices* provides you with the ability to choose how to spend your Benefit Dollars. You may choose a medical plan with a higher deductible, you may choose to make a deposit into a Health Care and/or Dependent Care Reimbursement Account, you may choose to buy additional life insurance or you may even choose to take some of your Benefit Dollars as cash. With your *Landmark Choices* comprehensive flexible benefits program the choice is yours!

You will need to read through each benefit area to fully understand each option. As you make preliminary selections, you can record these on the worksheet at the back of this workbook. This worksheet is similar to your personal enrollment form. You will probably change your mind several times as you work through all of the benefits and options. This is typical - selecting the benefit package that best meets your needs is not a quick process. Points that you should consider include:

- Your benefit needs today?
- Your short term future needs - for example, are you expecting a baby in the next few months?
- Your budget?
- Your long term future needs - for example, your retirement plans?

You should be aware that when you convert a portion of your pay to Benefit Dollars to purchase additional benefits, it reduces your Social Security (FICA) taxable income. This may have a slight effect on the benefits you and your family will receive from Social Security at retirement or in the event of your disability or death. Social Security amounts are determined using a formula that takes your FICA taxable income into account. **When you convert a portion of your pay to Benefit Dollars, you reduce your contributions to Social Security.**

The conversion of regular pay dollars to Benefit Dollars takes place before your pay reaches your paycheck and before withholding taxes are taken out. When we calculate your Federal withholding taxes, we do not include pay that has been converted to Benefit Dollars. Your total compensation stays the same, but the part that is taxable and printed on your W-2 form is less. Therefore, you pay fewer taxes and keep more of what you earn. For plan details, limitations, and exclusions, please refer to your Employee Handbook and Summary Plan Descriptions. In the event of any conflict between the information summarized here and the official plan documents, the plan documents will govern. The *Landmark Choices* plan has been designed to take maximum advantage of the current tax laws. Landmark Medical Center monitors the program to assure that it continues to meet the necessary legal requirements.

THE ADVANTAGES OF LANDMARK CHOICES

Landmark Choices was designed with several key points in mind.
- To provide employees the advantage of choosing benefits to meet their individual needs.
- To maximize the tax advantages available under the current tax laws.
- To offer the advantage of purchasing benefits at group rates and through payroll deductions.

With *Landmark Choices* you purchase benefits with non-taxable Benefit Dollars. You may choose to spend all of the Benefit Dollars allotted to you and even purchase additional benefits. To do this, you convert a portion of your pay to Benefit Dollars. The Benefit Dollars you use to buy benefits are not included on your annual W-2 form. This means you can purchase additional benefits and save tax dollars at the same time. Let's look at an example. Pat Smith is a Landmark Medical Center employee. Pat decides to spend allotted Benefit Dollars and elects to convert $500 of pay to Benefit Dollars to purchase additional benefits.

With *Landmark Choices*, the $500 of converted pay is paid before taxes are deducted from Pat's pay. The following illustration shows Pat's true costs under the *Landmark Choices* as compared to her costs for the same benefits purchased outside the plan at two different tax levels.

	Tax Rate 27%	Tax Rate 40%	*Landmark Choices*
Benefits Purchased	$ 500	$ 500	$ 500
Taxes	185	333	0
Actual Cost	$ 685	$ 833	$ 500

You can see how Pat saves between $185 and $333 (depending on her tax level) while choosing the benefits she wants through *Landmark Choices*.

Additionally, Pat probably has additional savings because pricetags are based on the group purchasing power of Landmark Medical Center.

Terms to Know

Some important terms which appear throughout your workbook and are used in the discussion of your *Landmark Choices* program are defined below.

Benefit Dollars - You purchase benefits with Benefit Dollars. Each year you receive a pool of money (Benefit Dollars) from Landmark Medical Center. When you spend Benefit Dollars on non-taxable benefits, the Benefit Dollars are non-taxable for Federal, State, and Social Security (FICA) tax purposes. When you spend Benefit Dollars on taxable benefits, the Benefit Dollars are taxable and included on your W-2 form at year end.

Options - A range of choices which you have to pick from in each benefit area. With some benefits, you have the option of taking No Coverage.

Pricetag - The cost of a particular benefit option. The pricetag represents the price of that benefit option for a one year period under **Landmark Choices**.

Plan Year - The **Landmark Choices** plan year is March 1 through the end of February each year. Eligible employees hired prior to January 1 of that year are qualified to participate. Eligible employees hired on or after January 1 of that year will receive a standard program of benefits until the following enrollment period, at which time they may enroll in the **Landmark Choices** customized program.

Core Benefit - A benefit in which all eligible employees must participate. The core benefits are Employee Life and AD&D Insurance and Long Term Disability Insurance.

Changes During the Plan Year

You will need to select your benefits and options carefully as the benefits will remain in effect for the entire plan year (through February 28, 1993). Changes are only allowed when there is a change in family status. The IRS defines a change in family status as:

- Marriage.
- Death of your spouse or dependent child.
- Birth or adoption of a child.
- Termination or commencement of employment of your spouse.
- A change from part-time to full-time employment (or vice versa) by you or your spouse.
- An unpaid leave of absence by you or your spouse.
- A significant change in the health coverage of you or your spouse attributable to your spouse's employment.

Any change to your flexible benefits must relate to a family status change. For example, if an employee has a baby, it would be appropriate to add dependent life insurance but not appropriate to add dental insurance. If you wish to make a family status change, you must complete a change request form within 30 days of the date of the status change. Forms may be obtained from Renee B. Rapko, Benefits Coordinator, or by calling Extension 2016.

Options, Pricetags & Benefit Dollars

This workbook describes all the benefit options available to you under your **Landmark Choices** plan. Your Personal Enrollment Form lists the options and pricetags for you. Some of the options do not have pricetags because they are accounts where you can deposit an amount of money for your use at a later time. Pricetags may be based on the number of hours you are scheduled to work and your base salary.

If you elect to use all the Benefit Dollars allotted to you under **Landmark Choices** and decide to purchase additional benefits, you can convert a portion of your current pay, which is taxable, to Benefit Dollars, which are not taxable, and not reported on your annual W-2 form. This means you can save tax dollars and purchase additional benefits at the same time.

You can convert unused Benefit Dollars to cash at $.50 for each $1.00 converted. When you convert an amount of Benefit Dollars to cash, it is taxable and is reported on your W-2 form for Federal, State, and Social Security tax purposes.

Medical Insurance

Medical benefits are a very important part of your *Landmark Choices* program. The substantial cost of medical services, and the impact which an unexpected medical expense may have on the financial security of a family, can be overwhelming. The *Landmark Choices* medical options allow you to choose a plan which meets your needs for health care protection.

As you review the options, you should consider the services you use and the way you prefer to receive the services. Classic BC/BS and ValueCare provide complete choice of provider. HealthMate covers some additional services and pays a higher level of benefits if you use a participating provider. HMO Rhode Island covers office visits with just a $5 copay but requires that you use participating providers. These options allow you to choose the plan that best suits your needs.

Terms to Know

As you select the medical plan that is right for you, you will need to review the benefits in each plan. Some important benefit terms are explained below:

Covered Services - services provided by a hospital or doctor that are allowed by the plan.

Deductible - the amount you pay up front before the plan starts paying for covered expenses.

Member Copayment - the dollar amount or percentage of covered expenses you pay.

Plan Copayment - the dollar amount or percentage of covered expenses the plan pays for services (after you pay any deductible).

Reasonable and Customary - charges for services that fall within an acceptable range based on the most common fees for similar services in a given local area.

Pre-existing Condition - a condition for which a covered person consulted a physician and was treated or took medication within the twelve months prior to becoming covered under the plan.

Medical Options

Landmark Choices provides five medical plan options. They differ in the method in which their services are delivered and the services they provide. They are:

A. Classic Blue Cross/Blue Shield Plan
B. ValueCare
C. HealthMate
D. HMO Rhode Island
E. No Coverage

Let's review each of your *Landmark Choices* medical plan options.

Remember, your contribution to this benefit is in Benefit Dollars. Benefit Dollars are **non-taxable**.

Classic Blue Cross/Blue Shield Plan

The Classic Plan provides Blue Cross/Blue Shield comprehensive medical protection against the high cost of serious illness or injury to yourself or your eligible dependents. This plan consists of two parts: basic services (paid at 100%) and major medical services (paid at 80% after satisfying an annual deductible of $100 per individual or $200 per family). This plan has a **Managed Benefits Program**. Effective January 1, 1992, major improvements have been made to the **Managed Benefits Program**. If services are rendered by a PARTICIPATING PROVIDER, employees and dependents will no longer be required to obtain pre-authorization for: non-emergency admissions to hospitals and other facilities; services like mental health or substance abuse treatment; out-patient surgery. In addition, second surgical opinions are no longer required. Further information about the Managed Benefit changes is available from the Benefits Coordinator. There is a $25 copayment for emergency room care. The copayment is waived if the services are provided by Landmark Medical Center or if you are admitted. Covered services include: 365 days (semi-private) in-hospital care, outpatient care, surgical and diagnostic services, maternity and nursing care, x-rays, laboratory tests and eligible emergency care. Well-baby care is paid at 100% after a $10.00 copay. Eligible dependents include your spouse and unmarried dependent children through the end of the year in which they turn age 19. Covered services are paid based on reasonable and customary charges. **Under this plan, you have complete choice in selecting your physician or hospital.**

ValueCare Plan

This option provides Blue Cross/Blue Shield comprehensive medical protection against the high cost of serious illness or injury to yourself or your eligible dependents. There is a $100 individual deductible on each inpatient hospital admission. Hospital charges, both in and outpatient, are paid at 80% (you pay 20%). There is an out-of-pocket maximum on these hospital charges of $1,000/year/person. Covered hospital expenses are then paid at 100% for the remainder of the year. The $100 inpatient hospital deductible does not apply to the out-of-pocket maximum. This plan has a **Managed Benefits Program**. Effective January 1, 1992, major improvements have been made to the **Managed Benefits Program**. If services are rendered by a PARTICIPATING PROVIDER, employees and dependents will no longer be required to obtain pre-authorization for: non-emergency admissions to hospitals and other facilities; services like mental health or substance abuse treatment; out-patient surgery. In addition, second surgical opinions are no longer required. Further information about the Managed Benefit changes is available from the Benefits Coordinator. There is a $25 copayment for emergency room care. The copayment is waived if the services are provided by Landmark Medical Center or if you are admitted. Physician charges for surgery, x-rays, tests, eligible emergency care and maternity charges are paid in full. There is a $200 individual annual deductible ($400 per family) on major medical services. Routine physicals and health checkups (excluding school, camp, employment, etc.) are covered under major medical. Well-baby care is paid at 100% after a $10.00 copay. Eligible dependents include your spouse and unmarried dependent children through the end of the year in which they turn age 19. All benefits are paid in accordance with Blue Cross/Blue Shield's established reasonable and customary charges. **You have complete choice in selecting your physician or hospital.**

HealthMate

HealthMate is a Blue Cross/Blue Shield program. Under your *Landmark Choices* HealthMate option coverage is provided for services such as hospital care, routine physical exams, well-baby care and eligible emergency care. Copayments of $10.00 are required for office visits, routine physicals and well-baby care. A $3.00 copayment for prescription drugs is required. This plan has a **Managed Benefits Program**. Effective January 1, 1992, major improvements have been made to the **Managed Benefits Program**. If services are rendered by a PARTICIPATING PROVIDER, employees and dependents will no longer be required to obtain pre-authorization for: non-emergency admissions to hospitals and other facilities; services like mental health or substance abuse treatment; outpatient surgery. In addition, second surgical opinions are no longer required. Further information about the Managed Benefit changes is available from the Benefits Coordinator. There is a $25 copayment for emergency room care. The copayment is waived if the services are provided by Landmark Medical Center or if you are admitted. Full coverage is provided for hospitalization (semi-private) at all Rhode Island hospitals plus three hospitals in Massachusetts. There is a 12 month pre-existing condition partial- copayment clause with this plan for any individual that has been hospitalized or had surgery. If you choose to receive your care from a non-participating provider, the plan will pay 80% of the reasonable and customary amount (you pay 20%). **You are responsible for any amounts that exceed the reasonable and customary charges.** Eligible dependents include your spouse and unmarried dependent children through the end of the year in which they turn age 19 (age 23 if full-time student). **Under this plan, you have the choice in selecting your physician or hospital. Remember, however, that benefits are paid at the lower level when you receive your care from a non-participating provider.**

HMO Rhode Island Plan
This plan is a Blue Cross/Blue Shield physician-based Health Maintenance Organization. Coverage is provided for the following medical services: office visits, well-baby care, maternity care, laboratory tests, x-rays, and immunizations. Visits to your primary care physician and specialists have a $5.00 copay. Hospitalization is covered in full. There is a $25 copayment for emergency room care. The deductible is waived if the services are provided by Landmark Medical Center or if you are admitted. Prescription drugs require a 20% copayment. There are no claim forms to complete. There is a 12 month pre-existing condition partial-copayment clause with this plan for any individual that has been hospitalized or had surgery. Eligible dependents include your spouse and unmarried dependent children under age 19 (age 25 if full-time student). **Except for an emergency, all services must be provided, authorized or referred by your primary care physician.**

No Coverage
Landmark Choices offers you a No Coverage option. This is available only to employees with other group medical coverage. If you are considering this option, be sure to check the policy carefully before you decide to select No Coverage. **Proof of other medical coverage is required.** The necessary waiver form may be obtained from the Benefits Coordinator. The Benefit Dollars you save by electing this option can be used to purchase other benefits or contributed to a reimbursement account.

Landmark Medical Center Discount Policy
Landmark Medical Center provides a generous discount to employees and their dependents who receive medical services at Landmark Medical Center. Landmark will write-off the dollar amount over and above what the Classic Blue Cross/Blue Shield Plan would pay on any hospital services for you, your spouse and dependent children. The employee, however, will be responsible for all copayments and appropriate facility charges. In addition, prescriptions filled at the Landmark Medical Center pharmacies are provided to you at cost plus $2.00 per prescription. Over-the-counter items are provided at cost plus $1.00 per item. **It is the responsibility of the employee involved to notify the Business Office when a member of his/her immediate family has received hospital service.**

Comparing the Plans

Consider your health care needs and those of your dependents carefully. Decide what level of health care protection you need and how you would like to receive those services. A "Medical Benefits Summary and Comparison" chart is provided on page 10. It highlights the benefits covered by each plan, the applicable deductibles and copayments. Review the comparison sheet carefully. It will help you choose the plan that is best suited for you and your family. If you are changing the type of coverage you presently have you must complete the respective enrollment form, which is available from the Benefits Coordinator.

Using Your Health Care Reimbursement Account

As you make your medical plan choices, do not forget your *Landmark Choices* Health Care Reimbursement Account. Deposits to your Health Care Reimbursement Account may be used to pay your medical plan deductibles and copayments, as well as many medical, dental, and optical expenses which are not covered or are partially covered by your selected plans. With your Health Care Reimbursement Account, you pay for needed health care expenses and save taxes too!

Eligible Employees

All employees who are regularly scheduled to work at least 20 hours each week are eligible for medical benefits.

Additional Information

For additional information regarding your *Landmark Choices* medical plan options, the benefits provided by each plan, its limitations and exclusions, **please review your benefit plan descriptions carefully**. They can be obtained from the Benefits Coordinator.

Pricetags

The pricetags listed on your *Landmark Choices* enrollment form represent the cost of providing this option to you for the plan year. You may purchase your elected Medical Insurance option using a portion of your allotted Benefit Dollars, or by converting pay to Benefit Dollars. **After you have chosen the Medical Insurance option that is right for you, write the appropriate letter and pricetag for that option on your worksheet. You must select one of the options**.

Medical Benefits Summary and Comparison

	Classic BC/BS • Plan	HealthMate Participating Providers	HealthMate Non-Participating Providers	ValueCare •	HMO Rhode Island
HOSPITAL SERVICES:					
Semi-Private Room	365 days	Unlimited	Unlimited / 80% of RC	$100 deductible/365 days	Unlimited
Inpatient & Outpatient	100% of RC	100% of RC	80% of RC	80% of RC	100%
Eligible Emergency	$25 if not admitted***	$25 if not admitted***	100% of RC	$25 if not admitted***	$25 if not admitted***
PHYSICIAN/SURGICAL CARE:					
Inpatient & Outpatient	100% of RC	100% of RC	80% of RC	100% of RC	100%
X-Ray & Tests	100% of RC	100% of RC	80% of RC	100% of RC	100%
MENTAL HEALTH:					
Inpatient	45 days	45 days	50% of RC / 45 days	$100 deductible / 45 days	45 days
Outpatient	80% participating doctor 50% non-participating doctor $20,000 lifetime maximum	$10 copay $1,000 annually	50% less $10 copay $1,000 annually	80% participating doctor 50% non-participating doctor $20,000 lifetime maximum	75% 20 visits per year
MATERNITY:	100% of RC	100% of RC	80% of RC	100% of RC	100%
MAJOR MEDICAL BENEFITS:	80%*	n/a	n/a	80%*	n/a
MAJOR MEDICAL DEDUCTIBLE:	$100 / $200	n/a	n/a	$200 / $400	n/a
PRESCRIPTION DRUGS:	80%*	$3 copay	$3 copay	80% *	20% copay
OFFICE CALLS/ROUTINE CHECK-UPS:	80% +*	$10 copay +	80% less $10 copay +	80% +*	$5 copay
WELL-BABY CARE:	$10 copay	$10 copay	80% less $10 copay	$10 copay	$5 copay
PLAN LIFE TIME MAXIMUM:	$250,000 **	Unlimited	Unlimited	$250,000 **	Unlimited
EYE EXAMS:	Not covered	$10 copay once a year	80% less $10 copay	Not covered	$5 copay 1 every 2 years
PRE-EXISTING CONDITION CLAUSE:	Yes**	Yes	Yes	Yes **	Yes

* - Deductible and plan maximum provision applies.
RC - Reasonable and customary charges.
+ - Frequency of covered exams is according to a schedule.

** - Applies to Major Medical Only (no maximum on other charges)
* - If a non-participating doctor charges you more than BC/BS regards as customary, you will be responsible for the amount above the reasonable and customary charge.
*** - $25 waived if services are provided by Landmark Medical Center.

Dental Insurance

Landmark Medical Center realizes the importance of good dental care in the maintenance of your overall health. Good dental care requires regular check-ups and preventive services. With **Landmark Choices**, you choose the dental coverage that is right for you. You should consider your past needs as well as future needs in selecting your option.

Terms To Know

Dental benefits are divided into four categories under your **Landmark Choices** program. These categories are described below:

Basic Services (Level I) - Oral exams, x-rays, fluoride, cleanings, fillings, biopsies of oral tissue, denture repairs, minor emergency treatment, single root canals, and simple extractions.

Additional Services - (Levels II & III) Endodontics, inlays and crowns, space maintainers, oral surgery, and periodontics.

Orthodontic Services - (Level IV) Braces and treatments. Orthodontic services are provided to eligible persons up to age 19.

Dental Options

Your **Landmark Choices** program offers three options to choose from in the dental area. A summary on **page 11** will help you review your choices. Remember, your contribution to this benefit is in non-taxable Benefit Dollars. Your Dental options are:

Delta Comprehensive Plan (Levels I - IV)
Exams, x-rays, fluoride treatment (under age 19), cleanings, fillings, simple extractions, crowns, oral surgery, and endodontic services are covered at 100% of reasonable and customary charges. Other items, such as periodontic treatment, bridges, and dentures, are covered at 50% of reasonable and customary charges. There are no copayments for the basic services. The annual maximum benefit paid per person is $1,200. Orthodontic services are covered at 50% of reasonable and customary charges. The lifetime maximum benefit paid for orthodontic services is $1,200 per eligible person. **You may select any dentist of your choice with this plan.**

Delta Preventive Plan (Level I)
Exams, x-rays, fluoride treatment (under age 19), cleanings, fillings, and simple extractions are covered at 100% of reasonable and customary charges. There are no deductibles or copayments for this plan. The annual maximum benefit paid per person is $1,200. **You may select any dentist of your choice with this plan.**

No Coverage

If you desire, you may choose not to participate in this benefit.

Who Is Covered?

You may choose dental coverage for yourself or yourself and your dependents. Eligible dependents include your spouse and children to the end of the year in which they turn age 19.

Eligible Employees

All employees who are regularly scheduled to work at least 20 hours each week are eligible to participate in a dental plan.

COMPARISON OF DENTAL PLAN OPTIONS		
	Comprehensive Plan Level (I-IV)	Preventive Plan Level 1
ANNUAL DEDUCTIBLE	None	None
PLAN PAYS		
BASIC SERVICES (Level 1)	100%	100%
Oral Exams / Cleaning / X-rays	100%	100%
Fillings	100%	100%
Simple Extractions	100%	100%
ADDITIONAL SERVICES		
Endodontics	100%	N/A
Inlays and Crowns	100%	N/A
Oral Surgery	100%	N/A
Periodontics	50%	N/A
PROSTHODONTIC SERVICES		
Bridges	50%	N/A
Dentures	50%	N/A
ORTHODONTIC SERVICES	50%	N/A
ANNUAL MAXIMUM PER PERSON	$1,200	$1,200
LIFETIME ORTHODONTIC MAXIMUM PER PERSON	$1,200	N/A

Additional Information

If you are changing the type of coverage you presently have you must complete an enrollment form, which is available from the Benefits Coordinator.

Pricetags

The pricetags listed on your *Landmark Choices* enrollment form represent the cost of providing each option to you for the plan year. You may purchase your chosen Dental Insurance option using a portion of your allotted Benefit Dollars or by converting pay to Benefit Dollars. **After you have selected the Dental Insurance option that is right for you, write the appropriate letter and pricetag for that option on your worksheet. You must select one of the options.**

Health Care Reimbursement

The **Landmark Choices** Health Care Reimbursement Account helps you save tax dollars. With this account, you can be reimbursed in non-taxable dollars for medical, dental and vision expenses that were not paid by insurance. Your tax savings can be significant. You will not pay Federal, State or Social Security taxes on your deposits to the account or on the reimbursements. This is a smarter way to pay for items such as eyeglasses, contact lenses, copayments and deductibles.

How It Works

The Health Care Reimbursement Account is very simple to use. It works like a bank account. You decide how much money to deposit to your account for the plan year. This amount will be deducted from your paychecks in equal amounts over the entire plan year. Then, as you incur eligible medical, dental or vision expenses, you submit claims for reimbursement. But, unlike a bank account, **your deposits and reimbursements are in non-taxable dollars.** You may deposit as little as $104 per year up to a maximum of $1,500 per plan year. Your deposit can come from your allotted Benefit Dollars, from pay converted to Benefit Dollars, or from both. Deposits made from your pay and converted to Benefit Dollars are made before taxes are calculated and subtracted from your pay.

How Much Should I Deposit?

You decide the deposit amount that is right for you. You will need to do some planning to determine your deposit amount. An easy way for you to plan is to review your checkbook entries for the past year or two. Note the expenses that you incur regularly which are not covered or not totally paid for by insurance. These expenses are typically ones that can be planned for and then reimbursed through your Health Care Reimbursement Account. We've included the following chart to help you review and list your expenses. Due to changes in the IRS rules, cosmetic surgery is no longer deductible unless it is to correct an abnormality or disfigurement. **Remember, IRS rules require that any money left in your account at the end of the plan year be forfeited.**

	Last Year's Expenses	Planned Expenses This Year
Vision exams	$_____	$_____
Glasses/contact lenses	$_____	$_____
Medical deductibles	$_____	$_____
Medical copayments	$_____	$_____
Dental deductibles	$_____	$_____
Dental copayments	$_____	$_____
Routine physicals	$_____	$_____
Well-child care	$_____	$_____
Orthodontic copayments	$_____	$_____
Hearing aids/exams	$_____	$_____
Prescription copayments	$_____	$_____
Other expenses	$_____	$_____
Plan Year Total	$_____	$*_____

*This total is the amount you may want to deposit to your Health Care Reimbursement Account.

This Account Can Save You Money

The following example compares actual costs at two tax levels to actual cost using the Health Care Reimbursement Account.

ALLOWABLE EXPENSES	27% TAX RATE	40% TAX RATE	Landmark Choices
Medical Expenses	$ 200	$ 200	$ 200
Dental Expenses	75	75	75
Routine Physicals	50	50	50
Eyeglasses	100	100	100
Eye Exam	50	50	50
Total Out-of-Pocket Expenses	$ 475	$ 475	$ 475
Taxes	$ 128	$ 190	$ 0
ACTUAL COST	$ 603	$ 665	$ 475

In this example, a savings of $128 or $190 could be realized through this employee's participation in the **Landmark Choices** Health Care Reimbursement Account.

Receiving Reimbursement

The reimbursement process is simple. In order to be reimbursed, you will need to submit to the Benefits Coordinator:

- A completed claim form.

- Copies of itemized bills or receipts showing date and type of service, name of person receiving care, fee or charge and name and address of the provider.

- A statement showing how much insurance paid, if applicable.

Reimbursement requests (in a minimum amount of $50) will be processed with your next paycheck, following receipt by the Benefits Coordinator. Remember, the dollars you deposit to your Health Care Reimbursement Account are **non-taxable**. The dollars you receive as reimbursement for medical, vision or dental expenses from your Health Care Reimbursement Account are also **non-taxable**.

Points To Consider

You will have until April 30, 1993 to submit expenses incurred within the plan year (March 1, 1992 - February 28, 1993). IRS rules allow you to change your deposit amount during the plan year when you have a change in family status only. The IRS also requires that any money left in your account at the end of the plan year be forfeited.

If you choose to participate in the Health Care Reimbursement Account and terminate your employment with Landmark Medical Center during the plan year, the following policies will apply:

- The unpaid balance of your annual contribution will be deducted from your final paycheck.

- You may continue to submit receipts and be reimbursed for eligible expenses incurred during the plan year as if you were an active employee.

After you have calculated the annual amount you wish to deposit into your account, write that amount in the space provided on your worksheet.

Dependent Care Reimbursement

The Landmark Medical Center Dependent Care Reimbursement Account was established to help you pay for dependent care expenses on a tax-free basis. Expenses that can be reimbursed through this account are expenses incurred for the care of your children, your incapacitated spouse or your dependent parent.

How It Works

Your Dependent Care Reimbursement Account is easy to use. Like the Health Care Reimbursement Account, it also works like a bank account. You decide how much money to deposit for your dependent care expenses. This money will be deducted from your paychecks in equal amounts over the plan year. Then, as you incur eligible expenses, you submit claims for reimbursement. Like the Health Care Reimbursement Account, **your deposits and reimbursements are in non-taxable dollars.** You may deposit as little as $260 per year up to a maximum of $5,000 per year. Your deposit to your account can come from your pay, your Benefit Dollars, or from both. Deposits made from your pay and converted to Benefit Dollars are made before taxes are calculated and subtracted from your pay.

Eligible Expenses

Your dependent care expenses can be paid through your account if they meet the following requirements:

- The services provided must enable you and your spouse to be employed.

- Eligible dependents are: your dependent children under age 13; physically or mentally impaired children age 13 or over; your incapacitated spouse or elderly parent.

- The amount to be reimbursed must not be greater than your income or that of your spouse, whichever is lower.

- If the services are provided by a day care facility that cares for six or more at the same time, the facility must be licensed.

- You will be required to provide the tax identification or Social Security number of your dependent care provider.

Providers

The care provided does not have to be through a licensed center unless the facility cares for six or more individuals at one time. The services may be as informal as your neighbor or mother caring for your child before and after school. However, you need to remember that you will be required to provide the Social Security number or tax identification number of your provider.

You may pay a relative to take care of your dependents. You may not pay a dependent to take care of another dependent. For example, expenses you incur by paying your teenage daughter to babysit for her younger brother or sister are not eligible under this plan. However, you may claim expenses you incur by paying your married daughter (not your dependent) to babysit her younger brother or sister (still your dependent).

How Much Should I Deposit?

You decide how much to deposit to your Dependent Care Reimbursement Account. You may deposit as little as $260 up to a maximum of $5,000 per plan year. It should be an easy process to determine your deposit. As you estimate your expenses, remember to exclude time for vacation, illness, etc., when you will not be required to pay dependent care expenses. This could be latchkey programs during the school year and full-time day care during vacation periods.

	Program #1	Program #2	Total Cost
Cost per week	_____	_____	
Times number of weeks	_x_____	_x_____	
Cost per program	_____ +	_____ =	*_____

This is the total amount that you may wish to contribute to your Dependent Care Reimbursement Account.

This planning step is important because the IRS regulations require that money left in your account at the end of the plan year be forfeited.

Tax Credit versus Reimbursement Account

If you use the **Landmark Choices** Dependent Care Reimbursement Account, you may not claim the same expenses for a tax credit. Most people get a greater tax savings with the Dependent Care Reimbursement Account. The tax credit applies only to Federal taxes while the Dependent Care Reimbursement Account saves you Federal, State and FICA taxes. The worksheets in your Reimbursement Account newsletter will assist you in deciding which method is best for you.

This Account Can Save You Money

If you are currently paying for child care expenses and not using the **Landmark Choices** Dependent Care Reimbursement Account, you are paying in taxable dollars and probably taking a tax credit at the end of the year. If you use the Dependent Care Reimbursement Account, you pay this expense in non-taxable dollars and **will not** be eligible to claim a tax credit for the same reimbursed amounts.

For most people, paying in non-taxable dollars is more advantageous. The following example compares total cost at two tax levels to total cost using the Dependent Care Reimbursement Account.

ALLOWABLE EXPENSES	27% TAX RATE	40% TAX RATE	*Landmark Choices*
Day Care Expenses	$ 2,000	$ 2,000	$ 2,000
Taxes	540	800	0
ACTUAL COST	$ 2,540	$ 2,800	$ 2,000

This working couple could save between $540 and $800 per year in taxes by paying for their child care through the Dependent Care Reimbursement Account.

Important Points

The deposit amount you decide on is for the entire plan year. The amount will be deducted in equal amounts each pay period. You will only be allowed to change a deposit if you experience a family status change. Only expenses incurred during the plan year can be reimbursed. You will have until April 30, 1993 to submit eligible expenses incurred within the previous plan year (eligible expenses for this plan year are those incurred between March 1, 1992 and February 28, 1993.) **IRS rules require that any money left in your account at the end of the plan year must be forfeited.**

How To Be Reimbursed

You are reimbursed from money in your account. In order to be reimbursed, you will need to submit to the Benefits Coordinator:

- A completed claim form.
- A copy of an itemized bill showing date and type of service, name of the person receiving care, fee or charge and signature of the provider.

Reimbursement checks (in a minimum amount of $50) will be processed with your next paycheck, after receipt by the Benefits Coordinator. Remember, the dollars you deposit to your Dependent Care Reimbursement Account are **non-taxable**. The dollars you receive as reimbursement for day care expenses from your Dependent Care Reimbursement Account are also **non-taxable**.

Annual Deposit

Remember, your annual deposit to your Dependent Care Reimbursement Account is in **non-taxable** dollars and will be deposited in equal amounts per pay period throughout the plan year. **After you have calculated the annual amount you wish to deposit to your account, write the amount in the space provided on your worksheet.**

Employee Life & AD&D Insurance

Employee Life and AD&D Insurance is a core benefit. This provides an important source of income for your dependents in the event of your death. It will pay the full amount to you if you suffer certain severe injuries such as the loss of two limbs or the sight of both eyes. One-half the insured amount will be paid in the event of injuries that cause the loss of one limb or the sight of one eye. The specific losses and benefits are described in your Group Insurance Benefit Booklet. With **Landmark Choices**, you prescribe your level of insurance protection. Your insurance planning will change as your financial and family responsibilities change.

How Much Life Insurance?

Only you can choose the amount of life insurance that is right for you. The following questions may help you decide how much life insurance you need:

- Would your family have to alter their standard of living without your paycheck?
- Is your income primary or secondary?
- Are your parent(s) depending on your support in their retirement years?
- Are there any major expenditures to continue, such as a mortgage on your house, consumer debt, or children's education?
- Would paying estate taxes force a liquidation of your assets?

Other aspects to consider in determining the proper amount of life insurance are the other resources that would be available at the time of such need.

- Social Security benefits.
- Individual Life Insurance Policies.
- Personal savings.
- Life insurance on your life provided through your spouse's employer.

Your **Landmark Choices** Employee Life and AD&D options are:

A.   1 x salary for both Life and AD&D (core benefit)
B.   2 x salary for both Life and AD&D (core benefit plus 1 x salary)
C.   3 x salary for both Life and AD&D (core benefit plus 2 x salary)

Tax Aspects

Your life insurance option is purchased in **non-taxable** Benefit Dollars. Benefits paid by the plan to your designated beneficiary are **non-taxable**, while AD&D benefits paid to you are considered **taxable** income.

An imputed income tax is incurred on life insurance coverage in excess of $50,000. Imputed income tax is a "user tax" and is required by tax regulations. It assigns a dollar value to life insurance amounts over $50,000 based on your age. The amount is added to your earnings over the year. This amount, if applicable, is shown on your enrollment form.

Other Considerations

If you are currently enrolled in **Landmark Choices** and choose a higher option than you selected last year, you may be required to prove that you are healthy. If this is your first enrollment in **Landmark Choices**, you may choose any option. If you choose to increase your level of coverage at a future enrollment, you may be asked to prove that you are healthy. If you are not actively working on the effective date, your current coverage will remain in effect until you return to work. If you are changing your life insurance amount you must complete an enrollment form, which is available from the Benefits Coordinator.

In order to provide the two times salary and three times salary options a participation level will be required. This means that a certain percentage of employees must continue to choose these options in order for the options to be offered.

Pricetags

The pricetags listed on your **Landmark Choices** enrollment form represent the cost of providing each option to you for the plan year. You have been provided with enough Benefit Dollars to purchase Option A. You may purchase your elected Employee Life and AD&D Insurance option using a portion of your allotted Benefit Dollars, or from pay converted to Benefit Dollars. **After you have chosen the Employee Life and AD&D Insurance option that is right for you, write the appropriate option letter and pricetag for that option on your worksheet. You must select one of the options.**

Dependent Life Insurance

Dependent Life Insurance provides you with an insurance benefit to help with the financial burden of a dependent child's or spouse's death. The plan choices offered cover both your spouse and children. A spouse is covered as long as Employee Life and AD&D Insurance coverage is provided to you as an employee. Children are covered from 14 days to 19 years of age, or age 23 if a full-time student. You are the beneficiary of record.

You should review your family's financial situation to determine if Dependent Life Insurance makes sense for you. This may be an easy and economical way to provide life insurance for the members of your family.

Dependent Life Insurance Options
You can choose one of the following levels of Dependent Life Insurance. Your **Landmark Choices** Dependent Life Insurance options are:

A. $10,000 spouse/$5,000 each child
B. $5,000 spouse/$2,500 each child
C.   No Coverage

Enrollment
There are no enrollment restrictions. This means you may drop, add or increase coverage during any enrollment period. Dependent Life Insurance covers your legal spouse and unmarried children who are your dependents for income tax purposes. If you are choosing this benefit for the first time or changing the amount of coverage, you must complete an enrollment form, which is available from the Benefits Coordinator.

Tax Aspects
Benefits paid by the plan to you are **non-taxable**. This benefit is purchased in taxable dollars.

Pricetags
The pricetags listed on your **Landmark Choices** enrollment form represent the cost of providing each option to you for the plan year. The pricetag will remain fixed during the year regardless of the number of dependents you have. **After you have chosen the Dependent Life Insurance option that is right for you, write the appropriate option letter and pricetag for that option on your worksheet. You must select one of the options.**

LTD Insurance

Your **Landmark Choices** Long Term Disability (LTD) Insurance is a core benefit for full-time employees with one year of full-time status. It provides you and your family with an important source of income should you become ill or disabled and unable to work for an extended period of time. The financial consequences of a disability can be disastrous. If you are disabled for an extended period of time, your Long Term Disability Insurance will pay you a percentage of your current income.

How It Works

LTD benefits begin on the 181st day of continuous disability and pay you 60% of your base pay to a maximum monthly benefit of $4,000. This is a benefit guarantee. Other benefits that Landmark Medical Center contributes to, such as Social Security and Workers Compensation, are taken into consideration in the calculation of benefits.

You have the choice of purchasing your LTD benefit in either taxable or non-taxable dollars. The difference is this: If you purchase the benefit in taxable dollars, the amount you collect if disabled is not taxable upon receipt. If you purchase the benefit in non-taxable dollars, the amount you collect if disabled is taxable upon receipt. Let's look at an example of what this means to you:

> Pat Smith, our Landmark Medical Center employee, becomes disabled. She is currently earning $20,000 per year. She selected Option B for her LTD coverage and paid for it with taxable dollars. This entitles her to 60% of her base pay, or $1,000 per month, received as **non-taxable** income.

LTD Options

Your **Landmark Choices** Long Term Disability options are:

A. 60% of base pay, purchased in non-taxable dollars, received as taxable income
B. 60% of base pay, purchased in taxable dollars, received as non-taxable income

Enrollment

There are no restrictions on the level of coverage you choose at this enrollment. This insurance will remain in effect for the plan year (March 1, 1992 through February 28, 1993). If you are not actively working on the effective date, your current coverage will remain in effect until you return to work.

Tax Aspects

If you choose, the Benefit Dollars that you spend on your **Landmark Choices** LTD benefit may be non-taxable and not included as income for Federal, State, or Social Security tax purposes. If you choose to purchase your LTD benefit in taxable dollars, all normal taxes will be deducted from your income before you pay for your LTD coverage.

Eligible Employees

All full-time employees scheduled to work 36 or 40 hours per week with at least one year of full-time employment are eligible to participate in this benefit.

Pricetags

The pricetags listed on your **Landmark Choices** enrollment form represent the cost of providing each option to you for the plan year. You have been given enough Benefit Dollars to purchase either option A or B. **After you have chosen the LTD option that is right for you, write the appropriate option letter and pricetag for that option on your worksheet. You must select one of the options.**

Vacation

We all need time off from work to relax at home, take a trip or complete personal projects. Paid vacation is an important benefit because it gives you a chance to relax and do the things you want to do. Each of us chooses what we want to do with our time off.

Landmark Choices allows you to sell some of your vacation time to use the dollars to buy additional benefits in the *Landmark Choices* program or to take as cash ($.50 per Benefit Dollar).

Vacation time is determined by the number of hours worked and seniority of each individual. Up to three days of earned vacation will be available in the *Landmark Choices* plan as options to sell. These days may be sold in whole day increments to purchase additional benefits, or you may take your vacation days as paid time off as usual.

Many employees do not work the same number of hours every day or do not work five days per week. Therefore, for the *Landmark Choices* plan, a vacation day is defined as 1/5 (20%) of the number of regularly scheduled hours per week as of December 31, 1991. Three of these days will be included in the *Landmark Choices* plan. You may sell one, two, three or none of the days.

Examples:

1. Mary works 8 hours each Monday through Friday for a total of 40 hours per week. For the plan, her vacation days are 8 hours each. The first 24 hours that Mary earned are part of the plan, and she may sell 8, 16, 24, or no hours.

2. Steve works 8 hours on Sunday, 7 hours on Friday and 5 hours on Saturday each week for a total of 20 hours per week. For plan purposes, Steve's vacation day equals 4 hours. The first 12 vacation hours are included on Steve's enrollment form, and he may sell 4, 8, 12, or no hours.

Vacation Options
Your vacation options are:

A. Retain your normal vacation
B. Sell one vacation day

C. Sell two vacation days
D. Sell three vacation days

Pricetags
If you choose to retain your vacation days, the pricetag is $0, as this is not a cost to you. If you choose to sell vacation days, the pricetag will be a negative number. **After you have chosen the vacation option that is right for you, write the appropriate letter and pricetag for that option on your worksheet. You must select one of the options.**

Enrolling

You have now reviewed your *Landmark Choices* benefit options. By using the worksheet on page 30 you can choose the benefits that meet your needs and your budget. Now it is time to transfer your choices to your Personal Enrollment Form. After you have copied each choice and recorded it properly on your Personal Enrollment Form **(using a number 2 pencil or blue/black ink only)**, add up the total dollars (except vacation) that you have spent for the plan year. Enter the sum total at the bottom of your Personal Enrollment Form on the line titled "Total Spent".

Then, write your vacation pricetag ($0 or a negative number) on the line marked "Vacation". Subtract the Vacation line from Total Spent and list the difference on "Subtotal".

Compare your Subtotal with your Total Benefit Dollars.

If your Subtotal is greater than Total Benefit Dollars, write the difference on the line titled "Difference" at the bottom of your enrollment form. This amount will be withheld from your pay in equal dollar amounts throughout the year.

If your Subtotal is less than Total Benefit Dollars, write the difference on the line titled "Difference" at the bottom of your enrollment form. Fifty percent (50%) of this amount will be added to your pay as taxable income, it will be paid to you in equal dollar amounts throughout the year.

Note: If you "cash out" your Benefit Dollars, they are paid at $.50 for each Benefit Dollar.

If your Subtotal equals Total Benefit Dollars, your pay will not be affected by your choices.

Before going any further, review the choices you have marked on your Personal Enrollment Form and make sure they accurately reflect your selections. Be sure that:

- The pricetags for the options you have chosen are correct.
- You have correctly added up the pricetags and deposits.
- You have correctly calculated the difference between Total Spent and Total Benefit Dollars.

Your Personal Enrollment Form

Give your Personal Enrollment Form a final check. When everything is in order, read the statement at the bottom of the form, fill in the date, and sign your name.

Save your workbook and your worksheet for your records. Separate the enrollment form. Keep the bottom copy and place the top two signed copies in the enclosed envelope. Please seal the envelope and send it to the Personnel Department.

After Your Form Is Submitted

We will check your Personal Enrollment Form to verify that it has been correctly completed and signed. If there is a problem, you will be called and asked to help clear it up. In some cases, you may be asked to complete a new Personal Enrollment Form. Assistance will be available should you need it.

Your **Landmark Choices** program has been carefully designed so you can take the maximum advantage of the tax laws governing flexible benefits plans. In some cases, these laws may change or limit how much salary you can convert to Benefit Dollars or the extent to which higher paid employees may participate in specific options. We will check the legal requirements. In a few cases, this check may require you to revise your choices. If so, you will be notified.

After your enrollment is completed and your choices are recorded by the Personnel Department, you will receive a Confirmation Statement. This statement shows which benefits you have chosen and verifies that they have been processed properly for the plan year March 1, 1992 through February 28, 1993.

If you are enrolling in a new benefit option you may have to complete the pertinent carrier enrollment form in order for coverage to commence in a timely fashion. The forms can be obtained from the Benefits Coordinator.

ERISA Information

The preceding pages of the booklet have presented some details, regarding how each plan works, the major benefits of each plan, limitations or restrictions that apply and so on. More information is available in the plan booklet provided for each benefit.

This section presents other information you are entitled to know regarding the plans:

- Your "ERISA" rights.
- How the plans are administered.

ADMINISTRATIVE INFORMATION

The Employee Retirement Income Security Act of 1974 (ERISA) regulates the following employee welfare plans which are detailed in this booklet. The official plan names and numbers are:

Name of Plan	Type of Plan	Plan Number
Group Life and AD&D Insurance Plan	Life	501
Group Health Insurance Plan	Hospital/Medical	502
Group Dental Plan	Dental	503
Group Long Term Disability Plan	LTD	504
Landmark Choices	Cafeteria	505

PLAN SPONSOR

Landmark Medical Center (Employer Identification Number, assigned by the Internal Revenue Service, 22-2921474), sponsors the above benefit plans for its eligible employees

> Landmark Medical Center
> 115 Cass Avenue
> Woonsocket, RI 02895

PLAN YEAR

The *Landmark Choices* plan is operated and records are maintained on a plan year basis by the Personnel Department. The plan year is March 1 through the end of February.

PLAN ADMINISTRATOR

The plans are fully insured by insurance companies. All claims are paid by the individual carrier. The plan administrator who is also designated as agent for service of legal process is:

> Stephen L. Hines
> Vice President, Human Resources and Public Relations
> Landmark Medical Center
> 115 Cass Avenue
> Woonsocket, RI 02895

YOUR RIGHTS AS A PLAN PARTICIPANT

As a participant in the Landmark Medical Center welfare plans, you are entitled to certain rights and protections under the Employee Retirement Income Security Act of 1974 (ERISA). ERISA provides that all plan participants shall be entitled to:

1. Examine, without charge, at the plan administrator's office and at other specified locations, all plan documents, including insurance contracts and copies of all documents filed by the plan with the U.S. Department of Labor, such as detailed annual reports and plan descriptions.
2. Obtain copies of all plan documents and other plan information upon written request to the plan administrator. The administrator may make a reasonable charge for the copies.
3. Receive a summary of the plan's annual financial report. The plan administrator is required by law to furnish each participant with a copy of this summary annual report.

RESPONSIBILITIES OF FIDUCIARIES

In addition to creating rights for plan participants, ERISA imposes duties upon the people who are responsible for the operation of the employee benefit plan. The people who operate your plans, called "fiduciaries" of the plan, have a duty to do so prudently and in the interest of you and other plan participants and beneficiaries. Your employer may not fire you or otherwise discriminate against you in any way to prevent you from obtaining a pension or welfare benefit or exercising your right under ERISA.

CLAIM ASSISTANCE

Appeals relating to a denial of benefits in whole or in part should be submitted in writing within 60 days of the denial to the Vice President, Human Resources and Public Relations, who will review the case and respond in writing within 60 days.

If your claim for a welfare benefit is denied in whole or in part you must receive a written explanation of the reason for the denial. You have the right to have the plan administrator review and reconsider your claim. Under ERISA, there are steps you can take to enforce the above rights. For instance, if you request materials from the plan and do not receive them within 30 days, you may file suit in a Federal court. The court may require the plan administrator to provide the materials and pay you up to $100 a day until you receive the materials, unless the materials were not sent because of reasons beyond the control of the administrator. If you have a claim for benefits which is denied or ignored, or if you are discriminated against for asserting your rights, you may seek assistance from the U.S. Department of Labor, or you may file suit in a Federal court. The court will decide who should pay court costs and legal fees. If you lose, the court may order you to pay these costs and fees (for example, if it finds your claim frivolous).

QUESTIONS OR CONCERNS

If you have any questions about your plan, you should contact the plan administrator. If you have any questions about this statement or about your rights under ERISA, you should contact the nearest Area Office of the U.S. Labor-Management Services Administration, Department of Labor.

As with any problem, Landmark Medical Center encourages you to discuss it with your supervisor or a representative of the Human Resources Department.

WORKSHEET

BENEFIT	OPTION LETTER	PRICETAGS
MEDICAL INSURANCE	☐	$_____
DENTAL INSURANCE	☐	$_____
HEALTH CARE REIMBURSEMENT	ANNUAL DEPOSIT	$_____
DEPENDENT CARE REIMBURSEMENT	ANNUAL DEPOSIT	$_____
EMPLOYEE LIFE AND AD&D INSURANCE	☐	$_____
DEPENDENT LIFE INSURANCE	☐	$_____
LTD INSURANCE	☐	$_____
SUBTOTAL		$_____
VACATION	☐	$_____
ADDING IT UP	**TOTAL**	$_____

Once you have completed this **Landmark Choices** Worksheet, copy your choices and their appropriate pricetags onto your Personal Enrollment Form. Retain this Worksheet for your records.

Appendix 3

Example of a Premium Conversion Plan: Salve Regina College

Source: Reprinted with permission from Salve Regina College, Newport, Rhode Island.

TABLE OF CONTENTS

ARTICLE I
PURPOSE OF PLAN

ARTICLE II
DEFINITIONS

ARTICLE III
PARTICIPATION

225

ARTICLE IV
BENEFITS AND CONTRIBUTIONS

ARTICLE V
NON-DISCRIMINATION

ARTICLE VI
ADMINISTRATION, AMENDMENTS AND TERMINATION

ARTICLE VII
GENERAL PROVISIONS

Salve Regina College
Premium Conversion Plan

ARTICLE I
PURPOSE OF PLAN

1.1 *PURPOSE.* The purpose of this plan is to enable the Participants to select from among the health and welfare benefits provided by the Employer in a manner best calculated to meet their particular needs. It is the intention of the Employer that the Plan qualify as a "cafeteria plan" within the meaning of Section 125 of the Code.

ARTICLE II
DEFINITIONS

2.1 "Account" means the record maintained by the Employer pursuant to Section 6.2.

2.2 "Benefit" means cash or coverage choices under the employee benefit plans set forth in Section 4.1.

2.3 "Code" means the Internal Revenue Code of 1986, as amended and the regulations issued thereunder.

2.4 "Dental Plan" means the Salve Regina College Dental Plan.

2.5 "Effective Date" means October 1, 1990.

2.6 "Elective Contributions" mean the amount of cash compensation a Participant elects, pursuant to Section 3.2, to forego in exchange for Benefits under the Plan. The amount of such cash compensation which may be foregone shall be limited to the total amount of Employee contributions required for participation in the Benefits set forth in Section 4.1.

2.7 "Eligible Employee" means any employee who has satisfied the eligibility requirements of the respective plan(s) listed in Section 4.1, under which the Employee is seeking coverage.

2.8 "Employee" means any employee of the Employer.

2.9 "Employer" means Salve Regina College.

2.10 "Highly Compensated Employee" means any person who is a highly compensated employee as defined in Section 414(q) of the Code.

2.11 "Key Employee" means any person who is a key employee as defined in Section 416(i)(1) of the Code.

2.12 "Medical Plan" means the Salve Regina College Medical Plan(s) including any health maintenance organization plan(s) offered by the Employer for each location maintained by the Employer.

2.13 "Participant" means any Employee who has elected to participate in the Plan in accordance with Article III and whose participation has not terminated.

2.14 "Period of Coverage" means the twelve month period coincident with the respective plan policy year. The first Period of Coverage shall be the short period from the Effective Date to the first day of the first respective plan policy year beginning after the Effective Date.

2.15 "Plan" means the Salve Regina College Premium Conversion Plan as set forth herein, together with any and all amendments and supplements hereto.

2.16 "Plan Administrator" means the Employer or the person or persons designated as the Plan Administrator by the Employer. The Plan Administrator shall be the named fiduciary of the Plan.

2.17 "Plan Year" means the calendar year except for the first Plan Year which will be from the Effective Date to December 31.

ARTICLE III
PARTICIPATION

3.1 *Commencement of Participation.* An Eligible Employee may elect to become a Participant in the Plan by completing an enrollment form and filing it with the Employer. In order to participate in the Plan for a particular Period of Coverage, an Eligible Employee must complete and file an enrollment form during the thirty day enrollment period designated by the Employer, which period shall end prior to the first day of such Period of Coverage. If a person becomes an Eligible Employee during a Period of Coverage, he or she may become a Participant as of the first day of the payroll period which follows the completion of the eligibility requirements in

Section 2.7 by completing an enrollment form and filing it with the employer prior to commencement of participation. In no event will a person's participation in the Plan commence unless the person is an active Employee on the date participation is to commence; if a person is not an active Employee on such date, participation will commence on the first day of the first payroll period after the date he or she returns to work.

3.2 *Enrollment Form.* In the enrollment form, the Employee shall designate the type of Benefits set forth in Section 4.1 which he or she wishes to receive, if any, and shall agree to a reduction in his or her compensation by an amount equal to the Employee's share of the cost of the available Benefits as determined by the Employer.

3.3 *Change of Election.* A Participant may change an election for a particular Period of Coverage by filing a new enrollment form prior to the beginning of the Period of Coverage. A Participant's election is irrevocable during the Period of Coverage except for a change on account of and consistent with a change in the Participant's family status, which change is sufficient to permit a change of election under regulations and rulings issued by the Internal Revenue Service, and reported by the Participant to the Employer within 31 days of the event.

A change in family status includes but is not limited to events such as the marriage or divorce of the Participant, the death of the Participant's spouse or a dependent, the birth or adoption of a child of the Participant, the termination or commencement of employment of the Participant's spouse, the switching from part-time to full-time status or from full-time to part-time status by the Participant or the Participant's spouse, and the taking of an unpaid leave of absence by the Participant or the Participant's spouse.

If any Benefit provided by an independent third-party provider is significantly curtailed or ceases during a Period of Coverage, or if the premium for such Benefit is significantly increased during the Period of Coverage, a Participant may revoke his or her election with respect to such Benefit and elect to receive, on a prospective basis only, coverage under another similar Benefit.

3.4 *Deemed Elections.* If a Participant fails to submit a completed enrollment form to the Employer during a subsequent open enrollment period, the Participant shall be deemed to have elected the same Benefit option and coverage under the Plan that the Participant was receiving during the preceding Period of Coverage and shall be deemed to have elected a reduction in compensation equal to the required Elective Contribution.

3.5 *Termination of Participation.* A Participant shall cease to be a Participant as of the earlier of (a) the date on which the Plan terminates (b) the date on which the Participant ceases to be an Employee eligible to participate or (c) the date on which the Participant fails to make the required premium payment with respect to a Benefit after separation from service. A former Participant who is rehired before the end of the Period of Coverage in which he or she separated from employment may not become a Participant again until the later of the date he or she meets the eligibility requirements of this Article III after reemployment or the first day of the next Period of Coverage following the original termination date.

ARTICLE IV
BENEFITS AND CONTRIBUTIONS

4.1 *Amount and Form of Benefits.* Each Participant shall designate on the enrollment form which of the following Benefits, if any, the Participant wishes to receive during the Period of Coverage, and the amount of Elective Contributions to be allocated to each such item:

(a) benefits available under the Medical Plan;

(b) benefits available under the Dental Plan;

A Participant's eligibility to receive benefits under the employee benefit plans set forth above, together with the terms of such benefits, are as specified in such plans, which are hereby incorporated by reference.

4.2 *Elective Contributions.* Pursuant to the election procedure set forth in Section 3.2, each Employee who elects coverage under an available Benefit shall elect to have his or her compensation reduced by the amount of the Employee's share of the cost of the selected Benefit as determined by the Employer, and to have that portion contributed by the Employer to the Plan on his or her behalf. Subject to the revocation procedures in Section 3.3, the amount of Elective Contributions elected by the Employee may increase or decrease during the Period of Coverage if the premium charged for the Benefit coverage by an independent third-party provider increases or decreases during the Period of Coverage.

4.3 *Maximum Benefit.* The maximum benefit provided under the plan shall be the employee's cost of each of the Benefits offered in Section 4.1 as determined from time to time by the Employer.

ARTICLE V
NON-DISCRIMINATION

5.1 *Non-Discrimination.* If, in the judgement of the Employer, the Plan may fail to meet any requirement of Section 125 of the Code (such as the prohibition of discrimination in participation in favor of Highly Compensated Employees or the limitation on benefits provided to Key Employees), the Employer shall take such action as it deems appropriate to assure compliance with such requirements or limitation. If, in the judgement of the Employer, the Plan or any of the employee benefit plans set forth in Section 4.1 may be discriminatory within the meaning of any section in the Code, the Employer shall take such action as it deems appropriate under rules uniformly applicable to similarly situated Participants. The action taken by the Employer pursuant to this Section 5.1 may include, without limitation, a modification of the elections of certain Participants, with or without the consent of such Participants.

ARTICLE VI
ADMINISTRATION, AMENDMENTS AND TERMINATION

6.1 *Administration.* The administration of the Plan shall be under the supervision of the Plan Administrator. It shall be a principal duty of the Plan Administrator to see that the Plan is carried out, in accordance with its terms, for the exclusive benefit of the persons entitled to participate in the Plan, without discrimination among them. The Plan Administrator will have full power to administer the Plan in all of its details, subject to applicable requirements of law. For this purpose, the Plan Administrator's powers will include, but will not be limited to, the following authority, in addition to all other powers provided by this Plan:

(a) To make and enforce such rules and regulations as it deems necessary or proper for the efficient administration of the Plan, including the establishment of any claim procedures that may be required by applicable provisions of law;

(b) To interpret the Plan, its interpretation thereof in good faith to be final and conclusive on all persons claiming benefits under the Plan;

(c) To decide all questions concerning the Plan and the eligibility of any person to participate in the Plan;

(d) To appoint such agents, counsel, accountants, consultants and other persons as may be required to assist in administering the Plan; and

(e) To allocate and delegate its responsibilities under the Plan and to designate other persons to carry out any of its responsibilities under the Plan, any such allocation, delegation or designation to be in writing.

(f) To obtain from Employees and Participants such information as shall be necessary to the proper administration of the Plan.

Notwithstanding the foregoing, any claim which arises under any of the plans listed in Section 4.1 shall not be subject to review under this Plan, and the Plan Administrator's authority under this Section 6.1 shall not extend to any matter as to which an administrator under any such other plan is empowered to make determinations under such plan.

6.2 *Accounts.* The Employer shall maintain an Account for each Participant for the purpose of recording the Participant's Benefit elections and allocations of Elective Contributions to particular Benefits.

6.3 *Examination of Records.* The Plan Administrator will make available to each Participant such of his records under this Plan as pertain to him, for examination at reasonable times during normal business hours. The Plan Administrator shall be responsible for complying with all notices, reporting, filing and disclosure requirements established by the Internal Revenue Service for Section 125 plans.

6.4 *Reliance on Tables, etc.* In administering the Plan, the Plan Administrator will be entitled, to the extent permitted by law, to rely conclusively on all tables, valuations, certificates, opinions and reports which are furnished by, or in accordance with the instructions of the administrator(s) of the Medical Plan or by accountants, counsel or other experts employed or engaged by the Plan Administrator.

6.5 *Nondiscriminatory Exercise of Authority.* Whenever, in the administration of the Plan, any discretionary action by the Plan Administrator is required, the Plan Administrator shall exercise its authority in a nondiscriminatory manner so that all persons similarly situated will receive substantially the same treatment.

6.6 *Indemnification of the Plan Administrator.* The Company agrees to indemnify and to defend to the fullest extent permitted by law any Employee serving as the Plan Administrator or as a member of a committee designated as Plan Administrator (including an Employee or former Employee who formerly served as Plan Administrator or as a member of such committee) against all liabilities, damages, costs and expenses (including attorneys' fees and amounts paid in settlement of any claims approved by the Company) occasioned by any act or omission to act in connection with the Plan, if such act or omission is in good faith.

6.7 *Amendment and Termination.* The Employer intends to maintain the Plan for an indefinite period of time. However, the Plan may be amended from time to time or terminated at any time at the will of the Employer. However, no such amendment or termination shall adversely affect the rights of any Participant hereunder with respect to any claims incurred prior to such amendment or termination for benefits under the employee benefit plans set forth in Section 4.1.

ARTICLE VII
GENERAL PROVISIONS

7.1 *Employment Rights.* The adoption and maintenance of the Plan shall not be deemed to constitute a contract of continuing employment between the Employer and any Participant. Nothing herein contained shall be construed to give any Participant the right to be retained in the employment of the Employer or to interfere with the right of the Employer to terminate the employment of any Participant at any time.

7.2 *Nonalienation of Benefits.* Except as otherwise provided in the Plan, no right or benefit under the Plan shall be subject to anticipation, alienation, sale, assignment, pledge, encumbrance or charge, and any attempt to anticipate, alienate, sell, assign, pledge, encumber or charge such right or benefit shall be void.

7.3 *Claims and Review Procedure.* If any person believes that he or she is being denied any rights or benefits under the Plan, such person may file a claim in writing with the Plan Administrator. If any such claim is wholly or partially denied, the Plan Administrator will notify such person of its decision in writing. Such notification will be written in a manner calculated to be understood by such person and will contain (i) specific reasons for the denial, (ii) specific reference to pertinent Plan provisions, (iii) a description of any additional material or information necessary for such person to perfect such claim and an explanation of why such material or information is necessary and (iv) information as to the steps to be taken if the person wishes to submit a request for review. Such notification will be given within 90 days after the claim is received by the Plan Administrator (or within 180 days, if special circumstances require an extension of time for processing the claim, and if written notice of such extension and circumstances is given to such person within the 90 day period). If such notification is not given within such period, the claim will be considered denied as of the last day of such period and such person may request a review of his or her claim.

Within 60 days after the date on which a person receives a written notice of a denied claim (or, if applicable, within 60 days after the date on which such denial is considered to have occurred) such person or a duly authorized representative may (i) file a written request with the Plan Administrator for a review of the denied claim and of pertinent documents and (ii) submit written issues and comments to the Plan Administrator. The Plan Administrator will notify such person of its decision in writing. Such notification will be written in a manner calculated to be understood by such person and will contain specific reasons for the decision as well as specific references to pertinent Plan provisions. The decision on review will be made within 60 days after the request for review is received by the Plan Administrator (or within 120 days, if written notice of such extension and circumstances is given to such person within the initial 60-day period). If the decision on review is not made within such period, the claim will be considered denied.

7.4 *Governing Law.* The Plan shall be construed and enforced in accordance with the laws of the State of Rhode Island, to the extent such laws are not preempted by applicable Federal law.

7.5 *Construction of the Plan.* The Employer may construe any ambiguous provisions of the Plan, correct any defect, supply any omission, or reconcile any inconsistency, in such manner and to such extent as the Employer in its discretion may determine; and any such action of the Employer shall be binding and conclusive upon all Participants. The masculine gender, whenever used herein, shall include the feminine, and the singular shall include the plural and vice versa, unless otherwise clear from the context.

7.6 *Plan Qualification Requirements.* The Employer intends that the Plan terms, including those relating to coverage and benefits, are legally enforceable. The Plan is maintained for the exclusive benefit of employees.

IN WITNESS WHEREOF, the Employer has caused this instrument to be executed this _____ day of September, 1990 to be effective as indicated herein.

Salve Regina College

by, _____

Title:

Appendix 4

Sample of a Request for Proposals

Source: Reprinted with permission of Martin E. Segal Company, from one section of a Request for Proposals for Health Care Services that was prepared for the purposes of comparing preferred provider organizations.

PPO Network

The Trust is requesting proposals for a Physician and Hospital PPO Network. There is currently only a discounted arrangement with Care Network. The cost for the PPO is $1.50 per employee per month.

Your proposal, including discounts, will be held in the strictest confidence and only accessed by the Trust and Martin E. Segal Company. Additionally, information developed for the proposals such as memoranda, bid analysis, etc. will not be released without the express consent of the proposers. No other firm bidding on this program will be allowed to review the material.

Your proposal should include a Physician and Hospital PPO Network. It is necessary that the chosen PPO Network have the ability to work with the Administration and Utilization Review firm selected by the Trust. It is anticipated that if a change in PPO's Networks were made, such a change would become effective July 1, 1991.

Identify the hospital facilities that are currently contracted with your network and indicate the discount arrangement you have with each facility in the following exhibit. If per claim, indicate by type of hospital confinement (i.e. S/P, ICU, CCU, Maternity, Med/Surg, etc.). If you use DRGs, please indicate such and enter an average discount received by the providers listed. Please complete the exhibit and include it in your proposal reflecting your discount arrangement by Hospital provider.

Hospital Discounts

				As of _____
_____				(Date)
Organization				
		*Arrangement**		
		1st $		*Dollar/%*
Hospital	*DRG*	*Discount*	*Per Diem*	*Discount*

*Check which arrangement applies to each hospital.

237

The following Exhibit represents the 25 most common surgical procedures by CPT code and HIAA prevailing fee based on the 90th percentile. Please fill in your reimbursement for each listed procedure and include it in your proposal.

Reimbursement of Physician Charges-Surgery

Procedure	CPT Code	HIAA Prevailing Fee*	Reimbursement
Cervical Cesarean Section	59501	$3,021	$
Forceps Delivery w/Episiotomy	59400	2,226	
Abdominal Hysterectomy	58150	2,650	
Vaginal Hysterectomy	58260	2,650	
Dilation and Curettage	58120	636	
Laparoscopy	258980	1,080	
Unilateral Simple Mastectomy	19180	1,166	
Left Cardiac Catheterization	93510	1,166	
Transurethral Prostatectomy	52601	2,120	
Cystoscopy	52204	424	
Total Cholecystectomy	47600	2,072	
Appendectomy	44950	1,266	
Tonsillectomy/ Adenoidectomy	42820	763	
Inguinal Hernia Repair	49530	1,749	
Knee Replacement	27447	4,823	
Bone Marrow Biopsy	85102	154	
ORIF Tibia/Fibula	27806	1,894	
ORIF Femur	27512	1,242	
Balloon Angioplasty	33970	1,272	
Total Hip Replacement	27130	5,099	
Coronary Artery Bypass (single graft)	33510	5,258	
Septoplasty	30520	1,802	
Exploratory Laparotomy	49000	1,696	
Vasectomy	55250	413	
Breast Biopsy (incisional)	19101	530	
Totals		$	$

*As of May, 1990.

How are Physicians reimbursed? Please explain your response in detail. Is it based on:

☐ Relative Value Scale (RVS)?
☐ Usual, Customary and Reasonable (UCR) charge system?
☐ Fixed fee basis?
☐ Physician UCR profile?
☐ Combination of the above?
☐ Other?

Organization

Date

Questions To Be Answered

PPO Background Information

1. Name of PPO:
2. Address of Principal Office:
3. Telephone Number:
4. Name (Title) and Telephone Number of Contact:
5. Name of Medical Director:
6. Date PPO was organized:
7. Date PPO became operational:
8. How was your organization financed initially? Who or what organization provided the financing?
9. Sponsorship of PPO (please check one of the following and state the name(s) of the sponsor(s)).
   [   ] Provider
   [   ] Purchaser (self insured/union trust fund)
   [   ] Blue Cross/Blue Shield
   [   ] Commercial Insurance Carrier
   [   ] HMO
   [   ] Individual Sponsor
   [   ] Business
   [   ] Benefit Consultants
   [   ] Broker
   [   ] Other—please explain
10. Provide a chart depicting the organizational structure of the PPO.
11. Are any of the owners, officers or board members connected in any way with your providers network? Please describe in detail.

12. Does the sponsoring organization participate in other alternate delivery systems (i.e. HMOs) besides the PPO?
    [   ] Yes   [   ] No   If yes, state the name(s) of this/these organization(s) and describe.
13. State the name(s) of the individual(s) who manages and/or administers the PPO and provide the name of their employer.
14. How many individuals are employed by the PPO (break out according to professional, clerical, etc.)? Are these individuals located in one or more geographic areas? Please state the geographic areas involved and the number of employees at each site.
15. What is the PPO's capacity for expansion? Will the PPO's current geographic area be expanded? If so, when?
16. Provide a copy of the PPO's liability policy. What are the limits of the PPO's liability insurance?
17. Does the PPO contract include a Hold Harmless clause to protect the plan sponsor?   [   ] Yes   [   ] No
18. Does the PPO arbitrate disputes between purchasers and physicians regarding quality of services and charges for delivery of care?
19. Is any of the PPO's revenue derived from providers of service? (Please describe.)
20. Do you require that your organization price all claims prior to being processed by claims payor?
21. If #20 above is yes, what is your current turn-around time for such pricing?

General Provider Service Information

1. List the type(s) of providers that currently have contracts with the PPO. Check and provide complete and detailed responses to any of the following that apply:
   [   ] Physicians only
   [   ] Hospital(s) only
   [   ] Physicians and Hospital(s)
   [   ] Specialty (please describe)
   [   ] Other health care professional network(s) available in addition to physicians and hospitals (plese describe)
2. a. How much advance notice must a provider give if terminating participation?
   b. How often are directories updated?
3. Are participating providers also enrolled in any other alternative delivery system programs which may or may not be sponsored by the PPO? [   ] Yes   [   ] No   If yes, please describe.

4. What credentialing process is followed by the PPO in the selection and enrollment of hospitals, health care facilities and physician providers? Describe and attach any necessary documentation.

5. How is cost efficiency/effectiveness of all participating providers measured? Describe the process used for hospitals, physicians, nonhospital providers.

6. How is the quality of care provided by each of the providers, described in #5 above, monitored?

7. How are physician practice patterns tracked/monitored? Is that data available to the Trust?

8. Are hospitals/health care facilities and/or physicians ever removed from your network? Under what circumstances would removal occur? How many were removed in 1988 and 1989?

9. What is the procedure for dropping from the network, either at the request of the PPO or the provider?

10. What is the rate of provider dropout (hospitals/health care facilities and physicians) and which providers have dropped out since the PPO's inception?

11. How often are directories updated?

12. How often are participating employers notified of changes in providers?

13. Are health education services available?   [   ] Yes   [   ] No
    If yes, please describe.

14. Are employee assistance programs available? [   ] Yes   [   ] No
    If yes, please describe.

15. Does the PPO include or is it able to assist in establishing discount arrangements for:
    [   ] Yes   [   ] No   Home care
    [   ] Yes   [   ] No   Hospice care
    [   ] Yes   [   ] No   Skilled nursing care
    [   ] Yes   [   ] No   Convalescent care
    [   ] Yes   [   ] No   Durable medical equipment
    [   ] Yes   [   ] No   Child care for sick children
    Please describe.

16. How are members identified as being enrolled in the PPO? How do providers handle patient eligibility? Please describe.
    [   ] ID cards
    [   ] Telephone verification
    [   ] Monthly/quarterly eligibility registers
    [   ] Other

17. For the last three years, what changes (increases/decreases) have been made to the reimbursement schedule and what was the basis for those changes?

Hospitals and Physician Provider Information
  Hospitals and Other Facilities

1. Please provide the names and locations of hospitals/health care facilities that have a contractual relationship with the PPO.

2. Do the above hospitals and health care facilities have multiple arrangements with alternative delivery systems other than your PPO? Please specify.

3. Are any of the PPO hospitals affiliated with any satellite clinics, outpatient surgery centers, emergency centers, etc.? If so, indicate location and description of services.

4. How often are contracts with hospitals and other facilities updated?

5. What type of cases or specialized treatment conditions *cannot* be provided by any of the hospitals in your network? Where can this/these service(s) be provided?

6. How long is the reimbursement rate for hospital(s) guaranteed?

7. If the discount amount(s) are changed, how much notice is given employer groups and how are they notified?

8. Does the method of reimbursement apply to inpatient, outpatient hospital, outpatient surgery and emergency treatment hospital services?

9. Please describe the reimbursement methodology to be used for outpatient services charges.

Appendix 5

Account Specific Analysis Program

Part I: Renewal Data, 1985-1988
Part II: A Comparison of Some Essential Data, 1987-1989
Part III: Analysis of Hospital Claims Costing More Than $100,000,
            2/1/89-1/21/90

Source: Prepared by Health Care Management Reports of Blue Cross/Blue Shield of Connecticut for the town of Old Saybrook, CT, February 1990.

PART I
Renewal Rate Data, 1985-1988

OLD SAYBROOK TOWN AND BOARD OF EDUCATION

RENEWAL YEAR	1988	1987	1986	1985
Hospital Rates	$61.10	$51.26	$49.34	$36.84
	122.20	102.52	98.68	73.68
	166.06	139.31	134.08	96.26
Loss Ratio	93.8%	93.6%	107.9%	91.5%
Trend cost of medication inflation	1.2234%	11.5%	1.1508%	1.1829%
Hospital				
Adjustment	3.62%	5.04%	5.78%	7.72%
Credit	13,283	15,572	18,687	17,784
Rate Adjustment	14.4%	7.4%	19.7%	9.5%
R.S.R. Info.				
Current Year	+57,159	51,088	−51,555	48,718
Prior Balance	+21,368	−29,720	21,835	−26,883
Cumulative Balance	+78,527	21,368	−29,720	21,835
Refund	None	None	None	None

245

PART II
A Comparison of Some Essential Data From 1987-88 to 1988-89

THE TOWN AND PUBLIC SCHOOL SYSTEM
OF
OLD SAYBROOK, CT

EXHIBIT I

INPATIENT HOSPITAL	PAID CLAIMS			% OF CLAIMS		# OF CLAIMS			LENGTH OF STAY/AVERAGE DAYS		
	1987-88	1988-89	INC/(DEC)	87-88	88-89	87-88	88-89	+/(−)	87-88	88-89	+/(−)
Surgical	$72,373	$158,973	$86,600	21%	33%	15	11	(4)	4.1	9.4	5.3
Psych/Alcohol	130,292	75,716	(54,576)	37%	16%	16	6	(10)	18.1	36.5	18.4
Medical	114,222	228,066	113,844	32%	47%	22	34	12	4.4	5.7	1.4
Maternity	34,805	19,577	(15,228)	10%	4%	7	7	0	3.7	2.7	(1.0)
Total	$351,691	$482,331	$130,640	100%	100%	60	58	(2)	7.9	9.2	1.3

EXHIBIT II

OUTPATIENT HOSPITAL	PAID CLAIMS			% OF CLAIMS		# OF CLAIMS		
	1987-88	1988-89	INC/(DEC)	87-88	88-89	87-88	88-89	+/(−)
Emergency Room	$12,692	$19,436	$6,744	9%	12%	98	127	29
Ambulatory Surgical	24,720	36,166	11,446	17%	22%	43	35	(8)
Diagnostic Services	22,988	70,670	47,682	16%	42%	143	206	63
Homecare	4,137	5,399	1,262	3%	3%	4	3	(1)
Medicare Supp.	585	307	(278)	0%	0%	4	6	2
Other Outpatient	25,707	9,255	(16,452)	18%	6%	64	35	(29)
Pre-Admit Testing	17,924	20,472	2,548	13%	12%	285	368	83
Psych/Alcohol	8,117	4,875	(3,242)	6%	3%	7	3	(4)
Hosp. Based Physician	25,125	N/A	N/A	18%	N/A	0	N/A	0
Total	$141,994	$166,579	$49,709	100%	100%	648	783	135

EXHIBIT III

MEDICAL/SURGICAL	PAID CLAIMS			% OF CLAIMS		# OF CLAIMS		
	1987-88	1988-89	INC/(DEC)	87-88	88-89	87-88	88-89	+/(−)
Chemotherapy	$1,530	$1,123	($407)	1%	0%	122	39	(83)
H&O Endorsement	77,665	89,952	12,287	30%	28%	2,349	2,524	175
H&O Surgery	23,971	35,792	11,821	9%	11%	330	445	115
In Hospital Surgical	43,980	56,885	12,905	17%	18%	82	74	(8)
Lab & Pathology	25,713	33,132	7,419	10%	10%	2,019	2,606	587
Medical Care	7,931	20,163	12,232	3%	6%	188	464	276
Obstetrics	9,598	12,893	3,295	4%	4%	11	19	8
Other	5,950	9,039	3,089	2%	3%	74	96	22
Pediatric Care	N/A	273	273	N/A	0%	N/A	12	12
Physical Therapy	10,554	15,372	4,818	4%	5%	543	770	227
Radiology	32,616	29,170	(3,445)	13%	9%	412	411	(1)
Testing	7,790	9,587	1,797	3%	3%	218	258	40
Vision Care	7,376	9,160	1,784	3%	3%	186	235	49
Total	$254,673	$322,541	$67,868	100%	100%	6,534	7,953	1,419

EXHIBIT IV

COVERAGE CATEGORY	PAID CLAIMS			% OF CLAIMS		# OF CLAIMS		
	1987-88	1988-89	INC/(DEC)	87-88	88-89	87-88	88-89	+/(−)
Female Employee	$280,362	$347,467	$67,106	37%	36%	2,672	3,451	779
Male Employee	94,964	116,151	21,187	13%	12%	1,156	1,220	64
Total Employee	$375,325	$463,618	$88,293	50%	48%	3,828	4,671	843
Female Spouse	$137,077	$122,055	($15,023)	18%	13%	792	1,058	266
Male Spouse	85,874	237,142	151,268	11%	24%	1,121	1,196	75
Total Spouse	$222,952	$359,197	$136,245	30%	37%	1,913	2,254	341
Children (M&F)	$150,081	$148,636	($1,445)	20%	15%	1,501	1,869	368
Total	$748,358	$971,451	$223,093	100%	100%	7,242	8,794	1,552

EXHIBIT V

MAJOR SERVICES	PAID CLAIMS			PCT CHNG	# OF CLAIMS			PCT CHNG
	1987-88	1988-89	INC/(DEC)		87-88	88-89	+/(-)	
INPATIENT HOSPITAL	$351,691	$482,331	$130,640	37%	60	58	(2)	-3%
OUTPATIENT HOSPITAL	$141,994	$166,579	$49,709	35%	648	783	135	21%
TOTAL HOSPITAL	$493,685	$648,910	$180,349	37%	708	841	133	19%
MEDICAL/SURGICAL	$254,673	$322,541	$67,868	27%	6,534	7,953	1,419	22%
TOTAL	$748,358	$971,451	$223,092	30%	7,242	8,794	1,552	21%

COVERAGE CATEGORY	PAID CLAIMS			PCT CHNG	# OF CLAIMS			PCT CHNG
	1987-88	1988-89	INC/(DEC)		87-88	88-89	+/(-)	
EMPLOYEE	$375,325	$463,618	$88,293	24%	3,828	4,671	843	22%
SPOUSE	$222,952	$359,197	$136,245	61%	1,913	2,254	341	18%
CHILDREN	$150,081	$148,636	($1,445)	-1%	1,501	1,869	368	25%
TOTAL	$748,358	$971,451	$223,093	30%	7,242	8,794	1,552	21%

PART III

The Town and Public School System
of
Old Saybrook, CT
Hospital Claims >$10,000
2/1/89 – 1/31/90

Condition	Claimant	Days Continued	Total Charges
Rheumatoid Arthritis	Spouse	38	$ 43,367
Neurotic Disorder	Child	105	42,285
Heart Disease	Spouse	17	42,131
Out-of-State Surgery	Spouse	25	34,282
Schizophrenia	Employee	49	29,917
Cancer of Colon	Employee	9	29,073
Cancer of Lung	Employee	42	28,310
Subarachnoid Hemorrhage	Employee	22	27,321
Osteoarthrosis	Employee	13	23,300
Heart Disease	Employee	10	15,945
Cerebral Artery Occlusion	Spouse	7	15,376
Traumatic Arthropathy	Spouse	8	15,092
Cancer of Uterus	Employee	10	13,798
Cancer Treatment	Employee	0	13,137
Displaced Intervertebral disc	Employee	11	12,740
Schizo-Affective disorder	Spouse	36	10,025
		402	$396,099

*Total large claims $396,099 represents 25.5% of total claims charged (14 individuals)

Hospital Pooling Point – $75,000

Appendix 6

Comparison of Coverages and Costs of Two Different Insurance Plans

Comparison of Benefits Offered by Two Insurance Companies

BENEFIT	COMPANY A	COMPANY B
Medical Insurance (1st Dollar)		
Surgical Benefits	Reasonable & Customary (R & C) Charge	Scheduled Amount*
Anesthesia Benefit	R & C Charge	Scheduled Amount*
Second Surgical Opinion	R & C Charge	Scheduled Amount*
Assistant Surgeon	R & C Charge	Scheduled Amount*
In-Hospital Physician	R & C Charge	Scheduled Amount*
Day Limit	120 Days	None
Out-of-Hospital Physician		
Deductible	$0	$0
Maximum per calendar year	$270*	$270*
Eye Exams		
Deductible	$10	$10
Benefit	R & C	Scheduled Amount*
Maximum per calendar year	$270	$270
Overall Medical/Surgical Maximum	N/A	$10,000 per year*
Diagnostic Lab and X-Ray	$500	Scheduled Amount*
Prescription Drugs		
Deductible	None	None
Basic Plan Maximum per year	None	$500*
Contraceptives	Not covered	Not covered

*The excess over these amounts are covered under major medical benefits.

255

BENEFIT	COMPANY A	COMPANY B
Dental Insurance		
Type I Benefits	100%	100%
Type II Benefits	100%	100%
Type III Benefits	50%	50%
Type IV Benefits	60%	60%
Deductible	None	None
Dental Calendar Year Maximum	$1,500	$1,500
Orthodontia Lifetime Maximum	$1,000	$1,000
Dependent Limiting Age	19	19
Full-time Student Limiting Age	25	25
Major Medical Expense Benefits		
Deductible per Calendar Year	$100	$200
Family Annual Deductible Maximum	$250	$400
Coinsurance	80%	80%
Maximum Out-of-Pocket Costs		
(including deductible)	$500	$600
Maximum Family Out-of-Pocket Costs		
(including deductible)	$1,000	$1,200
Lifetime Plan Maximum	$1,000,000	$1,000,000
Dependent Limiting Age	19	19
Full-time Student Limiting Age	25	25

BENEFIT	COMPANY A	COMPANY B
Psychiatric Care		
Outpatient benefit	50%	50%
Maximum per year	$2,000	$2,000
Inpatient limit per year	60 Days	60 Days
Coverage & Limitation Differences		
Professional nursing limit	None	$20,000 per year
Home health care deductible	None	$50 per year
Home health care coinsurance	80%	75%
Accident Benefit		
Maximum per accident	$300*	N/A*
Special Services Benefit		
Emergency hospital care	N/A*	Scheduled amount*

BENEFIT	NUMBER ENROLLED	COMPANY A MONTHLY PREMIUMS		COMPANY B MONTHLY PREMIUMS	
		Cost Per Employee	Total Cost	Cost Per Employee	Total Cost
All Medical Benefits					
Individual	17	$164.65	$ 2,799.05	$116.94	$ 1,987.98
Two Person	22	354.02	7,788.44	242.28	5,330.16
Family	31	424.22	13,150.82	312.89	9,699.59
Medicare Supplement	4	301.37	1,205.48	91.98	367.92
Medicare Supplement	3	606.85	1,820.55	183.96	551.88
Total Monthly Cost			26,764.34		17,937.53
Dental					
Individual	17	23.92	406.64	21.16	359.72
Two Person	22	80.12	1,762.64	64.31	1,414.82
Family	31	80.12	2,483.72	64.31	1,993.61
Total Monthly Cost			4,653.00		3,768.15
*Life and AD&D**					
Rate per $1,000			.45		.57
Volume			700,000.00		700,000.00
Total Monthly Cost			315.00		399.00
TOTAL MONTHLY COSTS			31,732.34		22,104.68
TOTAL ANNUAL COSTS			$380,788.08		$265,256.16

*Life rate has not been rated including retirees; final rates will be higher.

Summary and Comments

The proposed package of Company B saves close to $100,000 over Company A's existing rates. With Company A's renewal rates due to go up July 1, the savings will be even more impressive. Rates are increasing by about 20 percent for medical benefits and 11 percent for dental benefits.

The cost illustration has been revised to show correct Medicare supplement rates and proper enrollment. Prior cost pages did not add the major medical cost in Company A's Medicare supplement rate. The life rates have to be requoted to include seven retirees. The rate will go up; however, the overall cost difference to the package will be small. Company B must seek approval from its home office to insure the seven retirees for major medical benefits, but this should not pose a problem. Company B also has quoted rates that assume a 4/1 effective date. Major medical rates will have to be slightly adjusted to go to a 7/1 effective date.

As the comparison shows, coverages differ some, but overall, the contract is substantially the same. Dental coverage has been enhanced in the basic services area. Company A's plan did not cover work started prior to the plan's effective date, including bridges and dentures for teeth missing prior to the effective date. Company B's does include a three-month extended benefit for the following procedure if the work started prior to the plan's effective date: (1) fixed bridgework and full or partial dentures; (2) crowns, inlays, and onlays; and (3) root canals.

The only notable reductions in coverage are (1) the first-dollar prescription drug coverage now has a maximum limit, although costs over the maximum are covered by major medical; (2) the major medical deductible goes up to $200 for individual plans and to a $400 maximum for family plans. In addition, Company A reportedly allows more under their reasonable and customary (R & C) guidelines, since they update their schedules more often. As a result, out-of-pocket expenses, along with deductibles and prescription drug costs, will be somewhat higher with Company B.

Placing the major medical plan with an insurer other than Company B will require employees to resubmit uncovered medical charges. This requirement should not create too much hardship since employees are currently dealing with two insurance companies. Company C is a large insurer of superimposed major medical. Their claim office is very familiar with Company B.

Appendix 7

Health Care Cost Containment Measures Found in Labor Contracts

Source: Reprinted from Bureau of National Affairs, Inc., *Collective Bargaining Negotiations and Contracts* 44:551.

Health Care Cost Containment Measures

Hospitalization-Related Provisions

Cost-cutting measures found in hospitalization plans include deductibles, requirement for pre-admission certification or pre-admission testing, restrictions on emergency room use or weekend admissions, and employee rewards for detecting billing errors. Other provisions provide coverage for less costly alternatives to hospitalization, such as for care rendered at a convalescent nursing home, hospice, or birthing center, or at a patient's home.

Hospitalization Deductibles—

—Two hundred dollar individual ($400 family) applied to all basic plan expenses in each plan year

A $200 per individual ($400 family maximum) deductible will be applied to all covered basic plans' expenses in each Plan Year (July 1st through the following June 30th). These deductibles apply to the covered expenses for Hospitalization and Medical Surgical Benefits. . . . (H.J. Heinz Co., Heinz U.S.A. Div. *and* Food and Commercial Workers; exp. 3/94)

—Twenty-five dollars for each of first four days

There will be a twenty-five dollar ($25.00) per day deductible paid by the employee for each of the first four (4) days of hospital confinement, not to exceed one hundred dollars ($100.00) for each confinement. This deductible is not applicable under Major Medical. (Ohio Rubber Co. *and* Rubber Workers; exp. 1/92)

Pre-admission Requirements—

—First $100 of hospital charges forfeited for lack of certification

PAC/CSR REQUIREMENTS. Pre-Admission Certification (PAC) and Continued Stay Review (CSR) refer to the process used to certify the medical necessity and length of any Hospital Confinement as a registered bed patient. PAC and CSR are performed through a utilization review program by a Review Organization with which CG [Connecticut General Life Insurance Company] has contracted. PAC should be requested by you or your Dependent through your Physician for each inpatient Hospital admission.

Expenses incurred for which benefits would otherwise be paid under this plan will not include the first $100 of Hospital charges made for each separate admission to the Hospital as a registered bed patient unless PAC is received: (a) prior to date of admission; or (b) in the case of an emergency admission, by the end of the first scheduled work day after the date of admission, or as soon thereafter as circumstances would reasonably permit but in any event prior to discharge. (American Brass Co. *and* Steelworkers; exp. 3/93)

—Benefits reduced by 30 percent for failure to submit to review procedures

Pre-Hospital Admission Review;

Hospital confinement is to be evaluated for appropriateness of treatment, treatment site, and anticipated length of stay. Prior to admission (except in emergencies) covered employees and eligible dependents are required to submit a properly completed Request for Pre-Admission Review form to the carrier for review or contact the carrier by phone.

Covered employees and eligible dependents who do not contact the carrier for review will have the regular benefits provided by the plan reduced by 30% even if it is later determined that the confinement was medically necessary. (Services or supplies, including hospitalization, not ordered by a physician or not medically necessary are not covered charges under the health benefits program.) In emergencies, the Pre-Admission Review (PAR) unit must be contacted by phone within 48 hours of admission, or 72 hours over a holiday or weekend. (Miller Brewing Co. *and* Auto Workers; exp. 8/92)

—Non-certification results in $1,000 penalty

Pre-Admission Certification: If admission is not certified, a $1,000 penalty on allowable hospital charges will be assessed. This $1,000 will not count toward the deductible. (Babcock and Wilcox Co. *and* Boilermakers; exp. 8/92)

—Failure to comply with testing rule, results in forfeiture of first day's confinement payment

Pre-Admission Testing—must be done on an outpatient basis for all non-emergency admissions. If not performed on an out-patient basis the first day of confinement's charges for room and board will not be a covered expense. (American National Can Co. *and* Graphic Communications Union; exp. 6/92)

—Unnecessary testing in inpatient basis results in forfeiture of one-half of expenses payment

Preadmission Testing—Preadmission Testing controls ensure that needed tests prior to surgery are performed on an outpatient basis whenever possible. If such testing is done on an inpatient basis unnecessarily, only one half of the charges will be considered eligible expenses. (Miles Inc. *and* Steelworkers; exp. 3/92)

—Testing must be medically necessary to qualify for benefit

Pre-Admission Testing Benefit. Pre-admission testing is covered on a reasonable and customary basis at one hundred percent (100%). Charges for hospital admission for diagnostic purposes will be reimbursed if the admission is medically necessary, or if the tests cannot be performed on an outpatient basis. (Owens-Brockway Packaging Inc. *and* Glass, Molders, Pottery, Plastics and Allied Workers; exp. 3/93)

Emergency Room and Weekend Admission Rules—

—Plan will pay only 50 percent of emergency room expenses if treatment is not urgent

Non-Emergency Care in an Emergency Room

This encourages you to use the emergency room only in an emergency. When you have minor ailments, you shouldn't substitute the hospital emergency room for your doctor's office. It can cost up to four times more because of staffing and equipment.

If you are treated in a hospital's emergency room and the treatment is not emergency care, the Plan will pay only 50% of emergency room expenses. You pay the remaining 50%. This percentage will not count toward your stop-loss limit.

There are two exceptions:

* If adequate care is not available to you elsewhere, or

* If the treatment could not safely be performed outside a hospital. (Siemens Energy and Automation Inc. *and* Electronic Workers; exp. 3/93)

—*Urgent care facilities incorporated as substitute for use of hospital emergency rooms, where cost effective*

During the 1989 contract negotiations, both the Company and the Union expressed concern about the continuing cost increase of health care and in continuing efforts to control such costs. As a result, we have agreed to the following:

. . . .

To incorporate Local Urgent Care facilities as a substitute for use of hospital emergency rooms, where cost effective. (Dana Corp. *and* Auto Workers; exp. 12/92)

—*Friday or Saturday non-urgent admission results in forfeiture of benefits*

Weekend Hospital Admission (Mandatory)

Admission to a hospital on a Friday or Saturday in a non-emergency situation will result in the forfeiture of benefits covered by the medical insurance program. (JPI Transportation Products Inc., Heavy Bearings Div. *and* Machinists; exp. 9/92)

—*Benefit payment for unauthorized Friday or Saturday non-urgent admission reduced by 50 percent*

WEEKEND HOSPITAL ADMISSION LIMITATION PROGRAM

. . . .

PROGRAM REQUIREMENTS. An Inpatient Hospital Stay for a Non-Emergency Admission that starts on a Friday or Saturday must be approved by the Insurance Company under the Pre-Admission Hospital Certification program. The Employee or Dependent should inform the Insurance Company of the day of admission when requesting a Pre-Admission Hospital Certification.

The Insurance Company will inform the Doctor and Hospital by telephone of the approval or disapproval of the day of admission. This will be confirmed by written notice to the Employee, Doctor, and Hospital.

BENEFIT PAYMENT. In the event a Friday or Saturday Non-Emergency Admission is not approved, the Hospital room and board benefit payment for the unauthorized day(s) shall be reduced by 50%. . . . (NCR Corp. *and* Auto Workers; exp. 6/92)

—*Exceptions to prohibition of weekend admission listed*

Hospital benefits will be covered for Friday or Saturday admissions only when:·

The doctor determines that observation on Friday or Saturday is medically necessary.

Surgical procedure is to occur within 24 hours of admission.

Reason is given of medical necessity or treatment which could not have been performed on an out-patient basis for those days of admission.

Admission is indicated as medically necessary on the attending doctor's report and hospital records. (DynCorp., Fort Rucker Div. *and* Machinists; exp. 5/92)

Self-auditing Reimbursements—

—Thirty percent of hospital overcharges, with $1,000 maximum payment

The COMPANY's Group Insurance Plan will include the following special programs:

Self Audit of Billing: Employees will be allowed thirty (30%) percent of any dollar savings resulting to the COMPANY from their review of covered medical and/or hospital charges which uncover overcharges. The minimum eligible overcharge covered is $10.00 and the maximum payment to an employee in any one year shall be $1000.00 (Sloan Valve Co. *and* Steelworkers; exp. 9/92)

—One-half of recovered billing errors, up to $1,000

HOSPITAL COST AWARENESS REWARD PROGRAM

The Fund wants to catch not just billing mistakes, but bills for services that are unnecessary. If you help the Fund find a mistake, you can get half of what is recovered—up to $1,000.

Everything that happens in a hospital is open to this "amateur auditor" reward. Surgical and other medical procedures are included. Day-to-day hospital routines, like the scheduling of tests, surgeons, surgical assistants, administration of prescriptions, aspirin, mouthwash, and TV, can lead to cost which you—and the Fund—might consider avoidable. Take your complaint to the provider, and if the provider agrees, we can save ourselves unnecessary expense.

Here's what you do:

* Try to keep track of what happens in the hospital—what tests you have, your medications, services, etc. CARE has a form to help you do this called "Participant's Record." When you're discharged, request that an itemized bill be sent directly to you.

* If there's an error on your bill, or if you believe you've been charged for anything you consider unnecessary, ask for an explanation from the hospital. If the hospital agrees, have them correct your bill.

* Send the original bill and the corrected bill to the Fund office with an explanation of your "audit." We'll give you half of what you recover, up to $1,000. (Giant Foods Inc. *and* Food and Commercial Workers; exp. 9/92)

Alternatives to Hospital Care—

—Plan pays 100 percent of charges up to 100 days a year in a skilled nursing facility

Skilled nursing facilities offer an alternative to hospitals as a place where you can recuperate. The plan pays 100% of charges up to 100 days in a calendar year in a skilled nursing facility.

Covered charges in a skilled nursing facility include charges for semi-private room and board skilled nursing care, medical supplies and equipment, prescribed drugs and biologicals and other services ordinarily furnished. Custodial care is not covered.

Charges are covered only if both of the following conditions are met:

● A doctor recommends confinement to this type of facility.

● The patient would have to be confined to a hospital if the skilled nursing facility services were not used. (Chevron U.S.A. Inc. *and* Oil Workers; exp. 2/93)

—Convalescent nursing home charges paid up to a maximum $5,000 per year

Convalescent Nursing Home Care Benefits. In the event an Employee or dependent is confined in a Convalescent Nursing Home, charges made by the Convalescent Nursing Home will be considered provided:

(1) the confinement in the Nursing Home is upon written recommendation of the patient's attending doctor, and

(2) the doctor's recommendation must contain a certification to the effect that in the absence of a Convalescent Nursing Home qualified to treat the patient, the patient would have to be confined in the hospital.

Convalescent Nursing Home charges will be payable only while the person remains under the continuous care of an attending physician and only for the period for which the physician certifies that twenty-four hour a day nursing care is essential. Convalescent Nursing Home charges shall be eligible for benefits up to a maximum of five thousand dollars ($5,000) per Benefit Year. (BF Goodrich Co. *and* Rubber Workers; exp. 5/92)

—*Home health care provided for up to 90 days following stay in a hospital or extended care facility*

Home Health Care will be provided for up to 90 days following a stay in a hospital or extended care facility. 100% of reasonable and customary charges will be provided at home visits by. . . .

Registered Nurse
Licensed Practical Nurse
Licensed Visiting Nurse
Physical Therapist
Occupational Therapist
Speech Therapist
Health Aids in conjunction with nursing and therapy services
Oxygen and medical supplies
Medical Consultations

(General Cable Co. *and* Electrical Workers [IBEW]; exp. 8/92)

—*Plan will pay home care benefits for a maximum 200 visits in a calendar year*

We will provide home care benefits through a coordinated hospital-based home care program or Home Health Agency approved by us. The benefits will be provided in place of what would otherwise be a continued Hospital stay or a replacement for a Hospital stay. We will pay Benefits for a maximum of 200 visits in a Calendar Year. This benefit is dependent on the need for skilled nursing and, if necessary, any one or more of the following therapeutic services such as physical, speech or occupational therapy, dietary and medical social services, medical and surgical supplies, prescribed drugs, and laboratory services, as well as home health aides.

For home health aides, each 4 hour service will be counted as 1 visit. Benefits are limited to 80 visits in a Calendar Year. These 80 visits will be counted as part of the 200 visits provided for above.

If the Member is diagnosed by a Physician as terminally ill with a prognosis of 6 months or less to live, home health care benefits will be provided even if the Member wasn't hospitalized. We will allow up to $200 toward Medical Social Services. (A. Wimpfheimer & Bro. Inc. *and* Clothing and Textile Workers; exp. 5/92)

—*Payment made for actual expense of visiting nurse service*

VISITING NURSE SERVICE

Benefits are payable if following hospital confinement you or your Dependent receive the services of a Visiting Registered Nurse on account of the same injury, sickness, pregnancy, childbirth or a related medical condition for which benefits are payable under the In-Patient Benefits. Such services must be prescribed by the attending physician and provided by or through a hospital or non-profit visit nurse association.

Payment will be made for the actual expense of the charges for such nursing service but for not more than one visit on any day. Payment will not be made for more than 730 days of confinement under the In-Patient Benefits, the Out-Patient Benefits and the Visiting Nurses Services combined during one period of disability. Each visit under the Out-Patient Benefits and each visit by a Visiting Nurse shall be counted as one day of confinement. (Stanadyne Inc. *and* Mechanics; exp. 5/92)

—*Inpatient hospice care covered for up to 30 days; outpatient care up to a lifetime maximum of $5,000*

Hospice Care

Inpatient hospice care is covered for up to 30 days. Outpatient hospice care also is covered up to a lifetime maximum of $5,000.

The term "hospice" denotes a special establishment for the terminally ill—those with a prognosis of six months or less to live—which provides various combinations of medical care and emotional and spiritual support services to patients and their families. This benefit aims not only at reducing hospital costs, but at enhancing the quality of remaining life and helping the family cope with accompanying stress. (James River Corp., Flexible Packaging Div. *and* Western Pulp and Paper Workers [Ind.]; exp. 9/92)

—*Hospice benefits paid in full for up to 210 days; maximum $500 can be paid in bereavement counseling benefits*

Hospice Care. Applies to services of Medicare-certified hospices. Hospice is a special program designed to meet the needs of terminally-ill individuals and their families. The purpose of hospice is to offer a comfortable, caring environment during the final stages of a patient's incurable illness.

Hospice care is given primarily in a patient's home, with inpatient services as a backup, if necessary. Services for patients range from nursing to coordinating hospital services to housekeeping assistance to therapy and counseling. In addition, counseling and support services are available for a patient's family.

Hospice benefits will be paid under both medical plans in full for up to 210 days (excluding bereavement counseling for family members). In addition, a maximum of $500 can be paid in bereavement counseling benefits. (Corning Inc. *and* Flint Glass Workers; exp. 1/93)

—*Covered hospice care services listed*

Hospice Care Benefit

The Plan will pay one hundred percent (100%) of Covered Expenses for charges made due to a Terminal Illness for the following Hospice Care Services provided under a Hospice Care Program:

(a) By a Hospice Facility for Bed & Board and Services & Supplies.

(b) By a Hospice Facility for services provided on an outpatient basis.

(c) By a Physician for professional services.

(d) By a Psychologist, social worker or family counselor.

(e) For pain relief treatment, including drugs, medicines and medical supplies for such pain relief treatment.

(f) By a Home Health Care Agency for part-time or intermittent nursing or Home Health Aide services and laboratory services for purposes of palliative care. (Northwest Airlines Inc. *and* Transport Workers; exp. 12/94)

—Birth center benefits include those normally provided by hospital

BIRTH CENTER

Benefits will be provided for maternity services rendered in a Blue Cross Member Free-Standing Birth Center. Services include those which are normally provided by a hospital and for which the Birth Center is licensed to provide. . . . (Fisher and Porter Co. *and* Auto Workers; exp. 4/92)

—Birthing center benefit pays 100 percent of reasonable and customary charges

If a female employee, or a female dependent of a male employee receives obstetrical services in an approved Birthing Center, the Hospital ancillary services benefit under Hospital and Related Benefits is payable at 100% of the facility's Reasonable and Customary Charge for the delivery room, recovery room and other Hospital-type facility charges. A Birthing Center is a free-standing facility which offers comprehensive maternity care to carefully screened patients who are expected to have an uneventful pregnancy with a normal uncomplicated child birth. The facility must have a pre-arranged agreement with a nearby Hospital for emergency transfer of mother and/or infant if an unexpected complication occurs. The Birthing Center Facility must be approved by the Insurance Company. (Al Tech Specialty Steel Corp. *and* Steelworkers; exp. 9/93)

—Up to $500 paid for midwife service

Midwifery

The Fund has added benefits for services performed by a licensed nurse-midwife. Many healthy expectant mothers are deciding to deliver their babies at a birth center, hospital birthing room, or at home attended by a nurse-midwife. These facilities specialize in child birth in a home-like environment with limited medical attention. A nurse-midwife is a licensed specialist in non-complicated childbirth. In most cases, the cost of delivery by a nurse-midwife is less than half of the cost of delivery by an obstetrician. The Fund will pay up to $500 to a nurse-midwife for delivery services. Using a nurse-midwife can save money for you and your Fund. (Associated General Contractors of Maryland *and* Laborers; exp. 3/93)

—Home health benefits plus $100 cash incentive for mother discharged from hospital within 24 hours of delivery

MATERNAL-INFANT EARLY DISCHARGE PROGRAM

This program is available at most Vermont hospitals. It allows a mother to be discharged within 24 hours of a normal delivery, with approval by her physician, and provides additional home care benefits such as skilled nursing visits and homemaker services. Blue Cross and Blue Shield of Vermont is offering a $100 cash incentive as a reward for subscribers who choose this less costly method of health care. An additional reimbursement of up to $50 is available to cover the cost of prenatal instruction for those subscribers who choose to attend a course, and participate in the Maternal-Infant Early Discharge Program.

. . . .

This is an optional program which needs to be discussed with your physician. (Cone-Blanchard Machine Co. *and* Steelworkers; exp. 6/93)

—Medical case management program established to recommend treatment alternatives covered by the plan that can be significantly less expensive than a traditional hospital

Medical Case Management

Cases of critical or long-term injury or illness that are referred, screened and accepted for medical case management will be assigned to a medical consultant (at no cost to the employee) to work with the attending physician to evaluate and recommend treatment alternatives covered by the Plan that can be significantly less expensive than a traditional hospital setting. Examples of critical or long-term injury or illness include major head injuries, spinal cord injuries, multiple fractures, amputations, severe burns, high-risk new-born children, strokes, certain neuromuscular diseases, cancer and AIDS. Significant alternatives include home-health care, hospice or skilled nursing facilities. All charges other than the consulting fee incurred after the medical case management referral is accepted will be treated as covered charges subject to the usual deductible and copayment percentage. (Hercules Inc. *and* Operating Engineers; exp. 2/92)

—*Medical case management will allow plan to pay for items at 100 percent that are not currently covered to insure best care in least expensive setting*

Medical Case Management. This is a voluntary program that will allow the Plan to pay for certain items at 100%, that are not currently covered under our Plan, to insure that the patient receives the best care possible in the least expensive setting. The types of cases that will normally qualify for this special program include the following:

— major head trauma

— severe burns

— spinal cord injury

— acquired immune deficiency syndrome (AIDS)

— comatose

— selected blood abnormality (e.g., hemophilia)

— multiple amputations

— anorexia nervosa

— muscular/neurological disorders: muscular dystrophy amytrophic lateral sclerosis (Lou Gehrig's disease) paralysis (e.g., Guillain-Barre syndrome)

— diagnosis involving long-term IV therapy (e.g., osteomyelitis and endocarditis)

— severe rheumatoid arthritis

— selected osteoarthritis

— neonates with high risk complications

— crohn's disease

— bulimia

— births with multiple congenital abnormalities

— long-term ventilator dependent patients

— cerebrovascular accident (stroke) requiring long-term rehabilitation

— any condition resulting in an admission of over 30 days.

NOTE: The above list is subject to change as conditions dictate. (Fieldcrest Cannon Inc. *and* Clothing and Textile Workers, exp. 3/93)

Health Care Cost Containment Measures

___ *Surgical, Prescription Drugs, and Other Related Provisions* ___

Cost containment measures commonly found in surgical-medical plans include requirements that employees or dependents obtain second surgical opinions or use outpatient surgical facilities and generic drugs to qualify for full benefits.

Among other provisions designed to curb health care costs are those calling for establishment of joint cost containment committees, flexible spending accounts, and wellness programs.

Surgical Restrictions—

—Failure to obtain mandatory second opinion results in 20 percent penalty

If you or one of your dependents is advised by a surgeon to undergo any of the following surgical procedures, you or your dependents must obtain a second surgical opinion.

The elective surgical procedures requiring Second Surgical Opinions are:

Bunionectomy

Heart Surgery (Coronary Artery Bypass Surgery)

Cataract Surgery

Gallblader Surgery

Hysterectomy

Mastectomy

Hernia Repair (Inguinal Hernia Repair)

Prostatectomy

Tonsillectomy

Knee (except for diagnostic procedures) and other Joint

Surgery (Hip Joint Replacement)

Sinus and Nasal Surgery (Submucus Resection, Nasal

Polypectomy and Sinusotomy)

Spinal and Vertebral Surgery (Spinal Disc Surgery)

Hemorrhoidectomy

. . . .

Failure to obtain a mandatory second surgical opinion will result in a 20% penalty of the surgeon's fee with a maximum penalty per family of $300 per year. The penalty may not be used to satisfy any other deductible under your group insurance program. (Al Tech Specialty Steel Corp. *and* Steelworkers; exp. 9/93)

—Failure to obtain second opinion for specified procedures results in forfeiture of benefits

Second Surgical Opinion (Mandatory)

A mandatory second surgical opinion is required relative to the need or advisability of a surgical procedure in a non-emergency situation for the following:

Hernia Surgery

Removal of Bunions

Knee Surgery

Removal of Uterus (Hysterectomy)

Nose Surgery

Back Surgery

Removal of Tonsils and/or Adenoids

Removal of Breast

Cataract Surgery

Dilation & Curettage (D&C)

Prostate Surgery

Varicose Vein Surgery

Colostomy

Hemorrhoid Surgery

Hip Surgery

Gall Bladder Operation

The cost for the second surgical opinion will be paid for by the insurance coverage.

Failure to obtain a second surgical opinion will result in the forfeiture of surgical benefits covered by the medical insurance program. (JPI Transportation Products Inc., Heavy Wall Bearings Div. *and* Machinists; exp. 9/92)

—Second opinions may be voluntary or mandatory, depending on procedure

Second Opinion — Surgical Consultation Benefit

The Program will pay the reasonable and customary charges of a consulting physician for a covered surgical consultation, and the reasonable and customary charges for any laboratory or X-ray examinations made in connection with the consultation.

A "consulting physician" must be certified by the American Board of Surgery or other specialty board. Only consultations provided before the employee or dependent enters the hospital for the proposed surgery are covered under this benefit.

Benefits are not payable for consultations provided in connection with a normal obstetrical procedure, any procedure for which a surgical expense benefit would not be payable under the Program and the proposed procedure must require more than local infiltration anesthesia and be non-emergency in nature.

A second opinion is required for certain surgical procedures to receive the maximum surgical, hospital, etc. benefits. Such expenses will be covered at 80% if a second opinion is not obtained for such procedures. Other second opinions are voluntary.

A surgical consultation is not required, but may be requested by the employee, the dependent, or the operating physician when the proposed surgery is actually performed.

A third opinion will be covered on the same basis as the second opinion in those situations where the second opinion does not confirm the recommendation of the operating physician. (Ball-Icon Glass Packaging Corp. *and* Glass, Molders, Pottery, Plastics and Allied Workers; exp. 3/93)

—*Eighty percent coverage for in-patient surgery that could have been performed on out-patient basis*

Outpatient surgery is covered in the same manner as inpatient surgery. When non-emergency surgery can be performed on an outpatient basis and the physical and mental condition of the employee or covered dependent permits, such surgery will be covered at 80% if performed on an inpatient basis. (Owens-Brockway Packaging Inc. *and* Glass, Molders, Pottery, Plastics and Allied Workers; exp. 3/93)

—*Fifty percent coverage for procedures performed in hospital unless hospital confinement is medically necessary*

Surgeon's and Anesthesiologist's charges for the following procedures performed in the hospital will be paid at 50% of UCR unless hospital confinement is medically necessary. Benefits will be paid at 100% of UCR if performed in a Hospital outpatient department or a free standing surgical center.

Ingrown Toenail	Laproscopy
Pilonidal Cyst (Depends on Size)	Tonsillectomy-Adenoidectomy
Tumor-Biopsy-Breast	Cataract
Cystoscopy	D & C
Tubal Ligation	Myringotomy
Excision of Skin Lesion	Examination of Knee Joint
Plastic Surgery	Benign Lesion Excision up to ¼
Bunion Removal	inch (0.6 Cm.)
Biopsy of Breast-Needle & Incision	Walking Cast
Circumcision	Thoracentesis-Initial or
Myringotomy with Tube Insertion	subsequent
	Neuroplasty
	Carpal Tunnel

BIOPSY

Bronchoscopy	Colonoscopy
Peritoneoscopy	Sigmoidoscopy
Gastroduodenoscopy	Cystourethroscopy
Laprscopy	

The employee cost will not be applied to the Major Medical Plan deductible or Stop Loss. (General Cable Co. *and* Electrical Workers [IBEW]; exp. 8/92)

—*Out-patient surgery criteria listed*

Certain surgical procedures should be performed on an out-patient basis. When performed on an in-patient basis the reimbursement will be limited to 80% of the scheduled benefit. The criteria for out-patient surgery will be:

a. Patient's condition permits the surgery on an out-patient basis.

b. An out-patient facility is available.

c. The situation is a non-emergency.

d. It is not required that there be post operative observation by a nurse or skilled medical personnel.

e. A related surgical procedure which requires hospitalization is not being performed.

f. Appropriate home care is available.

g. It is not a two-stage surgical procedure.
(Corning Inc. *and* Flint Glass Workers; exp. 1/93)

—Services rendered in an ambulatory facility payable on same basis as inpatient services

Benefits shall be payable on the same basis as if the Employee or Dependent had been admitted to the Hospital as an inpatient for any services rendered to the Employee or Dependent in an Ambulatory Surgical Facility. (Aluminum Company of America *and* Aluminum, Brick and Glass Workers; exp. 5/92)

Prescription Drugs Restrictions—

—Lower deductible for generic drugs than for brand-name drugs

● Employee co-payments under the Mail-Order Prescription Drug Program to increase from $0 to $5 for generic drugs and from $5 to $10 for brand-name drugs per prescription. (Armstrong World Industries Inc. *and* Rubber Workers; exp. 10/92)

—Lower deductibles if mail order system or generic drug is used; benefit reduced to 75 percent of amount remaining after deductible if prescription filled by non-participating pharmacy

The benefit for each prescription or refill will be the amount charged by the physician, dentist, or participating pharmacy less:

$1.00 if the mail order system is used, or

$3.00 if a generic drug is used or there is no generic, or

$7.50 if a generic drug is commercially available, but not used.

If the prescription is filled by a non-participating pharmacy, the benefit may be reduced to 75% of the amount remaining after the respective deductible is applied. (Dana Corp. *and* Auto Workers; exp. 12/92)

—Charge for prescription drug waived if filled with generic drug

Drug Prescription Card. Each employee will receive a prescription drug card. This card may be presented at participating drug stores whereupon prescription drugs will be supplied for an individual prescription charge of *$4.00. In the event the prescription is filled with a generic drug, the *$4.00 charge is waived.

*effective 1/1/90-5.00   1/1/92-6.00

(Albany International Dryer Fabrics Div. *and* Textile Workers; exp. 6/92)

—Prescriptions obtained from mail order company supplied at no cost to employee

The prescription drug benefit is equal to the portion of the charge actually made to the employee or eligible dependent for each new prescription or refill for a covered prescription drug which is in excess of the deductible amount for each prescription. The applicable deductible amount (RX card contribution) is shown below:

8/20/89 - 8/22/92=$5.00

NOTE: The Deductible amount is not eligible as a Major Medical expense.

Effective 8/18/86, employees are eligible to obtain prescribed maintenance drugs from an approved Mail Order Drug Company. Any prescriptions obtained in this manner will be supplied at no cost to the employee. (Leeds and Northrop Co. *and* Auto Workers; exp. 8/92)

Joint Cooperative Commitments—

—Committee composed of two to four representatives each from employer and union shall continue

HEALTH CARE COST CONTAINMENT COMMITTEE

The joint committee which has been established for the purpose of investigating health care cost containment issues shall continue during the term of this Agreement: The committee shall be subject to the following provisions:

a. The committee shall be comprised of not less than two nor more than four representatives each from the Commonwealth and from the FOP.

b. The FOP representatives shall be granted time off with pay (unless a present or threatened emergency requires their services) as is reasonably necessary to complete the foregoing (including travel time). (Commonwealth of Pennsylvania *and* Police; exp. 6/92)

—Committee shall determine best way to mount campaign in support of national health insurance

NATIONAL HEALTH INSURANCE

The inflationary spiral affecting health care costs in the United States has caused the parties concern over the continued viability of their insurance program. Therefore, the parties agree that it would benefit the insurance program and the employees who are covered by this agreement if an appropriate National Health Insurance program is enacted. It is further agreed that the Joint Labor Management Committee shall meet to determine the best way to mount a joint campaign in support of the establishment of an appropriate National Health Insurance Program and to implement such a campaign. (Men's and Boys' Shirt and Nightwear Industry *and* Clothing and Textile Workers; exp. 8/91)

—Union and employers will seek to control costs and to work with health care community to provide quality care at reasonable costs

HEALTH CARE COSTS CONTAINMENT:

The Union and the Employers recognize that rapidly escalating health care costs, including the costs of medically unnecessary services and inappropriate treatment, have a detrimental impact on the health benefit program. The Union and the Employers agree that a solution to this mutual problem requires the cooperation of both parties, at all levels, to control costs and to work with the health care community to provide quality health care at reasonable costs. The Union and the Employers are, therefore, committed to fully support appropriate programs to accomplish this objective. This statement of purpose in no way implies a reduction of benefits or additional costs for covered services provided miners, pensioners and their families.

In any case in which a provider attempts to collect excessive charges or charges for services not medically necessary, as defined in the Plan, from a Beneficiary, the Trustees, the Plan Administrator or their agent shall, with the written consent of the Beneficiary, attempt to resolve the matter, either by negotiating a resolution or defending any legal action commenced by the provider. Whether the Trustees, the Plan Administrator or their agent negotiates a resolution of a matter or defends a legal action on a Beneficiary's behalf, the Beneficiary shall not be responsible for any legal fees, settlements, judgments or other expenses in connection with the case, but may be liable for any services of the provider which are not provided under the Plan. The Trustees, the Plan Administrator or their agent shall have sole control over the conduct of the defense, including the determination of whether the claim should be settled or an adverse determination should be appealed. (Bituminous Coal Operators' Association Inc. *and* Mine Workers; exp. 2/93)

—*Mutual responsibility of company and union to police all insurance usage*

To assure the greatest benefit for the money expended, it is a mutual responsibility of the Company and the Union to police all insurance usage. (Anchor Glass Container Corp. *and* Glass, Molders, Pottery, Plastics and Allied Workers; exp. 3/93)

—*Union agrees to make diligent efforts to get members to help slow or stop costs from escalating*

The Union and the Company recognize and agree that the rising cost of health care insurance has operated to the disadvantage of the Company and, in turn, to the employees covered by this agreement. In recognition of this fact and in a mutual effort to slow, or stop, escalating health care insurance costs:

1. The Union agrees that it will make all diligent efforts to get its unit members to help slow, or stop health care insurance costs from escalating and to minimize the likelihood of future increases in the cost of said insurance. (Holyoke Machine Co. *and* Electrical Workers [UE]; exp. 8/93)

—*Union agrees to work with management to identify administrative changes that would reduce costs and to establish preferred provider arrangement*

The Union also agrees to work jointly with Management to identify the administrative changes that would reduce the cost of providing health care while not reducing the negotiated level of benefits.

The Union agrees to work with Management and their insurance administrator to establish a preferred provider arrangement with medical providers to reduce cost for both the Company and the employees by March, 1991. (Cummins Engine Co. Inc. *and* Diesel Workers Union [Ind.]; exp. 4/93)

Flexible Benefit Accounts—

—*Employee contributions used to pay for deductibles, co-payments, and expenses not covered by insurance programs; remaining in account at end of year pooled with that of other employees and divided equally*

REIMBURSEMENT ACCOUNTS

There will be flexible spending accounts available which will provide reimbursement for health care expenses and dependent care expenses. An active employee ... may elect before the beginning of each calendar year to have up to $1500 for his health care reimbursement account and up to $3000 for his dependent care reimbursement account withheld from his wages through payroll deduction and deposited in the appropriate accounts. The moneys in an employee's health care reimbursement account shall be used to reimburse an employee for cash deductibles, co-payments, and expenses not covered by the Medical Care, Dental Care, and Vision Care Programs elected by the employee. The moneys in an employee's dependent care reimbursement account shall be used to reimburse an employee for expenses incurred in caring for a dependent child, parent, and/or disabled spouse so that the employee and/or the employee's spouse may be gainfully employed. Distributions for eligible expenses totaling less than $50 from the reimbursement accounts will be made after the end of each calendar quarter. Distributions for eligible expenses totaling more than $50 from the reimbursement accounts will be made after the end of each calendar month. In the second quarter following the end of each calendar year, any moneys remaining in an employee's reimbursement account will be pooled with the remaining amounts in all other employees reimbursement accounts and will be divided equally and distributed to all employees who had reimbursement accounts during such calendar year. (Timken Co. *and* Steelworkers; exp. 9/93)

—*Employee may direct up to $2,000 of pay before taxes to account and up to $5,000 to dependent care account; unused balance at end of year shall be used to reduce employee premium costs*

FLEXIBLE BENEFIT ACCOUNT

. . . .

C. Salary Redirection (Effective 7/1/86)

1. To the extent allowed by law employees may elect to redirect up to $2,000 of pay in to the Flexible Benefit Account to fund health care expenses with pre-tax dollars.

2. To the extent allowed by law employees may elect to redirect up to $5,000 of pay into a Dependent Care Account to fund Dependent Care expenses with pretax dollars.

D. With regard to funds in the Flexible Benefit Account and the Dependent Care Accounts:

1. They may be used throughout the year, on an income tax-free basis, for reimbursement of health care related or dependent care expenses, and

2. To the extent required by law any unused balance at the end of each year shall be forfeited and such forfeited monies shall be used to reduce the total premium costs paid by the employees, provided that dependent care forfeitures will be first applied to any dependent care program that may be implemented.

E. Health care related expenses for reimbursement from the Flexible Benefit Account include the following:

1. Medical and Dental Plan deductibles. . . .

2. Those Medical/Dental expenses which are not reimbursed in full. . . .

3. Other health care related expenses not covered by the Medical or Dental Plans, such as:

Routine medical check-ups

Eyeglasses

Hearing aids

Orthodontia

Cosmetic surgery (Xerox Corp. *and* Clothing and Textile Workers; exp. 3/92)

—*Allows employees to spend "benefit dollars" to buy combination of benefits that best meets individual needs.*

GROUP INSURANCE CONTRIBUTIONS

(a) The TWU recognizes that controlling the spiralling costs of health care has become a national priority and a critical mutual objective for both the Company and TWU represented employees.

In order to provide maximum flexibility and choice for individual employees, while helping to assure the Company's continued financial strength, effective January 1, 1990, the Company will implement a flexible benefits program which limits the impact of future health cost increases for both the Company and TWU represented employees as follows:

(1) The Company will provide "benefit dollars" which will allow each employee, in 1990, to "purchase", at no cost beyond those "benefit dollars", the basic Group Life and Health Benefits Plan as modified in the May 5, 1989 Letter of Agreement.

(2) Employees may spend their "benefit dollars" to buy that combination of benefits that best meets their individual needs — for example, more life insurance, but less health coverage.

(3) Employees may select a more limited benefit plan (such as a plan with a higher deductible), and receive cash in exchange for unused "benefit dollars". These cash payments will not increase other benefits (e.g., pension accruals or life insurance) and are subject to income and Social Security taxes. (American Airlines Inc. *and* Transport Workers; exp. 3/93)

Preventative and Other Measures—

—*Employees eligible to participate in Employee Assistance Program and Wellness Facility*

Wellness

(a) Employee Assistance Program:

(1) As part of a positive approach to Wellness by both the Union and the Company, it is agreed that employees and their dependents will be eligible to participate in the Company's Employee Assistance Program (EAP) so long as, and to the extent that the Company offers such a program in the general area and so long as all parties agree to continue participation.

(2) The EAP offers the employee or his dependents the opportunity to get professional help for personal problems. Medical problems such as alcohol or drug abuse are addressed, as well as mental, financial and legal.

(3) The EAP utilizes a local third party agency to ensure strict confidentiality.

(4) Utilization of the EAP program by employees and their dependents is on a voluntary basis.

(b) Wellness Facility:

(1) It is agreed that Union employees will be eligible to participate in the Company Wellness Facility on the same basis as other employees.

(2) The facility is designed to improve a participant's physical fitness and lifestyle and is to be available to a limited number of voluntary participants.

(3) It is understood that continuation of the Wellness facility is strictly at the Company's discretion and may be discontinued anytime. (Miles Inc. *and* Steelworkers; exp. 3/92)

—*Employee reimbursed up to $100 per year upon submittal of paid invoice for an approved wellness program*

The Company will reimburse employees up to $100 per year, subject to required Federal and State tax withholdings, upon submittal of a paid invoice for an approved wellness program, such as:

— Physical Recreational Club memberships.

— Smoking Cessation Programs.

— Diet Workshops.

— Routine Annual Physicals.

— Lamaze.

(Bath Iron Works Corp. *and* Independent Guards Association [Ind.]; exp. 9/91)

—*Company will pay 50 percent of the costs of a stop smoking program, up to $500*

Stop Smoking Benefits

To help employees and eligible family members, James River will pay 50% of the costs of a Company-approved stop smoking program, up to an individual lifetime maximum of $500. This benefit is not part of the group insurance coverage. It is sponsored solely by James River and is available to employees, no matter which type of health care coverage was chosen. Before starting a program however, employees must check with the benefits representative to make sure the program is on the list of approved programs. Benefits are paid upon completion of the program. (James River Corp., Flexible Packaging Div. *and* Western Pulp and Paper Workers [Ind.]; exp. 9/92)

—*Disease detection provision pays up to $75 per year for specified tests and procedures*

Disease Detection

Effective January 1, 1990, the Plan will pay for the following tests and procedures for the early detection of disease among eligible employees and Class I and II dependents, provided they are not otherwise eligible for reimbursement under the Well Child Benefit. Reimbursement is at 100% of reasonable and customary cost up to a total of $75 per year per participant for all such tests and procedures combined. Such reimbursement is not subject to Plan deductibles or copayments.

● Mammogram and interpretation by a radiologist once every other year from age 40 through 49, and annually thereafter.

● Fecal occult blood test once annually

● Total serum cholesterol once annually

● Blood glucose for diabetes once annually

● Sigmoidoscopy once every 3 years from age 50 through 59, and annually thereafter.

When experience dictates that additions and/or alterations should be made to the list of covered tests and procedures, the Company reserves the right, at its discretion, to make changes in this list when it deems necessary. (Michigan Bell Telephone Co. *and* Communications Workers; exp. 8/92)

—Annual $100 allowance to promote health check-ups

$100 Annual Preventive Medicine Allowance - To promote annual health check-ups, each employee and spouse will have an annual allowance of $100 toward the cost of Pap tests and gynecological exams, routine mammogram, prostate exams, and routine medical exams performed without medical diagnosis. This $100 is not subject to the deductible. After the $100 annual allowance has been used, the following services will be covered subject to the deductible and co-pay:

(1) annual Pap test;

(2) routine mammography exams:

age 40-49 — 1 time every two years

age 50 & over — 1 time every year

(3) 50% paid on annual medical exams for subscriber or spouse over 50 years when performed without medical diagnosis. (Teledyne Wah Chang Albany *and* Steelworkers; exp. 5/95)

—An employee who withdraws from or waives health insurance coverage will be paid $1,000 at end of fiscal year

Withdrawal from Health Care Coverage. Effective July 1, 1991, an employee who withdraws from or waives health insurance coverage under Blue Cross, Blue Shield and major medical or their health maintenance organization equivalent for an entire fiscal year will be paid $1,000 at the end of that fiscal year. Employees may enter or leave the plan at any time provided they must have not participated for an entire fiscal year to be eligible for the preceding payment and may be subject to proof of insurability on re-entry if required by the insurance carrier. Such payment will be subject to income tax deductions, but not to pension or any other payroll deductions unless specifically authorized by the employee or such deduction is required by operation of law. Such payment will not be considered wages or earnings in the determination of pension benefits. (City of Hartford, Connecticut *and* Hartford Police Union [Ind.]; exp. 6/94)

—Up to $5 of each benefit increase may be used for AIDS projects or funds

The Union may use up to $5.00 of each of the benefit increases in the last four years of the contract for AIDS projects or funds. (San Francisco Hotels *and* Hotel Employees and Restaurant Employees; exp. 8/94)

Appendix 8

Charlottesville, Va. Wellness Program

Source: Reprinted with permission from the *Employee Advisory Committee on Health Care Report* (Fairfax, VA: Fairfax County School System, 1990).

Employee Health and Fitness Programs—The experience at Charlottesville

Wellness Programs are primarily intended to promote healthy lifestyle behavior as a means of reducing health care costs but may have many other positive benefits. By changing behavioral patterns, employees are likely to have lower medical claim costs, reduced sick leave usage, and increased productivity levels.

The American Medical Association estimates that as many as 50% of all medical problems are lifestyle related, and that many catastrophic claims experienced by the study group can probably be attributed to lifestyle related illnesses.

Because of the potential long-term financial impact that Wellness Programs have on reducing health care costs, staff is recommending that the school board provide funding for a Comprehensive Wellness Program. As an example, we would like to cite the experiences of the City of Charlottesville, Virginia which implemented a Wellness Program, called Life Choice, in 1985. The following provides a brief discussion of how the program works.

The basic component of "Life Choice" is the health appraisal which every employee is required to complete. Aggregate data collected from a detailed computerized health risk appraisal, and Martha Jefferson Hospital's medical tests provide a valuable source of data on identifying the major health risks to City employees. Each employee receives a personal report on their current health status and recommendations for improvement in confidential meetings with a physician.

For an average cost to the City of just over $50 per person, all employees were given a mini-physical exam which tested for pulse rate, blood pressure, height and weight, glaucoma and visual acuity, hearing acuity, pulmonary function, and a basic blood test for cholesterols, heart disease, anemia and diabetes. Voluntary colon cancer test kits were included. A medical history was also taken to help the doctors evaluate the risks of certain hereditary diseases. Nurses from Martha Jefferson Hospital performed all tests on City premises for two years and at the Hospital during the third appraisal. A competitive bidding process was established to pick this Hospital as the provider of these services, and the Hospital has since gone on to promote and market similar services to other employers.

Employee morale has benefited significantly from the total Life Choice program, but the effect on productivity is difficult to measure. Sick leave utilization has begun to decrease, currently down from over 7.5 days per year per employee to approximately 7.0. Medical expenses provide a more quantitative yardstick. Medical costs per covered City employee are increasing at only one-third the statewide average and are, in fact, below the percentage increase in hospital and physician's fees around the state and the country. This means actual services utilized by employees are declining.

As a positive incentive to employees, their share of medical premiums, as well as the City's, was reduced for two years in a row. If medical expenses had increased at the rate anticipated by Blue Cross over the last three years, health plan premiums would have been 27% higher this year, not 10% lower. This difference is approximately $500,000, measured against less than $350,000 in expenses for the City's entire three-phase program over four years. A series of major hospitalizations in 1988 for cancer and heart disease increased medical costs to the City for the first time since 1985.

So that all factors are considered, it should be clear that four years ago the medical plan was redesigned to provide financial incentives for less costly outpatient treatment, and a thorough package of cost containment features was added. Yet the plan is still a generous 90/10 coinsurance design. It is impossible to segregate the effect of plan design from the educational and risk reduction effect of Life Choice, but we have not seen anywhere near this degree of financial success with other employers who have just made plan design modifications and added cost containment features without attempting to create a healthier workforce. It should also be noted that at first Blue Cross of Virginia was very skeptical about the impact of Life Choice on plan utilization. Now, Blue Cross has developed similar programs of their own.

Those individuals who have made substantial changes in their lifestyle, such as a major improvement in eating habits, or have stopped smoking, or who have joined the fitness program (unique in the City's willingness to pay the full cost for those who participate at least twice a week) will have a major impact on cost down the road. Smokers are estimated to generally cost 50% more in medical expenses than non-smokers and to use sick leave 30% more often. In the first health evaluation in 1985, 40% of employees were active smokers. This figure has dropped to 30% in 1988. A corresponding increase in those who classify themselves as former smokers verifies this figure.

The aggregate data produced by the health evaluations provides a valuable resource in designing risk reduction programs. This data does not in any way allow access to an individual's record. The clearly confidential nature of the health evaluation, reinforced by utilizing nurses and physicians to administer all tests and provide individual counseling, has gone a long way toward creating the positive attitude employees feel toward the program.

Risk reduction programs must be oriented toward significant behavioral problem areas. In order of importance, the major medical risks identified are:

- Heart Attack
- Stroke
- Cancer
- Motor Vehicle Accident Trauma

Risk reduction programs target these areas, and the City continually produces literature and posters that highlight these health concerns. Also, each month every City employee receives a copy of "Healthaction," one of the best health newsletters available, colorful and easy to read. Healthaction is mailed to every employee's home address.

The City also established an Employee Assistance Program to provide individual counseling to City employees and their dependents. All programs are coordinated through the City's Benefits Manager.

In the first year, there was some initial resistance to this program, but this quickly evaporated and now the program is a model in the community. Life Choice has even become an effective recruiting tool for new employees.

Appendix 9

The Massachusetts Health Security Act of 1988 and 1992

Basic Provisions of the Act as Adopted in 1988
(Fact Sheets #1–3)

FACT SHEET #1: Universal Health Insurance Provisions

The Health Security Act of 1988 gives Massachusetts residents the nation's first program to assure basic health security through universally available insurance. There are 600,000 uninsured Massachusetts residents—1 in 10 of our fellow citizens—who will finally be able to get affordable, quality health insurance.

The Act initially encourages and later requires employers to contribute to health insurance for their employees since two-thirds of the uninsured are working people and their dependents. Persons who are not covered by employers will be able to obtain health insurance through a number of new programs and through a new state agency at state-subsidized rates.

All Massachusetts residents will have health insurance available to them by 1992, according to the following schedule:

- *Disabled adults* who wish to work and *disabled children* of working parents will have primary and supplemental health insurance, with benefits up to Medicaid levels, available to them by the end of 1988;
- Child support and alimony laws have been strengthened to improve health insurance availability for *dependent children and former spouses*;
- Firms with six or fewer employees will be able to join a *new small business group insurance purchasing pool in 1989*;
- Phase-in initiatives offering health insurance and managed care to uninsured persons will be started in 1989;
- Beginning September, 1989, all *college and university students* studying at least three-quarter time will have health insurance coverage, offered through their schools;
- Beginning in 1990, a two-year *tax credit* will be offered to businesses with 50 or fewer employees which have not offered health insurance in the previous 3 years; the credit will equal 20% in year 1 and 10% in year 2;
- In 1990, *persons receiving unemployment insurance* will be eligible for employer-subsidized health insurance;

- In 1991, *persons receiving General Relief* from the state will be enrolled in prepaid health insurance plans;
- Beginning in January, 1992, most employers will be required to contribute to a state-administered *medical security trust fund* for the benefit of their full-time, permanent employees; employers who already contribute to their employees' health insurance will be allowed a deduction equal to these expenditures;
- By mid-1992, all Massachusetts residents who do not have health insurance through their employers will be able to purchase affordable health insurance through the *new Department of Medical Security*; the Department will offer managed care plans and will set premiums according to a sliding fee scale.

Employer mandates under the new law:

- The Act requires employers to contribute to the cost of health insurance:
  —beginning in 1990, employers will contribute an amount equal to .12% of the first $14,000 in yearly wages per employee (maximum = $16.80) to help finance health insurance for workers receiving unemployment insurance;
  —beginning in 1992, employers will contribute an amount equal to 12% of the first $14,000 in yearly wages per employee (maximum = $1,680) to help finance health insurance for their workers.
- The employer mandates apply to all Massachusetts employers except:
  —employers with five or fewer employees;
  —self-employed persons;
  —new businesses in their first year of operation (they are subject to one-third of each contribution in their second year; two-thirds in their third year and the full rate thereafter).
- Employer contributions are required for the following employees:
  —full-time employees working at least 30 hours/week after 90 days;
  —part-time employees working at least 20 hours/week after 180 days or after 90 days if they are heads of households.

- Employer contributions are *not* required for employees who are:
  —hired for less than five months, such as temporary or seasonal workers; or
  —have health insurance through another source, such as a spouse or parent.

New Hardship Fund for small employers:

  —employers with 50 or fewer employees who are severely impacted by the 12% contribution will be eligible for financial assistance;
  —the fund will pay contribution costs exceeding 5% of an employer's gross revenue.

FACT SHEET #2: Hospital Financing and Cost-Containment Provisions

In addition to assuring universal access to health insurance, the Massachusetts Health Security Act contains a four-year hospital financing arrangement that includes cost-containment measures, including arrangements that will bring about a closing or conversion of unneeded hospital facilities and beds.

Hospital Rate Increases are limited for the next four years:

- Aggregate increased hospital charges to private payors are limited to:
  $289 million in FY'88
  $262 million in FY'89
  $195 million in FY'90
  $195 million in FY'91
- These hospital rate increases represent medical inflation plus two percentage points dedicated to salary increases, adjust for prior period underfinancing among certain hospitals and also permit pass throughs for capital costs, government mandates, malpractice insurance costs, etc.
- The Commonwealth will help offset hospital losses attributed to federal Medicare cutbacks up to $50 million per year from FY'88 to FY'91.

Hospital Excess Bed Capacity will be reduced to eliminate extra costs carried in the industry:

- Hospitals with very low bed occupancy will be offered incentives to close, consolidate or convert to other community uses under the supervision of a new Acute Hospital Conversion Board.
- Allowable hospital rates will no longer cushion hospitals with falling occupancy.
- Special protections and assistance will be offered to hospitals serving remote areas.

- Retraining and job placement assistance will be offered to displaced hospital workers.
- Excess beds will be de-licensed, with a simple process available to relicense beds when needed.

Hospital Free Care/Bad Debt Pool

- The total obligation of private payors to the hospitals' free care/bad debt pool is capped and gradually reduced as follows:

  $325 million in FY'88
  $318 million in FY'89
  $312 million in FY'90
  $277 million in FY'91

- Although the free care/bad debt pool is expected to decrease as uninsured persons are enrolled in health insurance plans, the Commonwealth will fund the pool above the private payor cap up to 115% of that cap and will share any amounts greater than 115% with the hospitals.
- The Commonwealth will begin management of the pool in October, 1988.

FACT SHEET #3: How Much Will the Health Security Act Cost the Commonwealth?

	FISCAL YEARS—In Million Dollars				
	1988	*1989*	*1990*	*1991*	*1992*
Payments to Hospitals:					
Medicare Supplement	$34	$50	$50	$50	$16
UCP—State Share	—	20	50	50	—
Sub-total	34	70	100	100	16
Insuring the Uninsured:					
General Relief (beg. 1-1-91)	—	—	—	25	50
Tax Credit	—	—	1.	2.5	3.5
Phase-In Initiatives	—	10.	20.	30.	50.
Administration (including small business assistance)	.5	3.3	4.	5.	8.
Sub-total	.5	13.3	25.	62.5	111.5
Additional Programs:					
Disabled Adults & Children		10	18	20	22
Medicaid Expansion— Pregnant Women (net cost)	—	3.9	4.4	4.9	5.2
Medicaid Continuation— for ET	—	2.0	6.0	8.0	8.0
Sub-total	—	15.9	28.4	32.9	35.2
Total Costs:					
Gross Costs	34.5	99.2	153.4	195.4	162.7
less savings*	2.5	20.	—	—	—
Net Costs	32.	79.2	153.4	195.4	162.7
Range	31–33	79–82	150–165	185–205	155–175

*Savings are available in the '88 and '89 budgets due to higher prior estimates of Medicaid hospital rates.

The Health Security Act in 1992

FACT SHEET #4

Due to mounting fiscal concerns, the Legislature subsequently amended the law. The reimbursement system was totally overhauled in an effort to reduce excessive government regulation and to replace it with the cost control benefits derived from a competitive marketplace. The provisions designed to improve access to affordable health insurance also were pared back. For example, the effective date of the law's major mandate—a provision that would have required businesses to provide health insurance to employees or else pay into a special fund—was postponed from 1992 until 1995.

While greatly modified, the role of the Department of Medical Security continues to be significant; indeed, with passage of recent legislation to restructure the hospital reimbursement system, including the hospital free care pool, the department's activities in some areas are being expanded.

These are the department's chief responsibilities today:

A. Hospital Free Care Pool

The Hospital Free Care Pool is the Commonwealth's health care "safety net," which pays hospitals for free care they provide to low income persons without health insurance. The Hospital Free Care Pool is funded through an assessment—currently 9 percent—of every hospital bill paid for through health insurance. The amount collected is currently capped at $300 million.

The Department of Medical Security is responsible for tracking the free care provided by acute care hospitals, collecting payments to the pool and disbursing funds owed to hospitals.

B. Health Security Plan

The Health Security Plan provides temporary health insurance protection to qualified persons receiving unemployment compensation and their families. To qualify, family income one year prior to the date of layoff can not exceed 400 percent of the Federal poverty guideline. As of Feb. 15, the Federal poverty income guideline for an individual was $6810 a year and $13,950 for a family of four.

This means that in order to qualify for the Health Security Plan an individual can not have earned more than $27,240 ($6810 × 400 percent) the year prior to layoff and a family of four can not have earned more than $55,800 ($13,950 × 400 percent).

Administered under contract by the John Hancock Mutual Life Insurance Company, the plan offers two programs: 1) Direct Coverage and 2) The Continuation Plan.

Direct Coverage is a basic package of health insurance benefits with several deductibles, which means that a patient must pay some of the hospital and physician charges. In the case of hospital inpatient charges, there is a $300 charge, and for outpatient charges, there is a $150 deductible charge. These are the maximum, one-time charges for a full benefit year.

The Continuation Plan is for unemployed persons receiving unemployment compensation who have continued the group health insurance they had while employed under the Federal COBRA law (Consolidated Omnibus Budget Reconciliation Act). Under COBRA, an employer of 20 or more persons must continue group coverage for a laid off employee as long as the employee pays the premiums. The Continuation Plan provides partial reimbursement for COBRA premium payments.

Applications for the Health Security Plan are available at all Massachusetts unemployment offices or by calling the Health Security Plan Service Center toll free at 1-800-367-7781.

C. CenterCare

CenterCare offers primary health care services to low income individuals and families through independently licensed community health centers throughout the Commonwealth.

Through CenterCare, potential users of the Hospital Free Care pool can receive managed health care in a low cost setting, and community health centers can receive compensation for the free care they traditionally have provided.

D. Labor Shortage Initiative

The Department of Medical Security collaborates with the Massachusetts Hospital Association (MHA) in the planning and implementation of the Labor Shortage Initiative.

The Initiative provides funds for a variety of programs which, among other things, train health care workers, provide child care opportunities and support at hospitals and other health care facilities, and develop career ladders for the health care professions.

Funding for the Labor Shortage Initiative is generated through an assessment on each acute care hospital equal to one-tenth of one percent of the hospital's annual revenues.

E. Student Health Insurance

Since adoption of the Health Security Act of 1988, all full-time college students attending school in Massachusetts must either document that they have health insurance or else purchase it through the institution they are attending. DMS is charged with monitoring this provision of the law.

Appendix 10

Example of a Joint Labor-Management Study on Health Care: Fairfax County School System

Source: Reprinted with permission from *Report of the Employee Advisory Committee on Health Care* (Fairfax, VA: Fairfax County School Board, 1989).

I. Executive Summary

In July, 1989, the Fairfax County School Board authorized the formation of an Employee Advisory Committee on Health Care to make recommendation to the Superintendent on issues related to the employee's health benefit program. After three months of research and study, the committee has concluded that the issues involved in the field of health care are complicated and require further evaluation. Therefore, this report is considered to be the committee's interim report.

The recommendations of the committee fall into four areas: General; Short-Term (for consideration in FY 1991); Long-Term (those areas requiring further study and evaluation); and issues related to retiree health care. The committee's recommendations are as follows:

I. General Recommendation
   A. It is recommended that the Employee Advisory Committee on Health Care be continued, and that a minimal budget be provided that would permit additional consultants to give presentations and thus broaden the committee's perspectives and answer significant concerns.

II. Short-Term Recommendations
   A. Cost Containment
      1. Maintain the current level of employee cost-sharing in the health care programs for FY 1991.
      2. Introduce an employee incentive program for the review of medical bills.
      3. Continue the current pre-admission certification utilization review and case management programs.
   B. Alternative Delivery Systems
      1. Continue the current health plans offered by FCPS for at least another year.
      2. Develop an employee survey to determine employees likes or dislikes of their current health plans for use in future planning.

C. Communication/Information Programs
   1. Place packets that contain information on all existing health plans at each worksite.
   2. Produce a comprehensive booklet explaining and comparing the benefits of each health plan.
   3. Provide more wellness and health consumer information in current publications.
   4. Make use of existing resources to write health/wellness articles.
   5. Offer health information and wellness programs as part of inservice days.
   6. Give employees a clear overview of health benefits when first hired.
   7. Prepare benefit materials in the most common languages of employees hired.
D. Wellness Programs
   1. Funding in the amount of $116,864.22 be appropriated in the FY 1991 budget to implement a schoolwide wellness program.

III. Long Term Recommendations
   A. Study feasibility of introducing a non-smoker discount program.
   B. Study feasibility of an incentive or discount for infrequent use of the health care program.
   C. Continue the careful study of the feasibility of a managed care plan.
   D. Study area medical services, in coalition with other employers, with the aim of maintaining the highest level of quality.
   E. Make changes to the current health care alternatives only after an extensive information campaign.
   F. Develop a more extensive health publication that would serve as a guide to health plan usage and provide wellness information.
   G. Provide training and consider upgrading the position classification of those staff members providing benefit counseling.

IV. Retiree Health Care Recommendations
   A. Make no changes to the level of benefits, the method in which retiree premiums are established, or the eligibility for retirees to participate in a FCPS health plan until a more complete analysis has been conducted.

B. Provide more information to retirees on the value of the health insurance coverage they receive.

The committee's report contains background information and rationale for their recommendations.

The committee believes that the establishment of this process is valuable to employees and its continuance will foster better employee relations. The committee appreciated the efforts of staff to support the committee's work.

II. Status of FCPS Health Care Program

In Fall, 1988, the school system was advised by Blue Cross/Blue Shield that based on the first quarter FY 1989 claims experience of the FCPS group that the premium structure established by the school system for FY 1989 would be insufficient to cover the cost of claims and administrative expenses for the remainder of the year. The consulting firm of Towers, Perrin, Forster and Crosby (TPF&C) was requested to conduct a complete analysis of the FCPS health program and to make recommendations.

The consultants initially advised that indeed the premium level established was not only insufficient to cover the estimated cost of claims that would be presented for payment during the course of the fiscal year, but that no additional funding would be available for claims that would be incurred during FY 1989, but not reported until the next fiscal year (IBNR).

It was determined that a mid-year rate increase of 37.6% would be required to generate sufficient revenue to cover the expected health care cost for the remainder of FY 1989.

After an extensive and comprehensive study of the FCPS indemnity medical plan and its relationship with the Health Maintenance Organizations (HMOs) provided to active and retired employees, the consultants concluded that the FCPS indemnity plan was competitive with other public employer plans in the Washington, D.C. metropolitan area and provided a higher level of coverage than is typically provided by major private employers in the area. However, the consultants further concluded that the plan design of the FCPS health plan was incompatible with the need to control the rapid escalation of health plan cost.

The consultant's recommendations covered the areas of plan design, cost containment, retiree medical benefits, HMO pricing, funding, and plan administration. After presentation and discussion with staff and School Board, the changes approved for FY 1990 were:

—Increase the BC/BS premiums 20% for FY 1990;

—Increase the plan's current annual Major Medical deductible from $100 per individual and $200 per family to $200 per individual and $400 per family;

—Introduce a separate per-admission hospital deductible of $100;

—Introduce an annual out-of-pocket limit of $600 per person and $1200 per family under the Major Medical plan;

—Reduce nervous and mental benefits under major medical coverage from 80% of the first $10,000 and 50% of the next $20,000 to 50% of $30,000;

—Require that the indemnity plan assume that retirees aged 65 and older are eligible for Medicare and that Medicare is the primary payor of benefits; and

—Require HMO enrollees to pay the same percent of total HMO contributions that enrollees participating in the indemnity plan are required to pay for their coverage.

Additionally, the School Board approved a new funding arrangement for payment of claims and administrative expenses to BC/BS. As opposed to sending BC/BS on a monthly basis premiums collected (both employee and employer) the school system would establish an interest bearing trust account for deposit of premiums collected. BC/BS would be paid on a weekly basis for claim expenses and administrative cost. The objective of such an arrangement would be to have control over the health care expenses and to allow staff the ability to monitor and maintain a true accounting of revenue and expenses; and to avoid the need for future, unexpected health cost increases.

These changes were implemented July 1, 1989, and after one quarter, sufficient funds have been established for IBNR. Appendix A provides charts depicting first quarter FY 1990 analysis of the claim expenses of the BC/BS plan.

III. Establishment and Work Plan of the Health Care Advisory Committee

The changes made to the health plan in July, 1989, represented the first major restructuring of the FCPS health benefit program in years. Although, many benefit improvements and enhancements have been made to the indemnity plan, never had the level of benefits been reduced. As a result of these changes, there was a great deal of reaction from both active and retired employees.

In response to employee concerns regarding the lack of involvement in the changes made to the health benefits program, on July 20, 1989, the School Board approved the formation of a committee of Fairfax County Public School employees to advise the Superintendent, and in turn the School Board, on issues and alternatives relating to the health care benefits available to employees. The committee was to be composed of representatives of all categories of employees appointed by the various associations.

The committee was charged with gathering information and making recommendations in the following areas:

—health care cost containment
—alternative health care delivery systems
—employee information programs
—employee wellness programs

In August, 1989, the Department of Personnel Services requested that the various employee associations appoint the appropriate number of representatives to serve on the committee. The committee held its first meeting on September 1, 1989. The committee first defined its mission and objectives and established four subcommittees to focus on the four areas identified by the School Board.

The committee has met seven times since its establishment and plans to meet at least one more time after this report is submitted. Additionally, the various subcommittees have met as necessary. The committee has received presentations on the various topics:

—Review of TPF&C December, 1988, Study on the FCPS Health Plans
—Managed Care—presented by Katherine Kelly, consultant, TPF&C
—Overview of Indemnity Plans and BC/BS Triple Option Plan—Beth Corish, Account Executive, BC/BS

—Characteristics of Health Maintenance Organizations—Ann Roderick, Kaiser-Permanente
—Review of the FCPS Rating and Trend Analysis
—Retiree Health Care Issues

The committee also received information on the school system's staff proposal for changes to the health plan for FY 1991.

Additionally, the committee has reviewed numerous articles and studies related to health care issues. (See Appendix C)

The committee discovered very early that the three month period given to provide a report to the Superintendent would not be adequate to explore in detail all of the alternatives. Therefore, the primary focus has been on long-range objectives and goals.

IV. Recommendations

A. General

The field of health care is a very complicated area, particularly when exploring cost containment and alternative delivery systems. The committee has concluded that there is a great deal more that must be examined and evaluated before recommendations can be made regarding possible changes to the FCPS health care program.

The committee has identified the following areas of concerns which require further study; or additional information is needed.

1. Quality Assurance

    —Further study must be given to a medical quality assurance plan to accompany any managed care program. Where the provider has a financial incentive, it may be possible for that provider to deny needed services as a cost saver.

    —Certainly the greatest number of questions that employees will have if the structure of the FCPS employee health care program changes significantly will be concerned with the issue of quality. Consumers tend to think that the best medical care costs the most. This is not necessarily true. It is recommended that the features of a quality evaluation program be further investigated (e.g. MediQual Systems, Inc.).

Last year, only two area HMOs operated profitably. If FCPS opts to have a new health care program, the financial condition of any health care provider needs to be investigated. It also needs to be determined what information is available on the financial condition of the companies currently providing services.

–Consideration should also be given to the fact that any new health care plan should have a strong nervous/ mental/drug and alcohol treatment component. Medical plans have always been designed to encourage the hospitalization of patients for these services. This is expensive and often not as effective as outpatient care might be. The nervous/mental and substance abuse component should be centered upon a gatekeeper concept. This approach would provide for a physician, usually a psychiatrist, to manage all of the care being provided to an individual. The plan design should encourage outpatient over inpatient services with an effective follow-up counseling program.

2. Choice

–Approximately half of the FCPS employees participate with a Health Maintenance Organization with the other half participating with the Indemnity Plan. This clearly indicates there are features of both programs which employees desire. If FCPS moves to a three option model of managed care, careful consideration needs to be given to the construction of the plan so that choice is real. If the financial penalty to opt out of the more cost effective option is set too high, the ability to choose point of service will be fiction.

–Should consideration be given to a managed care health plan, the indemnity portion of that program should use the usual, customary, and reasonable (UCR) rate as the basis for reimbursement.

–Since one of the main issues in selection between indemnity and prepaid plans hedges around selection of physicians, there needs to be information about the stability of the staff of HMOs and similar plans.

–Employees need actual cost comparisons between plans, so that they can make enlightened choices.

–All health plans considered need to provide services to include physicians and medical providers outside of Fairfax County.

3. Additional Information Needed

–Before a final recommendation is made, the committee wishes to hear presentations from employers/employee groups who have actually implemented managed health care programs.

Based on the need to obtain additional information in order to complete a more comprehensive study, the committee recommends:

–That the Employee Advisory Committee on Health Care be continued, and that a minimal budget be provided that would permit additional consultants to give presentations and thus broaden the committee's perspectives and answer significant concerns.

It is anticipated that the committee would make its final recommendations to the Superintendent by early Fall, 1990, for inclusion in the FY 1992 budget.

B. Short-Term Recommendations

Although the need has been established for further study, each subcommittee has identified some short-term recommendations for consideration and inclusion in the FY 1991 budget.

1. *Health Care Cost Containment*

–Maintain the current level of employee cost-sharing in the health care programs for FY 1991.

Significant cost-sharing adjustments were made at the beginning of this fiscal year; the employee groups represented on this committee do not believe that additional cost sharing would result in cost containment.

–Introduce an employee incentive program for the review of medical bills for both in-patient and out-patient services.

Based on information made available to the committee, this type of program has potential for assisting in the overall goal of cost containment and should be tried.

–Continue the current pre-admission certification and utilization review programs which include concurrent review of claims, discharge planning, and large case management.

Since hospital costs are a significant factor in the current health care inflation crisis, this strategy belongs in every plan to assist in cost containment.

2. *Alternative Health Care Delivery systems.*

Fairfax County Public Schools and its employees/retirees face a major crisis in the ever-increasing costs of health care. This situation is not unique. All Americans face escalating costs for health care that far exceed the rate of inflation. These costs promise financial ruin to individuals or families faced with extended health care needs. According to research conducted by the U.S. Department of Health and Human Services and the AFL-CIO, 37 million Americans have no health care plan. Another 43 million have partial or minimal coverage. Both private and public sponsors of health care programs can not continue to contribute the same proportion of plan costs without making substantial changes to their budgetary funding levels or plan design.

This situation requires the Fairfax County Public Schools to reevaluate its health benefits program. It also underscores the need for Fairfax County Public Schools and its employees to be certain that maximum service and benefits are obtained for each dollar spent.

In the area of alternative health care delivery systems, a variety of mechanisms have been investigated. Presentations were received from the HMO with the largest FCPS employee participation (Kaiser-Permanente), and the indemnity plan (BC/BS). Also, a written discussion of the similarities and differences of HMOs, PPOs, and Managed Health Care plans was received. This was followed by a discussion of the mechanisms for controlling costs under managed care programs (TPF&C report "A Discussion of Key Aspects of a Managed Health Care Program," October, 1989). A breakdown on the usage and benefits paid for nervous and mental disorders of the FCPS group was received, which indicated that in the previous five years this diagnostic area has comprised as much as 52% of the major medical cost of the indemnity plan. Several articles explaining Managed Care, HMOs, PPOs, and other items related to health care plans in private industry have been reviewed. In addition, the consultant's report from Towers, Perrin, Forster and Crosby, dated December, 1988, was studied, as well as materials distributed by VEA and NEA concerning health care plans.

Some committee members attended health care conferences, and viewed presentations by nationally prominent consultants on health care issues, in addition to those available through the employee advisory committee, (FEA conference in Windmill Point, VA, Franklin Morris and Associates, MediQual Systems, Inc., Robert D. Sacks Associates).

One thing has become crystal clear to the committee: the more learned about health care systems, the more questions there were to be answered.

Some concerns are: 1) establishing a health center for FCPS employees, 2) joining a statewide plan, 3) combining school employees with the county employees to make one group. The Metropolitan Council of Governments Plan and the HMO-Pact were reviewed. It was determined that all aspects of this area needed to be studied to assure that employees do not lose benefits and that cost is contained.

Dr. James Kenney, executive director of health care purchaser services for MediQual Systems, Inc. (a national health care consulting firm with offices in Westborough, MA, and Minneapolis, MN) has stated that the health care industry needs to move from philosophies of cost containment and cost management to a philosophy of value purchasing. This shift in thinking is necessary because cost containment hasn't worked, and there is a growing need for provider selection. Also, current utilization controls and quality assurance methods are inadequate, and purchasers and consumers are demanding information and accountability.

By tracking physician and hospital patient outcomes, rating the severity of patient illness, and comparing costs of hospitals and physicians, Dr. Kenney has concluded that the most effective medical care is often the most reasonable in cost.

The recommendations regarding alternative delivery systems are:

–Continue the current health plans offered by FCPS for at least another year;

–Develop an employee survey to determine what employees like or dislike about their health plans and what they would like to have in such a plan. This survey would be particularly valuable should FCPS opt to go to a managed health care or construct a new plan.

3. *Employee Communication/Information Programs*

"If employees do not understand their benefits, they probably don't appreciate their total compensation, and that can affect productivity, attitudes and retention." This quote from Dickson W. Lewis, a vice president of IDS Financial Services in an article on benefits communication sums up a major problem in employee benefits.

A function of health insurance is to remove the financial worry that a disease, illness, or accident can cause. The employer is investing in a healthy, happy employee. When there are changes in store or the financial equilibrium is upset, employees become anxious and potentially dissatisfied. The employer has a diminished investment. All upsetting incidents with health insurance cannot be avoided, but the disruption can be minimized if employees are fully informed consumers, understand their plan, and have been given clear and fair reasons for change.

In communicating to employees, only part of the intended audience will hear the message from any one attempt; therefore, a communication program needs to be on-going, repetitive, and varied as to approach and media. The committee believes that wellness information as well as health plan information needs to be communicated.

In a review of the research, it was clear to the committee, that where employers wanted to convey a sense of responsible consumerism to employees in the use of health insurance plans, a positive on-going campaign was necessary. These campaigns reflected real concern about employee health through positive personnel policies, wellness programs, and clear multi-media information programs. Studies indicate that it was difficult to establish data on savings from such programs because less use is an unquantifiable situation. Most, however, do report fewer lost days of work by employees.

In the area of communications the committee proposes the following actions:

> **–Packets that contain information on all existing plans should be placed conveniently at each worksite.**

> **–Employees need one comprehensive booklet explaining and comparing benefits of each health plan.** (Current information makes it difficult for employees to make decisions. The booklet should also give additional information on using health care.)

> **–Current publications should provide more wellness and health consumer information.** The Supergram should be considered for this information, as employees see that publication as the official school publication and will take messages more seriously.

> **–FCPS should make use of existing resources.** The school system should offer a stipend for school dieticians, teachers trained in health or foods or others to write health-related articles that can be used in publications to staff to inform them of things individuals can do to be healthier.

> **–As part of inservice days, FCPS should offer health information and wellness programs.** This has been done at the Leadership conference, but similar programs should be offered to all staff on a regular basis. Such emphasis would convey the seriousness with which the school system views the health of its employees.

> **–Employees, when first hired, should be given a clear overview of health benefits.**

> **–Materials and videos prepared for orientations and for ongoing use at worksites should be on a regular schedule for updating with all responsible offices and media services.**

> **–Because more support employees are non-English-speaking, materials need to be prepared in at least the most common languages hired.**

> *4. Wellness Program*

The vast amount of reading material being produced in the private and public work sector relating to the subject of wellness is an indication that this subject is a priority for both management and employees. Data received and reviewed clearly shows that wellness programs, when implemented and available to all employees, have a positive effect in areas of reduction of absenteeism and improvement in job performance. In addition, the working environment is enhanced and health care costs go down.

FCPS is currently piloting a wellness program at a number of worksites. Funding by FCPS is necessary to ensure that this program may be expanded to remaining worksites not already included in the pilot program. Taking leadership in wellness through funding and support of the Wellness Pilot Program will act as an indicator to employees that FCPS as a progressive organization endorses the wellness concept with all its accompanying benefits.

Therefore, it is recommended that:

–Funding be appropriated in the FY 1991 budget to implement a school-wide wellness program as described in the Wellness Pilot Proposal.

The amount of funding needed to expand the Wellness Pilot Program to remaining worksites is $116,864.22. A copy of the program proposal is included in Appendix B to this report.

C. Long Term Recommendations

As has been indicated, the committee is requesting additional time to make final recommendations regarding long-range objectives of the FCPS health care programs. However, in the areas of cost containment and communication programs, specific areas of study and recommendations have already been identified.

–Study feasibility of introducing a non-smoker discount.

Time and information available were insufficient to determine if such a component would help in cost-containment. The committee feels that it should be studied.

–Study feasibility of an incentive or discount for infrequent use of the health-care plan.

As with the non-smoker discount, the committee feels that exploration about potential cost-containment factors should take place. In themselves, one such program may not do much to bring down costs, but together they might play an important part in accomplishing savings.

–Continue the careful study of the feasibility of a managed care plan with employee options.

This recommendation simply recognizes the trends over the last few years in both the private and the public sector. Careful evaluation and information about a proposed plan's effectiveness at containing costs, local market conditions, employee preferences, incentives, choice, and operational efficiency must precede the inauguration of any such program.

–FCPS should work in coalition with other employers to have a quality study done of area medical services.

This study should provide extensive information on health providers so that employees can be better informed consumers. It should include cost analysis, mortality comparisons, and frequency of use of medical procedures by different providers. Employees are concerned that changes in health care providers will reduce quality. Providing information on the quality of care provided by doctors and hospitals will satisfy this concern. Such a study should precede any major change in health care plans, including a managed care system.

–Any changes to current health care alternatives should be preceded by an extensive information campaign.

This campaign should include background information, clear statements of cost factors, and reasonable assurances on quality of care under any new plan. There is a need for direct presentation to staff on any change. At a minimum, the school system should develop video presentations that can be followed by question and answer periods.

–FCPS should develop a more extensive health publication that would serve as a guide to health plan usage and provide wellness information.

While the committee requested a publication that compares current plans in short-term goals, this long-term request is intended to go well beyond simple comparisons. Such a publication might include ways to cut cost through intelligent consumerism including use of generic drugs, acceptable out-patient treatment, questions to ask when surgery is suggested and ways to check hospital bills.

–Provide appropriate training and consider upgrading the position classifications of those staff members responsible for providing benefit counseling and assistance to employees with health benefits questions and problems.

V.   Retiree Health Care Issues

The committee received a detailed presentation from staff regarding the cost of medical insurance for retirees. Specific information was provided on the claim expenses of the retired group versus the premiums collected.

–Chart A shows the number of retirees as a percentage of all employees enrolled in the FCPS health plans.

–Chart B shows the number of retirees enrolled in each of the four health plans offered by FCPS.

–Chart C shows the number of retirees enrolled in the Blue Cross/ Blue Shield health plans as a percentage of the total BC/BS enrollment.

–Chart D shows the retiree premiums as a percentage of the total health insurance revenue from July 1–October 25, 1989.

–Chart E shows retiree claims as a percentage of total claims.

–Chart F compares premiums paid by retirees versus claims paid for the first quarter of FY 1990.

The committee was also provided information on various alternatives used by some employers in dealing with the rising cost of health care for retirees. Included in these alternatives were:

–requiring a minimum number of years of service or participation in a health plan to continue with health insurance coverage after retirement.

–providing a separate rating structure for retirees that would better reflect the true claims experience of this group.

–providing benefits for medicare-eligible retirees under a carve-out arrangement as opposed to coordination of benefits.

Of primary concern to the committee was the need to make certain that any changes made to the health care program would consider the fact that several FCPS retirees may live outside of the service areas of any type of HMO or PPO arrangements.

Because much more research and evaluation is needed to determine whether a different or more specific course of action should be taken regarding health insurance for retirees, the committee recommends that:

–No changes be made to the level of benefits, the method in which premiums are established, or the eligibility for health coverage for retirees until a more complete analysis has been conducted.

–Current retirees and those planning to retire should be provided information on all health plans and the value of the coverage retirees receive.

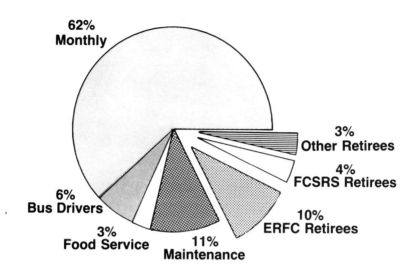

Chart A
Retirees as Percent of Total Census

62% Monthly

3% Other Retirees

4% FCSRS Retirees

10% ERFC Retirees

11% Maintenance

3% Food Service

6% Bus Drivers

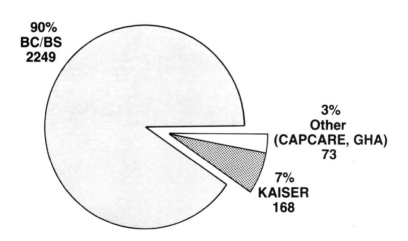

Chart B
Number of Retirees in Each Health Plan

90% BC/BS 2249

3% Other (CAPCARE, GHA) 73

7% KAISER 168

PARTICIPATION AS OF SEPTEMBER 1, 1989

Chart C
FCPS Retirees as a Percent of Total Participants in BC/BS Plan

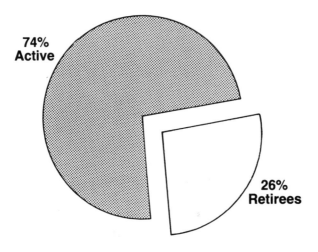

74%
Active

26%
Retirees

Chart D
Retiree Premium as a Percent of Total Revenue

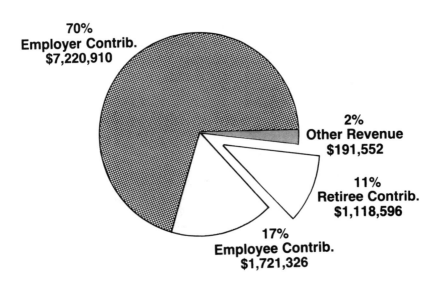

70%
Employer Contrib.
$7,220,910

2%
Other Revenue
$191,552

11%
Retiree Contrib.
$1,118,596

17%
Employee Contrib.
$1,721,326

For 1990 Fiscal Year as of Oct. 25, 1989

Chart E
Retiree Claims Compared to Total Claims

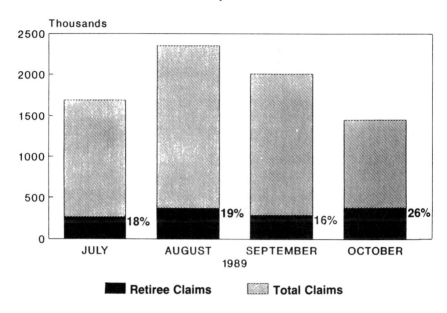

Based upon First Four Months 1990 FY

Chart F
Cash In/Cash Out for Retirees of FCPS Fiscal Year 1990

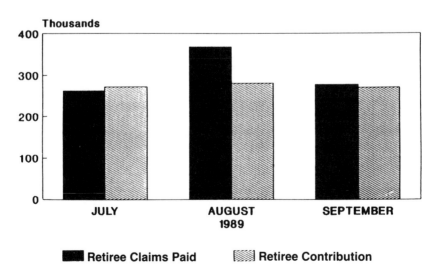

Appendix A

FCPS CLAIMS TREND ANALYSIS AND PROJECTIONS

(for BC/BS Health Plan Participants)

Claim Trend Projection
Fiscal Year 1983 Through 1989

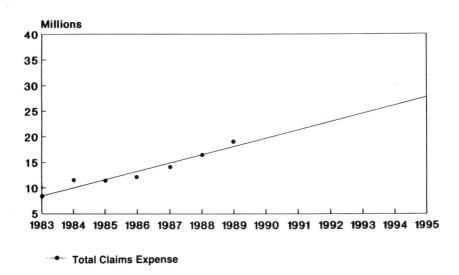

--•-- **Total Claims Expense**

Claim Trend Analysis
July 1987 Through September 1989

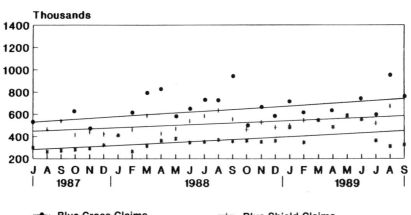

--•-- **Blue Cross Claims**   --+-- **Blue Shield Claims**

--*-- **Major Medical Claims**

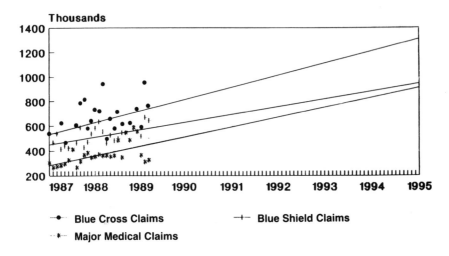

Claim Trend Projection
July 1987 Through June 1995

-•- Blue Cross Claims　　　-+- Blue Shield Claims
-*- Major Medical Claims

Top Line-BC; Middle Line-BS
Bottom Line-MM

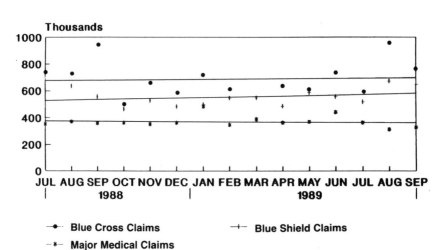

Claim Trend Analysis
July 1988 Through September 1989

-•- Blue Cross Claims　　　-+- Blue Shield Claims
-*- Major Medical Claims

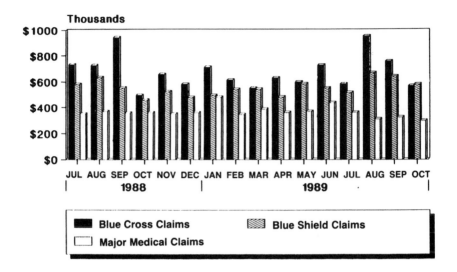

BC/BS Claims Paid
July 1988 Through Oct. 1989

Defined by Type of Payment

Index

About the Author

Suzanne Saunders Taylor is Executive Director of the University of Rhode Island Chapter, American Association of University Professors. She formerly worked in research, negotiations, and benefits for the Connecticut Education Association, an affiliate of the National Education Association. She has taught for several years at the University of Rhode Island Labor Research Center, where she currently teaches a graduate course in negotiating pensions and health insurance. Her first book was on the subject of public-employee pensions.